A STUDENT'S APPRO

RLD RELIGIONS

Buddhism

Denise Cush

SERIES EDITOR : BRIAN E. CLOSE

Hodder & Stoughton

A MEMBER OF THE HODDER HEADLINE GROUP

Acknowledgements

Several years have elapsed since the original idea for this book emerged out of my experience of teaching Buddhism at A level. As a result, the number of people who have contributed to making it possible are numerous. Among those who really must be mentioned and thanked are: St Mary's Sixthform College, Middlesbrough and Cleveland LEA for allowing me a term's secondment in 1985 to further my study of Buddhism. Andrew Rawlinson at Lancaster University for introducing me to Buddhism and supervising my study. Dawn Stewart for typing the first draft all those years ago. Peggy Morgan, Paul Williams, Anil Goonewardene and Arthur Giles for their helpful comments on the first draft. The Buddhism Resource Project for encouraging me to persevere. Jo Backus and David Francis for trying it out with their A level students. Bath College of Higher Education Faculty of Education for allowing me study leave to finish writing the final version. Professor Brian Bocking for his helpful comments on the final draft. All the students, whether in Middlesbrough or Bath, who have helped me test out my ideas for teaching Buddhism.

20 04001101

For David Francis

Orders: please contact Bookpoint Ltd, 39 Milton Park, Abingdon, Oxon OX14 4TD. Telephone: (44) 01235 400414, Fax: (44) 1235 400454. Lines are open from 9.00-6.00, Monday to Saturday, with a 24 hour message answering service.

British Library Cataloguing in Publication Data
A catalogue record for this title is available from The British Library

ISBN 0 340 54691 3

First published 1991
Impression number   14 13 12
Year   2004 2003

Copyright © 1993 Denise Cush

Printed in Great Britain for Hodder & Stoughton Educational, a division of Hodder Headline Plc, 338 Euston Road, London NW1 3BH by Athenæum Press Ltd, Gateshead, Tyne & Wear.

CONTENTS

CHAPTER ONE

INTRODUCTION

What is Buddhism?

Buddhism is one of the major religious traditions of the human race. It was estimated[1] that in the nineteenth century, Buddhism was a major influence on 40% of the world's population, and even after the upheavals of the present century, its adherents are estimated at about 500 million. Historically speaking, as far as this particular world is concerned, the Dharma (truth, teaching) was first proclaimed 2,500 years ago in India, where it continued to be a major influence until the twelfth century CE.[2] Countries where Buddhism has been traditional include Sri Lanka, Burma, Thailand, Cambodia, Laos, China, Japan, Korea, Mongolia, Tibet, Nepal, Sikkim, Bhutan, and Vietnam. Several of these countries, such as Burma, Thailand, Sri Lanka, Sikkim and Bhutan, still have a majority of the population loyal to Buddhism. In Japan, Buddhism flourishes alongside other religions, and even in the countries which have become communist there is evidence that the religion is still important to many people, for example in China, Laos and Tibet. In this century, especially the second half, people in 'Western' countries (ie America, Europe and Australasia) have taken an interest in Buddhism, and the number of adherents in these countries is growing year by year. 'Buddhism' is a Western term; it means the religion of the *Buddha* (enlightened one), a person who has woken up to the truth about life. Buddhists themselves usually describe their religion as the *Dhamma* (teaching) or *Buddha-dhamma*.

Buddhism is unique among the major world religions in that it is not based upon belief in a personal God, but on human experience and human potential. It is usually counted as a religion because it puts forward a goal for human life which transcends the material world that we perceive with the senses and presents life as having meaning and purpose that implies certain truths and ways of behaving. It is a very rich and varied tradition and has never had a set creed or list of beliefs to which all Buddhists subscribe, or centralised authority to enforce them. It has never been tied up with one particular nationality or culture and as it has spread to different countries and cultures, it has adapted and developed a variety of forms suited to a particular time and place. It has never demanded sole allegiance, and in many Buddhist countries followers of Buddhism also continue practices and customs from local religious traditions. In the opinion of Guy Claxton, 'Buddhism in Sri Lanka, Buddhism in Tibet, and Buddhism in Japan are as different on the surface as Christianity, Judaism and Islam'.[3]

This rich diversity of Buddhism reflects the attitude of the Buddha and his followers to what religion is for. It is not a matter of doctrines and commandments, but of finding practical ways for enabling spiritual progress to be made, by different people in different circumstances and at different rates. The Buddha stressed that his teaching was not to be taken as something sacred in itself, but as a means to an end. In one passage, he compares the *Dharma* (Buddhist teaching) to a raft that serves to carry a person from one side of a dangerous river to another, but which has then served its purpose and should be left behind. 'Using the analogy of a raft, I have shown you the Dharma as something to leave behind, not to take with you' (*Majjhima Nikaya* 1.134). The Buddha also stressed that any teachings, including his own, were not to be blindly accepted with faith and reverence, but should be tested out in experience. 'Do not go by hearsay, what is handed down by others, by what people say, or by what is stated in traditional teachings. Do not go by reasoning, or inferring, by argument, nor by reflection on an opinion, nor from respect for a holy teacher...' (*Anguttara Nikaya* 1.188). In other words, religion is not just something to believe in or discuss, but something to try out to see if it works, if it makes you a better person or takes you nearer to your spiritual goal. The Buddha's invitation was to come and see for yourself (*ehipassiko*). In the rich variety of teachings and practices that make up what we call Buddhism, the true teaching is to be distinguished as follows 'if these teachings lead to dispassion, detachment, decrease of materialism, simplicity, contentment, solitude, energy, and delight in good not evil... of these teachings you may affirm "this is the Dharma, the Master's message"' (*Vinaya* 2.10).

It might be helpful, before entering the complexities of the Buddhist tradition, to give a brief summary of the basics that most Buddhists share, and the major divisions into which Buddhism falls. This is bound to be oversimplified, but it is offered in the spirit of the raft - something that might help you to begin your understanding of Buddhism, but which should be thrown away once you've made further progress. In fact this applies to the whole of this book!

Some Basic Teachings of Buddhism

* Buddhism is about the quest for true happiness and peace for all beings.
* Life as most people live it is unsatisfactory, there is much suffering in the world, and nothing lasts.
* Much suffering is caused by the ignorance and selfishness of people, who are filled with greed for things that neither last nor bring real happiness, with hatred and with deluded beliefs.
* Like other things, human beings are continually changing. One of the deluded beliefs is in a 'real me' (self or soul) that never changes. This constant change applies from minute to minute, day to day and life to life.
* While we remain ignorant and deluded, when one life ends, another life will begin in the world of suffering. Thus most Buddhists believe in rebirth.
* The developments in our lives, and from life to life are the results of our own thoughts and actions. We make our own happiness and unhappiness.
* There is a way out of rebirth into an unsatisfactory world. If we can eliminate greed, hatred, delusion, selfishness and ignorance, by acting morally, training the mind and discovering the truth, there is an alternative state, nirvana, of perfect wisdom and peace. This is very difficult to imagine, and is understood and described in different ways by Buddhists, but basically involves perfect happiness and peace, understanding of life and unselfish love. It is the state Buddhists believe was achieved by the Buddha in the experience known as 'enlightenment'.

You may or may not feel, already, that some of these teachings relate to your own experience of life.

Theravada and Mahayana Buddhism

For convenience, people tend to divide the rich variety of Buddhism as it exists today into two main categories *Theravada* (pronounced Teravada) and *Mahayana*.

Theravada (the way of the elders) is followed in the more southern countries of Sri Lanka, Burma, Thailand, Laos and Cambodia. It is thus sometimes called 'Southern Buddhism' or 'Pali Buddhism', after the language of its scriptures. Mahayana (the great vehicle) is an overall term for the many varieties of Buddhism practised in the more

northern and far-eastern countries. These can be usefully subdivided
into Northern or Tibetan Buddhism, followed in Tibet, Mongolia,
Sikkim, Bhutan, and North-Western China; Eastern Buddhism,
followed in the rest of China, Japan, Korea and Vietnam. Tibetan
Buddhism is represented in four main tradition - Nyingma, Sakya,
Kargyu and Gelug. Among the better known varieties of Eastern
Buddhism are *Zen*, *Pure Land* and *Nichiren* Buddhism. 'Western'
Buddhists tend either to follow one of the traditional Southern,
Northern or Eastern varieties or else choose what they find helpful
from the various traditions, forming their own variety of Buddhism
(e.g. the Western Buddhist Order). This follows the pattern that
occurred as Buddhism spread from India to other countries and
cultures in the past (e.g. China), and reflects the practical orientation
of Buddhism.

Buddhist technical terms exist in many different languages,
including Sanskrit, Pali (the two classical scriptural languages)
Chinese, Japanese and Tibetan. I tend to use the term which has
become most common amongst Western and specifically English
Buddhist usage eg the Sanskrit 'nirvana' rather than the Pali
'nibbana', but the pali 'anatta' rather than the Sanskrit 'anatman'.
As you can see from these examples, the two classical languages
are sufficiently similar for an accurate guess to be made when
coming across an unfamiliar spelling. To avoid confusion, in the
text and glossary, technical terms will be followed in the
Glossary, and where appropriate in the text, by a letter or letters
to indicate their language of origin as follows:

C = Chinese	P = Pali	E = English
S = Sanskrit	J = Japanese	Sn = Sinhalese
K = Korean	T = Tibetan	M = Mongolian
Th = Thai		

---

1. by Rhys Davids in 1877, quoted by Bechert and Gombrich (1984)

2. The letters CE and BCE which appear after dates in this book denote Common
    Era and Before Common Era. These are considered preferable in Religious
    Studies to AD and BC as they avoid the specifically Christian claims contained
    in these abbreviations.

3. Claxton 1989

CHAPTER TWO

THE LIFE AND TEACHING OF THE BUDDHA AND EARLY HISTORICAL DEVELOPMENTS

The Historical and Social Context

The historical figure known as 'the Buddha', or 'Shakyamuni Buddha' (to distinguish him from other Buddhas) lived in Northern India, on the borders with Nepal, about 2,500 years ago. There is some dispute among scholars as to his exact dates. The most common dates quoted are 563-483 BCE, but some recent scholarship prefers 448-368 BCE (Bechert 1982). For our purposes, it is enough to know that there was an historical person who lived on this earth for eighty years somewhere between the 6th and 4th centuries BCE, and that we can know something of the sort of world he lived and taught in, the economic, political and religious background against which his life and teaching can be understood.

The Buddha's world consisted of the civilisation based on the Ganges plain. The people who lived here belonged to various tribal groups which had once been nomadic but were now settled in villages and towns. The ancestry of these people is a mixture of peoples indigenous to India, other groups whose origins may have been in Tibet or Burma and the Aryan (originally European) tribes who invaded North India a thousand years before and gradually imposed their culture and social organisation on the Indian population, without displacing many of the pre-Aryan beliefs and practices.

Compared with the Ganges plain today, in the 5th century BCE the population was far smaller and large areas were still forested. Land for crops could be obtained simply by clearing an area of forest and melting snow from the Himalayas meant that even in the Summer months the large rivers like the Ganges had plenty of water for irrigation purposes. There are three main seasons in this part of the world; from February to May, the hot, dry season; from June to September, the monsoon rains and from October to January the milder, warm, Winter period. This climatic background affected the lifestyle of the early Buddhist monks - it was common to sleep out under trees for most of the year with a minimum of clothing, but during the rainy season when travel was difficult, monks would take up a more permanent residence.

The economy of the Buddha's world was based on agriculture. The main crops grown were rice, millet, wheat, barley, bananas, mangoes, coconuts and dates. This economy was able to support the growth of towns and cities with the growth of trade groups such as wood, iron and leather industries, and there was sufficient wealth to support non-productive professions such as entertainers, intellectuals, and notably religious mendicants dependent on alms. Although the Buddhist scriptures mention a time of famine, there was normally enough food to support a growing population, and the upper classes appear to have lived in some luxury. The fact that life was fairly prosperous is attested by the number of people with the leisure to devote to religion and philosophical questions.

Merchants travelled from city to city with goods and information. The village dwellers lived a fairly simple agricultural life, but in the larger towns where the Buddha's teaching mainly took place, there was a complex society of nobles, businessmen, trade guilds, intellectuals and religious teachers, actors, musicians and dancers, places for drinking and gambling, and prostitutes, some of whom seem to have been quite wealthy and influential. Despite these settlements, there were still vast areas of forest, the home of wild animals such as tigers, monkeys and elephants, and a favourite retreat for the various types of holy men including the Buddha's followers.

Politically, the area was divided into small states. Some of these were simply areas claimed by tribal groups and governed by the leading families as a kind of aristocratic oligarchical republic, developed from the idea of tribal elders. Decisions were made by a regular assembly or 'sangha'. Examples of tribal groups with this kind of government were the Mallas, the Vajjians and the Shakyas to which the Buddha belonged. Other states were organised as monarchies with laws, police and army to back up the authority of the king. These were better adapted to the new urban conditions. In the Buddha's lifetime two powerful kingdoms were Magadha and Kosala. The Buddha was a personal friend of the kings of these states, Bimbisara and his son Ajatasattu of Magadha, and Pasenadi of Kosala. The monarchies gradually absorbed the tribal groups, and after the death of the Buddha, the Kingdom of Magadha expanded to take over the whole Ganges area, and by the third Century BCE became an empire covering most of India. Some scholars argue that the organisation of the Buddhist Sangha (order of monks) shows that the Buddha had a preference for the tribal-republican form of government, but as a matter of historical fact kings have always been very important in the spread of Buddhism from Bimbisara and Pasenadi through the famous third Century BCE Emperor Asoka to the modern King of Thailand.

Religious Background

The period within which the Buddha lived seems to have been a time of religious upheaval and innovation. Both from Buddhist scriptures and other historical sources, we gain a picture of much debate about the fundamental questions of human existence. Many different ideas were being put forward, old ideas questioned or reinterpreted, and new ideas advanced. As well as religious interpretations of life, there were materialists who rejected all spiritual teachings and practices, believing that this material world and what it had to offer in the way of happiness was all there was to life, and that there was no existence beyond this life.

This situation is thought to reflect the social changes from pastoral nomadic tribal groups to settled urban conditions. The pluralistic situation has often been compared to our present religious pluralism. The old traditions just were not appropriate to the new social conditions and new ways of life were being experimented with. Society was also peaceful and prosperous enough to allow people the leisure to discuss philosophical and religious issues.

The Buddha himself was brought up in the rich, privileged, ruling class, but exactly what beliefs he would have been taught as a child is not clear. Later accounts of his life tend to presume a classical Vedic or early Hindu education but it is not clear how far the Vedic culture had permeated the Eastern part of India. However, the religious background of the Buddha can, for convenience, be divided into three groups - the Vedic religion of the Aryan culture, ancient folk beliefs and the Shramana movement of non-conformist religious teachers.

The Vedic Religion

The official religion of the Aryan conquerors of India is referred to as the Vedic Religion after their holy books or *Vedas* (knowledge). The priests of this religion were known as Brahmanas or Brahmins and are often mentioned in the Buddhist scriptures. The Brahmins were very powerful in Aryan society and have retained this position in Hindu society up until modern times. However, we do not know whether they were totally dominant in the Buddha's world as it was a long way east of the centre of the Aryan culture in North West India - they seem more in the position of one influence among several. It is possible that the Buddha first met Brahmins only after leaving his Shakya homeland.

The Vedic religion consisted of the worship of a pantheon of gods who were mostly connected with forces of the natural world, especially those powers on which humans were dependent. There was Surya, the sun god, Indra the storm god, Vayu the wind god, Varuna the sky god, Agni the fire god, Brahma the creator god, and Soma the moon god. The list was traditionally considered to be 33 gods. Many of these are linguistically related to the names of Latin and Greek gods. It was felt necessary to keep these powers on the side of humanity by prayers, hymns and sacrifices. The hymns are recorded in the Rig Veda and are generally full of praise and flattery of the god in question, together with requests for worldly welfare such as good weather, success in agriculture and in battle, wealth, children etc. The gods were worshipped with elaborate rituals involving animal sacrifice, chants and complex techniques known only to the Brahmins. Some rituals involved the use of some intoxicating plant known as 'soma' which heightened the sense of communication with the supernatural powers.

By the time of the Buddha, this originally polytheistic religion was developing into a more pantheistic one. Even in the Rig Veda, although there are hymns to the traditional 33 gods, the gods are also said to number 330 or 330 million, and at the deepest level, one. 'They call it Indra, Mitra, Varuna, Fire...what is but one is called by many names." (*Rig Veda* 1.164.46). Sacrifices were beginning to be seen, not as presents to the gods, but ritual activities that themselves kept the cosmos going. The oldest sections of the Rig Veda, and practices like making offerings for ancestors seem to suggest that life after death was pictured as a heavenly realm. At the time of the Buddha, the religion of the Brahmins was beginning to absorb the concept of rebirth, found in the non-Aryan traditions.

As the only class who knew the vital rituals and formulae, the Brahmin class claimed top place in Aryan society followed by the Kshatriya or warrior class, the Vaishya or merchant/farmer class and the Shudra or servant class. This was the beginning of the later complex Hindu caste system, which was already developing in the Buddha's time as we find many references to class, and even to low persons considered 'untouchable'. However, the Brahmins may not have totally succeeded in imposing this system in the Buddha's world, as he and other Kshatriyas seem to have considered themselves more important than the Brahmin class.

The Buddha seems to have been most critical of the Brahmin tradition. He did not accept their superiority or authority in religious teaching. He taught that true nobility was not gained from birth into a particular class, but a matter of noble behaviour. He accepted people from any caste into his community, though in fact the majority seem to have come from Brahmin, Kshatriya or Vaishya backgrounds rather than the lower groups. He rejected the authority of the Vedic scriptures of which the Brahmins were custodians. He taught that animal sacrifices were both cruel and useless, and that using intoxicants, whether for religious or other reasons would confuse the mind rather than enlighten it. As regards the gods, he did not deny their existence, but did not see them as more than high beings, subject to the same laws of rebirth that apply to human and animal beings, and as therefore not of much help in the religious quest.

The Folk Traditions

Ordinary people were less influenced by the religion of the Brahmins than the dominant classes and had their own beliefs and practices, many of which were probably very ancient and pre-Aryan. These included beliefs about Spirits (either in nature or of the dead), devils, omens and spells, divination, etc. According to Trevor Ling, it was also the ordinary people who focused on the god Brahma, taking him not as one among many gods, but as the creator God who cares for us all, perhaps an idea found in non-Aryan religion. The Buddha was critical, but less severely so, of many of these folk beliefs. He did not reject them utterly but devalued their importance. Brahma exists, but is not as important as they think, he did not create the world and is only one among many Brahma gods. Spells and charms are forbidden to the monks but overlooked in lay people, and the practice of making offerings to the spirits of the dead (*pretas*) is continued but reinterpreted in Buddhism - pretas are one of the forms into which a person might be reborn.

From its beginning up to present times Buddhism has happily coexisted with folk beliefs as can be seen in Buddhist countries today - as long as the priority of Buddhism is clearly recognised, Buddhism is tolerant of such generally harmless practices.

The Shramana Movement

A Shramana, in contrast to a Brahmin, was a type of wandering freelance mendicant philosopher who taught alternative beliefs to those taught by the official Brahmin priesthood. It seems that many people were not satisfied with the established religion which seemed out of date and it became fairly fashionable in certain circles to retire from worldly society to seek for religious truth. The impetus for this trend was probably social change, but perhaps also revival of ancient pre-Aryan traditions such as yoga. Many of the leading figures seem to have belonged to the Kshatriya class, and may have been rulers displaced by political conquest. Some of these 'renouncers' were solitary, others formed organised groups. It is into this movement that the Buddha and his followers fit. There were many different ideas being discussed by the Shramanas, favourite topics being the soul, rebirth, release from the material world, detachment from society. Fashionable methods for finding the religious goal were techniques of yoga and meditation, and the mortification of the material body through acts of extreme asceticism and restraint, renouncing all luxuries. (An ascetic is someone who deliberately lives a life of severe discipline such as fasting, wearing little or no clothing, keeping the body in one position, and other physical hardships.)

The different groups of Shramanas taught different beliefs. Some sought to be loyal to the traditional religion, but reinterpreted it. This tendency is seen in the Hindu scriptures, the Upanishads. The authors of these scriptures saw their meditation and renunciation as the true meaning of sacrifice. They saw Brahman, the holy power or ultimate reality, in all things including the soul or self of human beings. They sought union with this power through knowledge and meditation, thereby freeing their soul from rebirth.

These religious thinkers and their ideas were taken up by the official religion of the Brahmins, transforming it with many ideas such as yoga and rebirth which may have come from the indigenous traditions of India. Although the Upanishads reflect similar concerns to the Shramanas of the Buddhist scriptures, they probably developed in different areas of India, as they show no knowledge of each other.

The Buddhist scriptures themselves mention six teachers by name, whose theories the Buddha criticised. They are interesting because they show some of the ideas Shramanas were putting forward. Nigantha Natapputta has been identified with Mahavira the founder of the Jain religion which has continued until today. The Jains believed that we each have a soul which is imprisoned in a material body and held captive by *karma* (the effects of our actions). The soul could be set free by refraining from actions, living a life of great restraint and austerity. Jains were very strict, taking great care not to harm the tiniest of insects; and many practised extreme asceticism. Ajita Kesakambalin was a materialist who taught that there was no punishment or reward (*karma*) from our good or evil actions and that death was the complete end of us. Makkhali Gosala taught rebirth like the Jains but did not believe in *karma*. In our course of reincarnations, we are totally ruled by fate and must just submit to what happens to us. Purana Kassapa taught that nothing we do with our body can at all affect our soul. Pakudha Kaccayana taught a theory of separate elements which cannot affect each other. Therefore, the soul cannot be killed. These last three are thought to be part of a larger movement which was influential in India up to the middle ages and whose adherents are known as Ajivakas. They believed in reincarnation and fatalism and practised extreme asceticism, perhaps from the idea that each person is destined to a certain quota of suffering which no action of his can avoid. Therefore, asceticism gets it over with quickly and hastens the final deliverance. Sanjaya Belatthaputta would not commit himself to any particular view and was agnostic and sceptical with regard to the possibility of having knowledge of ultimate reality and truth.

✳ The Buddha shared with other Shramanas the ideas of rebirth, the quest for transcendental peace, karma, meditation, detachment and self-discipline, but was very critical of other beliefs. He was particularly critical of belief in an individual separate soul which remained unchanged within a person, and of extreme asceticism and self-torture. He criticised the materialists who felt death was the end, as well as those 'eternalists' who believed in an immortal unchanging soul. He particularly disliked ideas which resulted in morality being irrelevant as in materialism and Ajivaka fatalism. He had no time for the noncommitted sceptics whom he called 'eelwrigglers' as he felt they were refusing to see what was true, and simply displayed their ignorance.

Among this welter of beliefs and opinions, the Buddha taught that he was the only one of his era to base his teaching not on views or speculations and opinions but on direct personal experience of the truth. This direct personal experience is referred to as his 'enlightenment'. Buddhists believe that not only his earlier life, but countless previous lives, prepared the ground for this total insight into reality. After his enlightenment, the Buddha's task was to try and share this insight with others.

The Life of the Buddha

That the man known as the Buddha was a real historical person is not seriously disputed nowadays. However, it is very difficult to establish the exact details of his life history 2,500 years after it happened. The earliest full length biography known to us is the *Acts of the Buddha* written by the first century CE Indian poet Ashvaghosa[1]; it is not surprising to find that after five hundred years legendary and mythological details have found their way into the story. An earlier source is the Pali Canon of the Theravadins, which relates many events from the Buddha's life, but incidentally because of some teaching related to the event, and not in chronological order. Even this source, though reputedly collected together about 3 months after the Buddha's death, was not actually written down until the first century BCE. Thus our story of the Buddha's life is obtained partly from the Pali Canon and partly from later commentaries and legends. It is impossible to separate out fact from legend, but most people are tempted to try to do so, from our knowledge of how legends and myths tend to develop. By 'legend' is meant stories with some possible factual basis, which have been embroidered as they have been passed down. What tends to happen is exaggeration, details are added for ulterior motives, misattribution of events that happen to one person to another, and stereotyping of the story into a neat pattern. By 'myth' is meant stories where meaning is to be sought not in the literal sense, but in a deep symbolic understanding of a truth which was difficult to express other than in this dramatic form. Another sense of the word 'mythological' is to refer to beliefs taken for granted in the world-view of the storytellers which do not figure in our current world view; examples of these would be gods that figure in the Buddha's life story, the heavens and hells, and miraculous powers.

Thus we can either accept uncritically one of the versions of the story, or restrict ourselves to the events related in the Pali Canon only, or attempt some literary criticism and 'demythologising' and reconstruct our own life of the Buddha. It must be remembered that this reconstruction is subjective and provisional; and influenced by current ideas of what is possible and impossible which may themselves be shown to be wrong in the future.

The personal name of the man who became known as 'the Buddha' was Siddhattha Gotama (Pali), Siddhartha Gautama (Sanskrit) - Siddhattha of the Gotama Clan. He belonged to a tribal group known as the Shakyas who inhabited an area in the North East of India on the present day border with Nepal in the foothills of the Himalayas. He belonged to the Kshatriya class, or ruling nobility. All forms of the legend claim that his father was a King, and this is claimed by the Buddha in the Pali Canon: 'A King Suddhodana by name was my father. A Queen Maya by name was the mother that bore me. The royal capital was the city of Kapilavatthu.' (*Digha Nikaya* 14) However, modern scholars believe that the Shakya tribe was ruled by an assembly of tribal elders, evidence for which is found in the Pali Canon itself, therefore Suddhodana was probably 'the elected head of an aristocratic hereditary ruling class' (Ling *The Buddha*, 1976, p 108) - a local leader rather than a very great king. This exaggeration is a natural way for the legend to develop, especially as monarchies took over from republics as the form of government in the centuries following the Buddha.

From the commentary and legends we learn that the Buddha was born (on the full moon of May according to Theravada tradition) in a garden called Lumbini. At the time of his conception ten months earlier, Maya dreamed that a white elephant entered her womb. Even in the Pali Canon it is suggested that this conception occurred miraculously through the *bodhisattva* ('Buddha-to-be') descending directly from the heaven where he spent his penultimate life into his mother's womb, with no mention of his father being involved. Some versions (eg *Lalitavistara*) stress that the Queen conceived while undertaking a temporary vow of chastity, but Ashvaghosa's version suggests that the conception was more normal. Other miraculous details of the birth, found even in the Pali Canon, include a 10-month pregnancy, miraculous jets of water, birth from her side while standing, totally clean; his immediately taking seven steps and proclaiming his mission; a shining light and an earthquake; the attendance and homage of deities. This story is a good example of myth, meaning that the message of the story is symbolic - that this was no ordinary man, but one unique in our world.

Maya is said to have passed away seven days after the birth, and to have been reborn in a heaven. The bodhisattva was cared for by Mahapajapati Gotami, his mother's sister who was also married to his father. His future destiny was foretold at his birth by an old Brahmin sage called Asita, and at his naming ceremony on the fifth day, by eight Brahmins. The legend refers to a prophecy that the boy would grow up to be one of two things: a universal emperor, or a Buddha (enlightened teacher) depending on whether he ever stopped to think about suffering. As a result, his father tried to keep all knowledge of suffering from him.

To his childhood and youth there are only two references in the Pali Canon. We are told that he was brought up in luxury and refinement and that once as a young man he sat under a roseapple tree while his father was working, and in this peace achieved the first level of meditation. This story is told in various forms in the later accounts, where is explained that the 'King' was involved in ceremonial ploughing during an agricultural festival and where the *bodhisattva*'s age varies from infancy through teens to twenty-nine. Other stories from later legends include the two which show his sensitivity and compassion even when young. In one story he is taken to see the beauty of the countryside, but he notices the reality - that the peasants and their oxen are exhausted by their work, and that small creatures like frogs, worms and insects are killed. In another, his cousin

Devadatta, who later figures as his main enemy, shot down a swan which was hurt but not killed. Against Devadatta's plan for a meal, the bodhisattva rescued the swan and, nursing it back to health, set it free. In later legends he is assumed to have been a brilliant child with knowledge of many languages as well as the warrior skills of his class. Some scholars question whether writing was known in this culture, but we do know from archaeology that scripts had developed by the next century or so.

He was married at 16, according to the legends, to a neighbouring 'princess' whose names is usually given as Yasodhara. Following the customs of the time, he won her hand in a contest of warrior skills - archery, fencing and riding. In some versions he also had a harem of dancing girls.

The Four Signs

The time when he really began to think about life occurred at the age of 29.[2] According to the commentaries and legends, the young 'prince' had led a very sheltered life, with all possible luxuries, deliberately kept away from all experience of sickness, old age or death in an attempt by his father to prevent him renouncing the world as the prophecies had foretold. However, on excursions from the palaces with his charioteer Channa, he saw four sights that changed his life. These were a tired, wrinkled, worn-out old man, a man in great pain with a diseased body, a corpse being taken to the cremation ground, and a religious ascetic. In Ashvaghosa's account, these figures had to be conjured up by the gods, as the 'King's' plan for removing such sights had been so successful. However, in the Pali Canon, there is evidence that this story really represents an event which occurred in the bodhisattva's own mind; and the story as it is told in the legends has an artificial, stereotyped form which is difficult to accept literally - for example, could anyone have reached the age of 29 without ever experiencing any pain or illness? Thus this story is myth dramatising the gradual dawning on the bodhisattva of the reality of suffering 'Whilst I had such power and fortune, yet I thought when an untaught ordinary man, who is subject to ageing sees another who is aged, he is shocked, humiliated and disgusted, for he forgets that he himself is no exception. But I too am subject to ageing, not safe from ageing, and so it cannot befit me to be shocked, humiliated and disgusted on seeing another who is aged. When I considered this the vanity of youth left me.' (*Anguttara Nikaya* 3:38) Similarly, he lost the vanity of health on considering sickness, and the vanity of life considering the inevitability of death. It is possible that if he had been brought up to believe in Brahma, the creator God, he abandoned the belief at this time. The 'sight' of the ascetic represents

his decision to renounce the transient pleasure of his life and seek a
solution to sickness, old age and death in religious asceticism. The
Pali Canon tells us that he decided to seek after 'the unborn,
unageing, unailing, deathless, sorrowless, undefiled supreme
surcease of bondage, nibbana' (*Majjihima Nikaya* 26) and that 'while
still young, a black haired boy blessed with youth and in the first
phase of life I shaved off my hair and my beard -though my mother
and father wished otherwise and grieved with tearful faces - and I put
on the yellow robe and went forth from the house life into
homelessness.' (*Majjihima Nikaya* 36) The later legends make the
story of the Great Renunciation more dramatic. The prince became
thoroughly disgusted with his life of pleasure, and his beautiful
dancing girls looked ugly to him, asleep after a party. The Great
Renunciation took place on the same night as Yasodhara bore him a
son, Rahula. It is said that the bodhisattva left home secretly in the
middle of the night, and crept in to his wife's bedroom to glimpse his
new-born son. However, he deliberately avoided waking his wife or
looking at the baby's face in case it weakened his resolve. This is
symbolic of the complete detachment necessary for enlightenment.

The *bodhisattva* left home and became a wandering, possessionless
ascetic as many others were at that time. Many current teachers were
claiming to offer the answers to life's questions and practical methods
for achieving peace of mind and salvation. Common practices were
extreme asceticism or self-torture, and various meditational or yogic
techniques. One common theory was that such practices could set
one's eternal soul free from the confines of the material body into
eternal peace. The Canon records the names of two teachers from
whom the bodhisattva learned techniques of meditation, Alara
Kalama and Uddaka Ramaputta. From these teachers the *bodhisattva*
learned how to achieve advanced levels of meditative states, known
in Buddhism as the mental state of 'nothingness' and of 'neither
perception-nor-nonperception'. However, the bodhisattva had not
yet found the complete release he was looking for and moved on from
these teachers. It is possible that with these teachers he first discussed
the ideas of rebirth, *karma*, and release as we know from Hindu and
Jain sources that such ideas were current amongst ascetics at the time.

He then decided to attempt extreme asceticism as a method of
completely destroying attachment to transient existence and breaking
through into eternal peace. Many of the ascetic groups believed that
harsh treatment of the body would lead to liberation of the soul for
example the Jains. Some of these ascetic practices are followed by
'holy men' of India even today. According to the Pali Canon the
bodhisattva spent six years as an ascetic following practices that sound
quite horrific. He either went without clothes or with rough clothes

made of materials like horsehair. He either went without washing for long periods or tried constant bathing. He spent long periods in one position without moving, like standing or squatting or holding one arm above the head. He pulled out his hair and beard. He deliberately lived in places like wild animal infested forests or cremation grounds, laid on beds of thorns to sleep, sought out the hot sun or the cold snow, lived at times in total solitude, tried to stop or slow his breathing, fasted, ate excrement and finally stopped eating altogether. Such practices are bound to teach you something about yourself and have some effect on the mind. Possibly some practitioners did have hallucinations brought on by deprivations and felt that they had reached divine realms.

Gautama himself found that he learned great self control, how to conquer fear, desire and disgust, and have much greater control over the mind. However, none of these practices really got him anywhere on his quest for the truth about life. So when, just about exhausted by his final fast, he decided to give up these austerities and accepted a meal of milk rice brought to him by a girl, and decided to concentrate on meditation instead. His ascetic companions left in disgust at what they saw as weakness. This six years of trying himself to the limit was perhaps an important psychological preparation for his enlightenment experience, which follows soon after this decision. The *bodhisattva*'s rejection of the extreme ascetic path is highly significant for Buddhism, which advises the middle way between self indulgence and self torture. Buddhists believe in strict self control, but not pointless suffering, helping others rather than total solitude, working to improve the world as well as yourself. It probably influenced the Buddhist rejection of a separate inner 'soul' substance untouched by what happens to the body, as the bodhisattva found by experience that physical sufferings do affect the mental or psychic parts of a person; a human being is not a soul imprisoned in a body but a psychophysical unity.

The Enlightenment

After five premonitory dreams and on the same night as accepting the meal, refreshed in mind and body, the bodhisattva sat under a tree in Bodhgaya and spent the whole night in meditation, during which he gradually gained insight into the nature of human existence and actually realised his goal of perfect peace. It is said that he decided to do this in recalling the sense of peace he had had years before sitting under a roseapple tree. He vowed to himself to make one last effort and that he would not move from the spot until he had found the answer he was looking for.

The myth relates that he was tempted by Mara (the Buddhist personification of change and death, often called 'the evil one') not to go through with this effort. The temptations represent his fears, doubts and desires to return to worldly pleasures. However, the bodhisattva had gained enough merit and self control to conquer these temptations. Mara, in desperation, is said to have tried to dispute the *bodhisattva*'s right to the piece of earth he was sitting on, but the *bodhisattva* touched the earth and called the earth goddess to testify to his right to sit there. Mara fled defeated and the bodhisattva went into a deep meditative state. The enlightenment experience is stereotyped into the four stages of the night. In the first watch of the night (6 to 10 pm) he successively reached the four stages of *jhana* ('absorption or deep meditative state') reached in Buddhist meditation. Such experiences are difficult to describe in words, but the traditional description of the four jhanas is that the first stage is a kind of detached and calm thinking, where one feels joy and rapture and is only just one remove from everyday consciousness. The second *jhana* is more detached and ordinary discursive thinking (the 'chatter' of the mind) fades away leaving joy and rapture. The third *jhana* reaches a purer joy. In the fourth *jhana* even joy fades away leaving a mind peaceful, tranquil, clear, a sharp tool ready to pierce into reality. With his mind prepared in this way, the *bodhisattva* went on to 'superknowledges'. The first of these occurred in this first watch of the night when the *bodhisattva* began to recall all of his past existences. These memories are believed to be normally locked away in the subconscious mind, but the successful meditator (and occasionally people who are hypnotised) can bring them into the light of consciousness. The *bodhisattva* recalled thousands and thousands of lives in details as if living them over again. Buddhists claim that some of these lives are retold in the Jataka tales of the Pali Canon. Full of compassion his next thought was that all other beings have to go through this process of life after life, getting nowhere fast, and how empty and pointless it all seemed.

Then in the next watch (10 pm to 2 am) he gained another superknowledge, known in Buddhist terminology as 'the heavenly eye'. This is the clairvoyant ability actually to see other beings coming to be and passing away, in and out of all the different possible realms of existence - not just human lives, but animals and beings that dwell in different dimensions like the so-called gods, ghosts and inhabitants of hells. In all this coming and going, beings made their own suffering through their own behaviour. This observation is called in Buddhism 'the law of *karma*'. The *bodhisattva* was full of pity for all beings who went through this time and time again without knowing why or what to do about it.

In the third watch (2 am to 6 am) he achieved the highest superknowledge which is synonymous with perfect wisdom: 'the knowledge of the destruction of the *asavas* (outflows)'. This means the end of all worldly desires, wrong views, ties to the process of becoming and - most of all - the end of all ignorance.

There are various ways of describing what the knowledge gained in enlightenment is: it is complete understanding of how beings come to be as they are and what can be done about it, along with knowing that you yourself have actually achieved liberation from the state of ignorance and suffering. The knowledge has been formulated in various ways - as the four noble truths which explain why life is suffering and how we can be released from it, or as the 12 interrelated conditions that cause our suffering lives, and can be undone to release us from it. The Four Noble Truths and the 12 conditions will be described later in dealing with the Buddha's ways of putting his experience into words in order to share it with others (see page 27). The exact nature of the personal experience of the Buddha ('the enlightened one', as he is now entitled to be called), cannot be known by the unenlightened or described in words. It consisted of perfect peace, utter conviction that he had finally reached the truth, and the experience of actually having broken away from the karmic chain of existence and through into a state of no more suffering, known to Buddhists as *nibbana* (P) or *nirvana* (S). Symbolically, this breakthrough coincided with the rising of the sun at 6 in the morning. There are verses in the Buddhist poem called the Dhammapada which are traditionally held to describe the Buddha's feelings at this time:

> Seeking but not finding the House Builder
> I travelled through the round of countless births
> O painful is birth ever and again.
> House Builder you have now been seen
> You shall not build the house again
> Your rafters have been broken down
> Your ridge pole is demolished too.
> My mind has now attained the unformed nibbana
> And reached the end of every craving.
>
> (*Dhammapada* verses 153-4)

> I have conquered all; I know all, and my life is pure.
> I have left all, and I am free from craving.
> I myself found the way.
> Whom shall I call Teacher?
> Whom shall I teach?
>
> (*Dhammapada* verse 353)

This last verse expresses the special status of a Buddha - one who has found the truth for himself without reliance on any guru (teacher).

Teaching Ministry

After that morning, the new Buddha spent some time assimilating his experience in great bliss and deep meditation. This time has been stereotyped into a period of seven times seven days.

During this time, the Buddha received his first disciples who were significantly laymen. Two passing merchants offered him food and formally 'took refuge' in the Buddha and his teaching. (Modern Buddhists take refuge in the Buddha, his teaching and the community, but at that time there was no Buddhist community). A third story tells us that the Buddha was inclined to dwell by himself in this attainment, because it would be almost impossible to explain what he had discovered to anyone else, being something beyond reason and words, and totally opposed to most people's interests. (This story is reassuring for anyone finding teaching or learning about Buddhism difficult!) However, prompted by the Indian god Brahma, who appears as a kind of good angel, he decided out of compassion for all beings to make an attempt at teaching, because some might be able to profit from it. Having made this decision, Buddha first thought of his old meditation teachers who seemed to have got nearest to the truth, but on discovering that these were dead, thought next of his five ascetic companions and set out for the Deer Park in Benares where they were living. The Pali Canon records the name of a man he met on the way who missed his big chance to become the first **monk** disciple of the Buddha - Upaka, who just shrugged his shoulders in an agnostic response to the Buddha's announcement that he had conquered the Truth.

Upon reaching the Deer Park, the five ascetics were prepared to ignore him but were soon impressed by his manner, and to them he preached his first sermon, which is known as the Deer Park Sermon, or the 'Setting in Motion of the Wheel of the Law', explaining the Four Noble Truths. His preaching was so powerful that one of the five gained immediate insight into the truth that 'all that is arising is subject to cessation' - an intuitive grasp of the Buddha's teaching known technically as the 'Dhamma vision' (literally: 'eye of the *Dhamma*). He formally committed himself to following the Buddha and his teaching, as did the other five. After a further sermon on the nature of the self, the five completely broke through into full knowledge and liberation and became enlightened like the Buddha. They are not however called Buddhas, as they were dependent upon someone else to teach them. They are called *arahats* (P) or *arhats* (S), which means 'worthy ones'.

The Buddha spent the next 45 years travelling around North-East

India teaching people from all walks of life, disregarding caste distinctions and gaining followers in four categories, monks, nuns, laymen and laywomen - the four-fold *sangha* (community). During his lifetime he enabled many other people to gain the enlightenment that he had gained, often quite quickly, as with the first five arhats. By the time he died he left a considerable following, including hundreds if not thousands of enlightened people. We have no connected chronological account of how he spent his 45 years ministry, but there are many events that deserve mentioning. Later commentators have arranged the events in a possible chronological order, especially for the first twenty years of the ministry.

The events attributed to the first year are the conversion of a young nobleman called Yasa, who like himself had become sickened by the worldly pleasures. Yasa became the seventh arhat and joined the order of monks, and Yasa's Father, Mother and wife became the first laymen and laywomen to formally take refuge in the Buddha, his teaching and his community. Many of Yasa's friends left home, shaved their heads, donned the yellow robe and joined the emerging order. When the number of *arhats* reached 61, the Buddha sent them out to preach, and when their converts reached such large numbers that it was difficult for the Buddha to ordain them personally, he gave his monks (*bhikkhus*) the power to ordain others themselves with a simple ceremony.

The purpose of the order, or monastic *sangha*, is to spread the message of the Buddha and thus enable people to gain enlightenment. Over the years, in response to situations that cropped up, the Buddha made further rules and regulations for his order, both moral and practical, which are remembered in the *Vinaya* or discipline section of the scriptures.

Also during the first year, he converted thirty people on a picnic who had lost their valuables by preaching on the theme that they would gain more by seeking for themselves rather than the thief; and a large group of fire-worshipping ascetics by performing greater wonders than their leader, controlling fire and water, and by preaching to them on the theme of fire - the fires that we should be concerned about are not sacrificial ones but the inner fires of the lusts and hates associated with the six senses. By this time the group is reputed to be a thousand strong and to have reached Rajagaha, capital of Magdha, where the King Bimbisara was converted and donated a Bamboo Grove as a dwelling place for the monks. Soon after this two of his most famous disciples, Sariputta and Moggallana, were converted and gained the Dhamma-vision immediately upon hearing a monk preach, and were *arhats* within 14 and 7 days respectively. Sariputta is famous for his great wisdom and Moggallana for his psychic powers. Other famous disciples include Kassapa and Ananda, who was a relative of the Buddha and his constant companion in later life. Ananda is famous for his soft heart and his good memory. Later he was important for the recitation of the Buddha's teaching after the Buddha's death.

In the Spring following his enlightenment, the Buddha returned home to visit his family. In order to convince them of his attainment, he had to display miraculous powers causing jets of fire and water to flow from his limbs. The Buddha is credited with many miraculous abilities such as being able to read minds, see events around the universe, visit other dimensions, walk through walls, etc but these are mostly down-played. These are considered psychic rather than supernatural abilities, and there are no healing miracles of the type seen in the Christian gospels. He was reconciled with his father (who died an *arhat* four years later) and his aunt, and he ordained his seven year old son, Rahula, into the order when sent by his wife to claim the inheritance due to him. After his father's death, his aunt Mahapajapati became the first nun, after much persuasion of the Buddha who, according to the story, was reluctant to ordain women. Buddhist feminists have often attributed this reluctance to the prejudice of later celibate monks rather than the enlightened one himself.

During the third year of his ministry, he was given another park by a rich man called Anathapindaka, in Savatthi in Kosala country. The Buddha is often shown spending the rains retreat or preaching in this park and the Bamboo Grove given by King Bimbisara.

Every year the community would spend the months of the monsoon - July, August, September - in one place. This custom started not only because it is hard to travel about in the rains, but also because it is the growing season and travelling monks could interfere with agriculture by trampling down the newly-sprouted crops. While staying in Savatthi, the other major power in the area, Pasenadi, King of Kosala, was also converted to Buddhism.

Events in the next few years include the incident of Nanda, his aunt's son, who found it impossible to meditate because of thinking of the beauty of his ex-girlfriend. The Buddha showed his skill at teaching by showing Nanda a vision of the heavenly nymphs he could attain if he paid attention to his meditation -of course, upon attaining arhatship he no longer desired such things and so did gain 'as many girls as he wanted'. Such skilful techniques are called in Buddhism *upaya-kausalya* (skill in means), one of the qualities of an enlightened person. Another achievement of these years was the prevention of a war between the Sakya and Koliya clans about irrigation of a river, by pointing out the superior value of human life over bits of land. According to tradition Buddha spent the 7th retreat of his ministry preaching to his mother in the heaven she was reborn into.

The tenth year of the ministry saw the first quarrel in the community of monks over a trivial matter. After preaching on the way to live together, the Buddha went off alone to find peace. In the fourteenth year, his son, Rahula, was old enough to receive full ordination (20 years old). In the seventeenth year, the Buddha is reputed to have refused to preach until a poor hungry peasant was fed. This story is remembered by those who argue that Buddhism implies social action. In the twentieth year, the Buddha converted a famous robber called Angulimala (garland of fingers of his victims). Courageously the Buddha went to his den alone, and when Angulimala tried to pursue him, the robber found he could not catch up with the monk. The Buddha explained that although outwardly he seemed to be moving fast, inwardly he had come to a stop. In order to find this calm, Angulimala became a monk and later an arhat and has become patron saint of childbirth because he once took pity on a woman in a difficult labour. He is also remembered by those who work with offenders.

By this time the Buddha's fame led to jealousy and attempts were made to discredit him by other sects. For example, one woman claimed to be pregnant by him, another claimed that he had raped and killed a nun. However, none of these stories had any success.

For the last 25 years of his life, Ananda became his permanent attendant. During this time, many more rules and regulations became necessary for the monastic *sangha*. Apparently the first rule - no sexual intercourse - came about when a monk visited his ex-wife because she wanted a son. The rules for helping the sick came about when the community neglected a diseased monk. The Buddha on this occasion taught by example, cleaning up the mess and tending the monk himself. Regular meetings began to be held to recall the rules; eventually, this became once a fortnight. Things were learned as the community went along. For example, moderation in meditation was realised after 30 monks committed suicide after too much meditation on the theme of disgust for the body. The Buddha himself always got involved, as when he tested out the adequacy of the triple robe on the coldest night. He was a gifted teacher and always taught at the level of his listener. When he saw boys illtreating fish he asked them how they would like it and told them about *karma*, that your actions will bear fruit in your later life or lives.

He often taught in parables such as the famous parable of the blind men and the elephant. In it, blind men are led into a room and asked to describe an elephant. As each is touching only one part of the elephant, they all come to different conclusions - an elephant is like a brush (the tail), a plough (the tusk), etc and eventually come to blows. This story was told to illustrate why religious teachers disagree.

Throughout his life the Buddha is shown in disputes with teachers of other sects: Brahmins, Jains, Ajivakas and materialists. He criticised their ideas of sacrifice and ritual, of an eternal unaffected soul, and that moral behaviour doesn't matter, either because there is no *karma* or life after death, or because of the fatalistic view of the Ajivakas.

His skill with individuals has been shown in the case of Nanda and Angulimala, and also in the story of Kisagotami. This lady came to the Buddha distraught after the death of her baby, perhaps hoping that this holy man could bring her baby back to life. As she was in no state to listen to a sermon on the impermanence of all things, the Buddha said he would save her baby if she could bring back a mustard seed from a house where no-one had died. As she went on her quest Kisagotami found out for herself that death is present everywhere. She went on to become a nun.

Death

Towards the end of his life the Buddha was saddened by the deaths of his two loyal friends Bimbisara and Pasenadi. He also had to contend with the plots of his cousin Devadatta who tried to kill him in various ways. However, all would-be assassins were converted by the Buddha's charm. Devadatta set up a rival order with stricter rules, but it did not prosper. Both Sariputta and Moggallana died before the Buddha, the latter violently.

Finally, aged 80, the Buddha became ill and died. The tradition maintains that he could have lived for an aeon if Ananda had only taken the hint and asked him to. He became ill after eating a meal of 'sweetpig' which is thought to be either pork or some sort of mushroom. He was in great pain but remained calm and in control, thinking of others. For instance, he tried to reassure the man who provided the meal that it was not his fault. It is significant that he died in an obscure place - Kusinara - which shows his humility and desire for people to listen to his message rather than make a fuss about his person. He criticised Ananda for being upset and said that this showed he had not been listening all these years to his teaching that all things are impermanent. He said that the *Dharma* (S) should now be their teacher and asked for last-minute questions. His last •

words were to remind them that 'subject to decay are all compounded things, so be mindful and vigilant in working out your own salvation.' He finally went into deep meditation and is said to have spent his last conscious moment in the fourth *jhana* of total peace and calm. This event is known as the Parinirvana or final passing into nirvana.

After his death, there was a wake of six days of music and reverence and then he was cremated. The bones remained unburned and were distributed as relics between the rulers of the different tribes and kingdoms. Stupas or burial monuments were built over these relics and veneration of them began. It is significant that the relics were given to the lay people rather than the monks who should not be concerned with such externals. The places of his birth, enlightenment, first sermon and death soon became places of pilgrimage.

Other Lives and Other Buddhas, Other Realms and Other Worlds

The preceding section gives some idea of who the Buddha was, at least, if by the Buddha is meant Siddhartha Gautama, Shakyamuni, the wise man of the Shakya tribe. However, when looking at pictures in temples or books it can be confusing to find that these represent not Shakyamuni but either some event in his previous lives or some other Buddha altogether. To understand this it is necessary to look at the Buddhist cosmology or world view.

With regard to time, the ancient Indian view, which probably goes back into prehistory, is that time, like the sun and the seasons, moves in cycles rather than straight lines. Beings die only to be reborn again and repeat the cycle of birth, growth, decay and death seen all around us in nature. More than this, holy men like the Buddha claim to have gained the power or superknowledge to recall these lives, which in most people are subconscious. There are hundreds of *Jataka* (birth) stories in the Pali Canon which claim to be stories of the *Bodhisattva's* previous births. In the main body of scriptures these previous lives are always human - in the Jataka collection they may be animal, or in the form of a tree spirit. Some of the stories may really have been told by the Buddha as stories of his previous lives, others are possibly parables which have been mistaken for Jataka stories. Others are good folk stories which have got themselves added to the collection. Whatever the source, the main function of these stories is twofold - to impress upon the audience the extreme effort needed to become a Buddha, thousands of lives of striving, and secondly to teach a specific virtue. They are very popular ways of teaching virtuous behaviour to children.

One of the most famous of all is the story which is supposed to represent the Buddha's last-but-two-life (the last-but-one was spent in a heaven world) as Prince Vessantara. This Prince was so generous that he gave away everything he possessed. First he gave away the most precious possession of his kingdom - a white elephant with the power of guaranteeing rain. For this he was exiled from the kingdom and before leaving he gave away all his money and possessions. In exile he gave away his children to a Brahmin who needed servants, and finally gave away his wife to a man who was luckily the god Indra in disguise. Indra rewarded his generosity by returning his wife, the family were finally reunited and lived happily ever after.

Another story illustrates compassion. The *Bodhisattva*, as a young prince, slits his own throat in order that a starving tigress with seven hungry cubs might live by eating his flesh.[3]

These stories are obviously much more dramatic and interesting than these brief summaries suggest. They are acted out and painted as friezes. They are not meant to be taken as literal models to follow, but to show the kind of attitude Buddhists should have. Other stories illustrate other virtues. Once when the *Bodhisattva* was an ascetic, he practised the virtue of patience even when a wicked king cut his body into pieces bit by bit. He felt no hatred, only pity for the king. The virtue of silence is shown by the story of a partridge who was only caught when he made a noise. The virtue of respect for seniority is shown by the story of the partridge who was revered by the much larger elephant and monkey, because although they remembered a great tree when it was just a sapling, he remembered eating the seed! Another favourite is the story of the Monkey King, who died to save his fellow monkeys.[4]

The Buddhist worldview considers that our dimension of humans and animals is only one among many. There are altogether 31 different planes of existence, divided into three realms. The lowest realm, of desire, includes humans and animals, demons, hells, *pretas* (spirits of the dead) and six different levels of gods including the 33 Vedic gods like Indra (level 2). Above this is the realm of form, consisting of 16 increasingly rarified forms of gods, with the Brahma-type gods at the lower end. Above this is an even more rarified realm, the formless realm, where the form of existence is unimaginable. The Buddhist goal of nirvana is beyond even these rarified forms of existence. In the process of rebirth, we may find ourselves in any of these realms, depending on our *karma* (actions).

Just as beings live over and over again, so does the world-system. Other Buddhas taught in previous world systems, millions of aeons ago. Their message was identical to that of Shakyamuni, but in each age there is a need for a new Buddha to teach all over again. The Pali Canon originally listed 6 previous Buddhas, but it soon expanded to 24. One of the previous lives of our Buddha is said to have taken place during the time of the 24th-before Buddha, Dipankara, when inspired by this example, the being who was much later to become Shakyamuni first made the decision to strive for Buddhahood. There will be another Buddha, called Maitreya, in the next age. His time is expected to be a 'golden age' when life will be better, and it will be easier to attain enlightenment. Many modern Buddhists aspire through their good works to be born in his time. At present he is believed to live in the 4th desire-realm heaven, Tusita, as do all *bodhisattvas* in their penultimate life.

Mahayana Buddhists have an even larger view of the universe. As well as Buddhas in previous ages, there are countless Buddhas in all directions in other world systems, existing simultaneously. Some of these have names, and many of the Buddha statues commonly seen are of these cosmological Buddhas rather than the historical one, for example, Amida Buddha who dwells in a world system to the West. The fat, jolly Buddhas seen in Chinese tradition are representations of Maitreya, the Buddha to come. More of the Mahayana worldview and Buddhology will be explained later in chapter 4. The important thing to remember about Buddhist cosmology is that the world we experience with the senses is just one small part of the lowest realm of one world system among many. Buddhists believe that in advanced meditation other realms and even worlds can be experienced.

What the Buddha Taught

The message of the Buddha is known as the *Dharma* (S) or *Dhamma* (P), a word which is hard to translate but covers the meanings of teaching, truth, law, order, duty, righteousness. It is the Buddhist word for Buddhism.

The exact content of this message is a matter of controversy. There are vast scriptures claiming to be the word of the Buddha, with some contradictions, especially between the scriptures of the Theravada and Mahayana traditions. Here we concentrate on the basics that no

Buddhist would deny, even though some Mahayanists would see them as only preliminary teachings.

Although the Buddha taught with great authority as one who was utterly convinced he had actually experienced the truth, he stressed that people should not believe just because he said so, but should test out his words by thinking things out for themselves, and in their own experience in both meditation and daily life.

Most accounts of the Buddha's teaching begin, logically, with his First Sermon on the Four Noble Truths. However, this sermon was given to five ascetic religious specialists and can sometimes give people the impression that Buddhism is (a) rather gloomy and depressing, and (b) intellectual and difficult. When talking to ordinary lay people the Buddha did not start with the Noble Truths but with 'morality, giving, heavens and detachment'. He taught about *karma* and rebirth, and how we could prepare for a better rebirth in a heavenly realm by living a moral and responsible life, not seeking happiness in transient material goods, and by unselfish kindness to all. Although there are many moral guidelines, the Buddhist attitude to life, like the Christian one, is not based on rules but on an unconditional love for all beings. This is expressed in the wish of the *Metta Sutta* (discourse on love) most characteristic of Buddhism, 'May all beings be happy and at their ease' and the advice that 'Even as a mother watches over and protects her child, her only child, so with boundless mind should one cherish all living beings, radiating love over the entire world, above, below, and all around without limit'. (*Suttanipata* 5:143)

Only on the basis of this preparation were people ready to understand the deeper teachings of Buddhism, expressed in such teachings as the Four Noble Truths. These teachings are preserved in the form of formulae such as the 'Four Truths' and the 'Twelve links of dependent origination', but these should be seen as convenient ways of remembering the Buddha's teaching and not the only way of expressing it - the Buddha himself felt that no words and formulae could really capture the experience he was trying to share.

The Four Noble Truths

The Buddha's first sermon is known as the Deer Park Sermon, or the Setting in Motion of the Wheel of the Law. In this sermon, the Buddha explained what he had discovered in terms of Four Truths, which function as a kind of doctor's diagnosis of the human condition - what is wrong with life, why it is wrong, the announcement of the good news that something can be done, and finally the prescription or way of life that will bring about the cure.

His sermon began by explaining to the ascetics that he had found by experience that both a life of hedonistic (pleasure seeking) self-indulgence and extreme self-mortification (denial of pleasure) were harmful and that the way of life that led to his insight, peace and enlightenment was a life of moderation, the Middle Path, which had enabled him to see clearly the Four Truths.

The First Truth

'This is the Holy Truth of Suffering: birth is suffering, ageing is suffering, sickness is suffering, death is suffering, sorrow and lamentation, pain, grief and despair are suffering, association with what is loathed is suffering, dissociation from the loved is suffering, not to get what one wants is suffering -in short, the five categories affected by clinging are suffering'. (*Samyutta Nikaya* 5:421-3)

The first truth is the statement that there is something fundamentally wrong with life as most beings experience it. The word translated by 'suffering' is *dukkha* (P), a word which does mean illness or pain but also a more basic unsatisfactoriness. There are said to be three forms of *dukkha* - plain ordinary suffering such as the examples listed above, pain and death, frustration of desires, having to watch the suffering of people we love. The more thoughtful and sensitive a person is, like the young bodhisattva, the more suffering one is aware of - the sufferings of other people in situations of poverty, famine and war, the sufferings of animals. Even without all the suffering caused by people's evil deeds, nature itself seems built on a system of competition, exploitation and suffering; animals prey on one another, disease and disaster occur through no one's fault. Then there is the suffering inherent in all pleasant situations because of the fact that everything changes all the time. The word for impermanence in Buddhism is *anicca* (P), one of the fundamental characteristics of life. Life does have many beautiful and enjoyable aspects, but these also cause suffering because they do not last and the more beautiful and enjoyable, the more suffering occurs when they pass. All beautiful things decay, our loved ones die, and even if the things and people remain, sometimes it is we who change and suddenly we are bored with something or someone that once gave us great pleasure. This is why even people who outwardly seem to have everything are still unhappy. The third form of *dukkha* is a more subtle dissatisfaction with life itself rather than any specific problem - a sense of frustration at the limitations of human existence, our limited powers, our lack of knowledge, the way we never really know what any of our actions are going to lead to, how we cannot really plan for the future, and that it is all going to end in death anyhow, which makes it seem pointless. A psychological term for this general insecurity is *angst* or anguish; a

Buddhist image is that life is 'as unsubstantial as the pith of a plantain tree' (ie empty). The Indian world-view, which involves our having to repeat this seemingly endless cycle of birth, growth, decay and death, over and over again, makes the prospect even more depressing. Buddhists feel that this first truth is undeniable to anyone who stops to think, and that in Buddha's enlightened experience, he actually saw this situation in its fullness, applying to every living being.

The Second Truth

The second truth asks what causes this suffering. The Buddha's answer was that suffering (ie existence in this world) is caused by our own *tanha* (craving) or selfish desires, which themselves spring from our *avidya* (ignorance) of the whole situation. This is not to say that every specific evil that occurs to us is traceable to a specific selfish desire on our part, but that our being here in such a state at all is attributable to our own fault.

'This is the Noble Truth of the Origin of suffering: It is craving which produces renewal of being, is accompanied by relish and greed, seeking its delight now here, now there, in other words craving for sensual experience, craving for being (ie eternal life), craving for non-being (ie oblivion).' (*Samyutta Nikaya* 5)

It is easy to agree that in some cases selfish cravings lead to suffering, as in excessive drinking leading to hangovers, but the Buddha attributes our being here at all in such a world to our own selfish craving. This is not so easy to understand for Westerners who do not share the Indian view of the cyclic nature of life. Put simply, it is as if we are addicted to worldly life, as to cigarettes or heroin. It only brings us suffering and can never bring us satisfaction, yet each time we die we crave for more. This craving is of three kinds - for more experience of the senses, or simply to continue existing, and even craving for oblivion brings us back to this world, as this suicidal desire is simply another sort of selfishness, wanting to avoid trouble. The chain reaction of our desire and cravings leading to further unsatisfactory experience is called *punabbhava* (rebecoming). Rebecoming happens from moment to moment, as what we do in one moment leads to consequences for what we are and how we feel in the next. Rebirth is simply a more outwardly observable moment of rebecoming, when one physical body is outworn. The whole cycle of rebecoming from moment to moment and life to life is called *samsara*. The force which keeps the cycle of *samsara* in motion is *karma* (S), *kamma* (P), literally 'action', meaning cause and effect. One of the insights of the enlightenment was that the Buddha could see in detail exactly how craving and *karma* lead to constant rebirth. It is recalled in a formula called *paticcasamuppada* ('dependent origination', 'conditioned co-production', or how various causes and conditions work together to produce effects). There are usually said to be 12 basic causal links, but there are lists in the Canon of 9 or 10 basic links. Thus it is perhaps more important to grasp the general principle of how one thing leads to another than worry too much about the individual links. (See table below)

Starting at the end, which is the situation of dukkha we find ourselves in, the twelve causal links are:

Link	Pictorial Symbol in 'Wheel of Life'
12. SUFFERING DECAY AND DEATH is dependent on	A corpse
11. REBIRTH into samsara ('this world') is dependent on	Childbirth
10. Being involved in the process called 'BECOMING' is dependent on	Pregnant woman
9. GRASPING (at life, sense pleasures, etc) is dependent on	Man picking fruit
8. CRAVING (for experience, more life or even oblivion) is dependent on	Man takes drink from woman (thirst)
7. FEELING (either pleasant, painful or neutral) is dependent on	Man with arrow in his eye
6. Coming into CONTACT with objects (of feelings) is dependent on	Man and woman embracing
5. Having the SIX SENSE FIELDS - sight, hearing, touch, smell, taste and mind is dependent on	House with six apertures
4. Existing as NAME AND FORM, ie in the psychophysical form is dependent on	Boat and four passengers (five components of a human being)
3. CONSCIOUSNESS, ie the 'life force' which continues from the previous life is dependent on	Monkey in a flowering tree
2. KARMA-FORMATIONS, ie the impulses or tendencies resulting from our actions or thoughts are dependent on	A potter
1. Our IGNORANCE (of the basic nature of life as analysed by the Buddha)	A blind man

This causal formula is rather difficult and has been interpreted in various ways. Some have seen it as showing what happens over three lifetimes:

No. 1 - 2 refer to one life,
No. 3 - 10 to a second life, and
No. 11 - 12 to a third life.

It can be drawn as a circle rather than a straight line, whereby suffering, decay and death leads back to more ignorance and so on, *ad infinitum*.

It has been suggested that it can be seen as two halves - half being what a human being is made up of, ie impulses, consciousness, name and form, senses, contact and feelings and half being the unhappy consequences this makeup can, but need not, lead to - craving, grasping, becoming, rebirth and suffering/death. Whichever way it is viewed, the important idea is that our human condition with its suffering, death and constant rebirth was brought about by a collection of interrelated causal conditions. It did not just happen by random chance, nor is there need of an external explanation such as God. And the most important thing of all is that if we can understand the causes of our situation, we can then go about tackling these causes and solving our problem. If we could break even one of the links in the chain, we could prevent the other consequences. The links that stand out as the ones we could possibly break are craving and ignorance, though we could also try to minimise contact and feeling. This idea that having understood the causes of our condition, we can actually do something about it takes us to the third Holy Truth.

The Third Truth

'This is the Noble Truth of the cessation of suffering; it is the remainderless fading and ceasing, the giving up, relinquishing, letting go and rejecting of that same craving.' (*Samyutta Nikaya* 5:421-3)

Having identified the cause of our suffering, if we can eliminate this cause, we can eliminate our suffering. The Buddha's message is that we can because he did. It is actually possible to eliminate craving and ignorance and the rest of the causal links. The question that arises is: What are we left with if we eliminate craving and ignorance? The answer is that for the rest of our time on earth we still have a consciousness, body, senses, contact and feelings, but these are no longer associated with any craving, grasping, becoming, suffering, and after death, there is no more rebirth into this situation ever again.

Nirvana

The Buddhist name for the state where all craving, ignorance and suffering has been eliminated is *nibbana* (P) or *nirvana* (S). It is a state which is said to be indescribable in our human words which are only designed to describe the samsaric human condition, which is why even the Buddha found it very difficult to express. There are two stages to *nirvana*, the stage where the mind and heart has achieved nirvana but the body still exists, and nirvana-after-death.

The word literally means 'blown out' - the burning fires of greed, hatred and delusion are extinguished. It often sounds rather negative, and some people have taken *nirvana* to mean that we escape suffering in the sense of shooting an animal to put it out of its misery - ie because we cease to exist altogether. Phrases that make *nirvana* sound like this are descriptions such as 'unborn', 'unbecoming', 'extinction', 'cessation', desireless'. yet although at times we feel that total annihilation would be preferable to our life, to most people this would hardly be a goal worth striving for, and it was one that the Buddha saw as one of our selfish cravings 'craving for extinction'. He criticised the materialists who taught extinction after death as much as those who preached about the immortal soul, and there *are* positive descriptions of *nirvana*. The most important is his statement that *Nirvana* is something which is: 'There **is** brethren an unborn, un-brought-to-being, an unmade, an unformed. If there were not, there would be no escape made known here for one who is born, brought to being...' Positive descriptions include Peace, Truth, the Everlasting, Supreme bliss, Purity, Freedom, independence 'The island, the refuge, the shelter, the harbour, the beyond.'

It may be infinite, beyond time and space, beyond even existence or non-existence as we know them, but we can obtain an idea of what it is like embodied in human form from the lives of the Buddha and the *arhats* who are happy, peaceful, energetic, never apathetic or boring, always knowing the right thing to do, still feeling all the pains and pleasure of other human beings but not being affected by them in the same way. Thus, while the liberated person is still physically alive, *nirvana* could be described as a different state of consciousness. Whether we can talk of consciousness after death is debatable; the Buddha refused to answer the question of whether an enlightened person existed or not after death; the impression given is that the dead arhat does exist in a sense, but a sense so different from what we know as existence that it is not worth using the same word. 'There's no measure to him who has gone to rest; he keeps nothing that could be named.'

Some people feel that the deepest states of 'mystical experiences' (where people report a loss of individual separateness in a greater unity beyond time and space, deep happiness, peace and conviction that they've reached the true reality) can give a foretaste of *nirvana*, others feel that even these experiences are part of this world rather than 'the beyond', maybe an experience of one of the higher realms. *Nirvana* cannot be understood, only experienced - to talk about it is like talking about colours to a blind person, or dry land to a fish. For more on nirvana in the Theravada tradition see page 68.

The Fourth Truth, the Eightfold Path

The Fourth Holy Truth is the practical one, the method by which we can attack craving and ignorance, and it is a whole way of life called the 'Middle Path' or the 'Noble Eightfold Path' because it has been summed up as eight factors that must be cultivated in life.

In some part of the Canon the path is a tenfold one, but the eightfold form is the most common.

'This is the Noble Truth of the Way leading to the Cessation of Suffering: It is this Noble Eightfold Path which consists of right view, right intention, right speech, right action, right livelihood, right effort, right mindfulness, and right concentration'.

The two extra factors sometimes found are right knowledge and right liberation. This way of life can be summed up as one of morality, meditation and wisdom. The whole Buddhist way of life both monastic and lay is simply a living out of this path; in the present context we will explain each aspect briefly.

Right view: means having the correct outlook on life, accepting the Buddha's analysis of human existence, etc. Without an initial acceptance no one would bother with the rest of the path.

Right intention: means having the right attitude to life, basically seeing one's goal as enlightenment and unselfish love for all beings. In Buddhist ethics, actions are judged by intention.

These two could be called 'initial wisdom'.

Right speech, conduct and livelihood: refer to moral behaviour. The basic moral code of Buddhism is enshrined in five precepts; to avoid killing, stealing, false speech, sexual misconduct and intoxicants but more basically to take responsibility for one's actions and do nothing to harm, only to help, others. Speech is singled out in the eightfold path as one of the most common ways of harming or helping others - wrong speech includes lies, gossip, harsh words, timewasting chatter.

There are far more opportunities of hurting people with words than actual physical blows. 'Right speech' includes helpful advice, teaching, words of consolation etc. The Buddha often stressed the value of silence, where no useful speech could be made. 'Right livelihood' is taken separately because people with blameless 'personal morality' in their private lives do not always apply this to their business dealings. To be a right livelihood, one's way of earning a living must not harm beings; you could not be a butcher, weapons manufacturer, purveyor of alcohol or drugs, or in any business that exploited people or animals in any way - by poor wages for example. Even agriculture is forbidden to Theravada monks, as many small creatures are destroyed; no wonder Theravada Buddhist monks leave the earnings of 'livelihoods' to the lay people.

The next three are to do with the discipline of the mind.

Right effort: is the initial discipline of being aware of the good and bad factors in one's personality and working hard to eliminate the negative and accentuate the positive.

Right mindfulness: is a technical Buddhist term for the deliberate cultivation of calm and awareness, especially of one's own body, sensations, feeling and thoughts with a view to having more knowledge of and control over them.

Right concentration: is formal meditation, the practice of techniques designed to lead the mind into the states (called *jhanas*) achieved by the Buddha, which prepare the mind for insight into the truth.

Right knowledge and **right liberation**: could be described as 'ultimate wisdom', the complete understanding of the Buddha's message achieved by the lesser wisdom, morality and meditation combined and identical to the Buddha's enlightenment experience.

The eightfold (rather than tenfold) path can be followed on two levels - on a worldly level people can accept the Buddha's teaching with pious faith, try to be more moral, meditate to improve the mind, and so on. This leads to a happier rebirth but not to *nirvana*. This is the attitude of the majority of Buddhists today. In the time of the Buddha and for Buddhist saints the path becomes a supramundane (above this world) path that really leads to attainment of enlightenment. This begins with a real breakthrough into understanding what Buddha taught, called in the Canon the '*Dhamma* vision'. This led swiftly on to full enlightenment. Those with '*Dhamma* vision' are divided into four categories; the 'stream entrant' who will gain *arhat* status in less than seven more lifetimes, the 'once returner' who will need only one more lifetime, the 'never-returner' who will not have to be reborn as a human again but will reach enlightenment in some higher dimension and the *arhat* who actually reaches enlightenment in the present life, as did hundreds of the Buddha's followers.

Again the eightfold path, like the 12 links, should not be taken too dogmatically as the only way of expressing the way to *nirvana*. There are alternative formulae found in the Pali Canon such as the 'seven limbs of enlightenment' - mindfulness, correct doctrine, effort, joy, tranquility, meditation and even-mindedness, or the 'five powers' - faith, vigour, mindfulness, concentration and wisdom. If these lists in the scriptures are added together one arrives at more than 37 factors of enlightenment, interesting for scholars, but not what the Buddha intended as is obvious from the fact that the same factors exist in different lists. There is also a positive version of the 12 links, whereby the human condition of suffering, instead of leading us through ignorance into craving and rebirth can cause us (as it did Siddartha Gautama) to think, pass progressively from faith through delight, enthusiasm, rapture, tranquility, bliss, concentration, disgust, dispassion and liberation to total knowledge and enlightenment.

From this analysis of the Buddha's first sermon we see that although Buddhism starts with a view of the human condition that at first sight seems quite negative and depressing, it does so only to show people that they themselves can take responsibility and do something to alter this condition, and in its concept of the final goal of human life is as exalted and positive as it is possible to be.

'No Self' and the Analysis of the Human Personality

Another Buddhist way of analysing the human condition is the 'three marks of life'. Human life is characterised by *anicca* (P), impermanence, *dukkha* (P), suffering and *anatta* (P), lack of self or essence. The first two marks have been dealt with under the First Noble Truth, but the third is less obvious and is perhaps the most vital Buddhist concept to grasp, as a real knowledge of 'no self' is another way of describing enlightenment. 'No self' was the subject of the Buddha's second sermon to the five ascetics, after which all five became enlightened *arhats*.

Our summary of the First Noble Truth referred without comment to 'the five categories affected by clinging'. This is a translation of *upadana-khandha*, the five grasping *khandas* (P) or *skandhas* (S), 'heaps' into which Buddhism analyses the human being.

A human being is made up of five categories of elements; FORM (the physical elements that make up the human body); SENSATIONS (the feelings we have as a result of the senses contacting the outside world); PERCEPTIONS (what we become aware of as a result of the senses contacting the outside world); MENTAL FORMATIONS or IMPULSES (resulting from our internal will) and CONSCIOUSNESS (the basic awareness of being alive with thoughts and feelings). Each of these five *skandhas*, or any of their component elements, are impermanent, constantly changing, and tend to be associated with clinging and grasping (as the First Noble Truth points out). Apart from this conglomeration of physical, emotional and mental bits and pieces, which come together at birth only to fall apart at death, there is nothing else to a human being. In particular, there is nothing corresponding to the concept of 'soul' or 'true self'. This denial of the 'self' was one of the issues which divided off the Buddha's teaching from that of many other *shramanas* in his day.

Many religious teachers believed firmly in an entity or substance which was called *atman* (self) often translated in English as 'soul'. This was defined as eternal, permanent, unchanging, perfectly pure, self-contained and not dependent on the body or the environment. This was identified as the 'real' you which either by accident, fate or *karma* had become imprisoned in a material or psychophysical organism with which it had no necessary connection. It was believed that if only this soul could be freed from the material prison it could dwell in eternal peace. This was the goal behind the popular practices of mortification of the body, yoga and meditation. The mystical experiences gained in meditative states were interpreted as experiencing the soul freed from the body. Thus, although the outer person might be impermanent and suffering, the inner self was untouched by this. The Buddha taught that this belief was a dangerous illusion. Not only was it not borne out by experience and reason, but it could lead to dangerous consequences such as total self obsession in the quest to liberate one's own soul, in disregard of other people, or a down playing of the importance of moral behaviour (as you cannot really hurt another person's 'self', nor is your 'self' really affected by evil deeds). In other words, belief in a 'self' can lead to selfishness - if you don't believe in a 'self', there is no point in being selfish.

The Buddha did not teach as a dogma to be accepted 'there is no *atman*', rather he pointed out that nothing can be found in experience that corresponds to the concept. He found, while undergoing severe asceticism, that physical, mental and spiritual aspects of a human being all affect each other. In his second sermon he asked the five ascetics to analyse the human being. Physical form cannot be our 'self' because it changes and suffers, is affected by the outer environment and is not under our control. The same applies to our sensations, our perceptions, our impulses and even our basic consciousness, and what else is there? Thus we can use the word 'self' for convenience, to refer to the current state of our ever-changing psychophysical personality, but this must not trick us into thinking there is actually an entity, over and above all the bits and pieces, called a 'self'. The idea of two levels of truth is important in Buddhism. Although on an everyday level we can talk about my 'self', on the level of ultimate truth no such entity exists.

The teaching of *anatta* (no self) is not just an interesting piece of Buddhist philosophy, but a vital necessity for Buddhist salvation. for it is the belief in ourselves as separate selves that leads us to distinguish between ourselves and others, to seek our good rather than theirs, to grasp things as 'mine' and remain blind and ignorant of the true nature of existence. Complete loss of this delusion of self is equivalent to enlightenment: 'seeing this, *bhikkhus*, a wise noble disciple becomes dispassionate towards material form, becomes dispassionate towards feeling, becomes dispassionate towards perception, becomes dispassionate towards formations, becomes dispassionate towards consciousness. Becoming dispassionate his lust fades away; with the fading of lust his heart is liberated; when liberated there comes the knowledge; 'It is liberated'. He understands, Birth is exhausted, the Holy Life has been lived out, what was to be done is done, there is no more of this to come.' (*Sutta Nipata* 3:66)

People with Western backgrounds often find it difficult to see how Buddhists can believe in rebirth but not in a soul. We are familiar with materialists who don't believe in a soul, but they think the organism ends at death; and most people's idea of rebirth is the Hindu or Greek idea of reincarnation - an eternal immortal soul getting a new body like a new set of clothes. The Buddhist view is that the whole person is constantly involved in rebecoming, our body, thoughts, feelings, etc change from moment to moment. Over the years these little changes form big changes, as when an adult compares herself with her baby photographs. What you are now is not the same as what you were before, but something that has developed directly out of what you were before as a result of all the outside influences and inner decisions of the will that have occurred in between. Death and rebirth is simply a rather more dramatic part of this process. As a result of the causal process, a moment comes when the bits and pieces that form a given psychophysical organism fall apart. However, the momentum built by the impulses, cravings, etc of this organism (the *karma*) directly causes a new psychophysical organism to start to grow, which bears the same relationship to the dead person as adult to child. Buddhists deny that any 'thing' passes on from one life to the next; the relationship is one of cause and effect. The connecting link is that of consciousness, which is more fundamental to a personality than physical body, feelings, etc. Not that an unchanging 'thing' called a 'consciousness' passes from one to the next, rather, the last act of consciousness in the old life and the first in the new life are consecutive moments in an uninterrupted sequence -this is the theoretical basis for being able to remember 'our' previous lives in the same way that we recall 'our' childhood. For more on *anatta* in the Theravada tradition, see page 66.

The Buddha's Basic Teaching: a Summary

The Buddha taught that by direct experience he had come to understand the human condition, and had discovered a means of transcending (going beyond) it. The human condition is one of continual rebirth into *samsara*, a state characterised by suffering, impermanence, and 'no self' or essence. Within this cycle our experience in the various states of being - human, superhuman, animal, unhappy spirit, or hell - is not fate, but directly conditioned by our own previous actions and thoughts. He found that what keeps us in this state is our own craving and ignorance of the true nature of things. If one can eliminate these things one achieves a state of perfection, liberation and peace known as *nirvana*, and one never has to be reborn in *samsara* again. The method of eliminating ignorance, craving and belief in a separate self is a threefold one of responsible moral behaviour reflecting unselfish compassion, discipline of the mind through meditation techniques and insight into the truths he discovered by reason, experience and meditation. It is not so much a philosophy about life as practical advice on how to live life based on the Buddha's own personal experience.

Questions the Buddha Refused to Answer

In the Pali Canon, we read about several questions that were left by the Buddha as 'undeclared'. These were questions of the type under discussion by shramanas at the time, and are on four basic issues:-
1. Whether the world can be said to be eternal or not - in other words, did the universe have a start in time, or has it always been here, simply changing state, and will it have an end in time?
2. Whether the universe is finite or infinite - does it have spatial limits? Can you arrive at the edge of the universe?
3. Is the 'life' of a human being to be identified with the physical being, or is it something separate from the physical being?
4. When an enlightened being or *Tathagata* (one who has gone) dies, can he be said to exist, or not exist, or both exist and not exist, or neither exist nor not exist?

On one occasion a follower of the Buddha puzzling over such issues decided to give up Buddhism unless the Buddha could answer these questions.[5] However, the Buddha refused to answer and explained why. The main reason is that such issues are irrelevant to the main purpose of life which is to eliminate craving and ignorance and achieve wisdom, peace and nirvana. Knowing the answers to these questions would not help us at all and thinking about them is merely a waste of time. On a deeper level, these questions are not answerable in the form in which they are asked - if an omniscient (all knowing) person did try to explain, he could not say simply 'yes' or 'no' but would have to undo the presuppositions about time, space and existence held by the questioner. Thirdly, if an omniscient person did attempt to explain, it would be impossible for an ordinary limited mind, with its words and ideas formed within the limitations of samsara, to cope with the answer - we would not be able to understand it anyway, and could be dangerously confused.

Of particular importance is the fourth issue of whether an enlightened person exists after death. Our human word 'exist' is just not applicable to the state of an enlightened being after death, and all four possibilities would give the wrong impression to the unenlightened mind. Enlightened people who had died do 'exist' in a sense, but in a sense so different from the normal meaning of this word that to use it is wrong.

The Buddha always claimed that he taught his followers everything they needed to know, ie the Four Noble Truths. In the Pali Canon it is claimed (probably by pious followers rather than the Buddha himself) that the knowledge he disclosed measured against what he actually did know could be compared to a handful of leaves against a forest full - but we have everything we need for all practical purposes.

In relation to this topic the Buddha told one of his famous parables:- the man asking such questions is like a man who was shot with a poisoned arrow and refused to let the surgeon remove the arrow until he had the answers to everything about it - the make of arrow, of arrowhead, the colour, height and family background of the man who shot the arrow, what the bowstring was made of, the type of bow used, etc. While asking these irrelevant questions the man would die - similarly one could spend one's whole life on philosophical questions about the nature of the universe and die without having got a step nearer to renouncing craving and ignorance and achieving nirvana.

Historical Developments in India After the Buddha

When the Buddha died, according to the Pali Canon, he died confident that his followers had been told and had assimilated everything they needed to know. The Dharma had been preached for 45 years and was well established in oral tradition, there were hundreds of enlightened arhats who could guide the community and the monastic sangha was well established, organised and competent to preserve the teaching. Immediately after the Buddha's death it is said that a Council of 500 arhats was called at Rajagaha with the purpose of collecting the authentic teaching of the Buddha. Upali is said to have recited the *Vinaya* (P) or material on monastic discipline, and Ananda the *Sutta* (P) or teachings. Although nothing was written down until several centuries later, the Theravadins believe that this material is faithfully recorded in their scripture, the Pali Canon.

The Buddha did not appoint a successor other than this oral tradition of the *Dharma*. Given the lack of written scriptures, and the fact that the monastic *sangha* was organised in self-contained local units with no centralised authority, it is not surprising that differences in practices and teaching began to creep in. During the first few centuries different schools of thought emerged and sometimes there were splits in the *sangha* over monastic practice. Buddhism as a whole seems to be tolerant of the first, but sees the second as a sad event. Although scholars talk of different 'sects', monks from different groups could be found living side by side in the same monastery, and the differences may have been irrelevant to many lay Buddhists.

The history of the early disputes is far from clear. It seems that a second Council was held at Vesali about 50 to 100 years after the Buddha's death when differences were beginning to be felt. The main dispute seems to be over monastic practice, with some groups of monks having a more lax interpretation of the vinaya than others. One example is that some were accepting money from lay benefactors. Either at this council, or some decades later at a further council in Paliputra, the *sangha* split into two groups, the Sthaviravadins 'those who follow the teaching of the elders' and the Mahasanghikas 'the great assembly'. According to which side you were on, the Sthaviravadins were keeping the original rules laid down by the Buddha, and the Mahasanghikas were becoming lax; or the Sthaviravadins were adding stricter rules to the Buddha's teaching, whereas the Mahasanghikas were keeping to the original simplicity. Either at the same meeting(s), or at others around the same time, there was also discussion about doctrinal points. One debate was over the nature of *arhats* - the so-called 'five points of Mahadeva' cast doubt on their perfection (eg they could still have erotic dreams; they were not all-knowing; they could still have doubts). The Mahasanghikas seem also to have had a more 'supramundane' view of the Buddha - he was no ordinary human being, but perfectly pure, never really dirty, ill or ignorant.

Further divisions occurred within each of these wings of Buddhism. Within the Sthaviravadin wing in the third century BCE, the Pudgalavadins put forward a belief in a 'person' other than the five skandhas in the human being, whereas the others thought this was dangerously close to an atman or 'self'. Then the Sarvastivadins and the Vibhajhavadins divided over whether the dhammas (momentary events that make up experience) could be said to really exist or not. The Sarvastivadins taught that past, present and future dhammas had real existence, whereas the Vibhajhavadins did not. (For more on dhammas see page 52). The Sarvastivadins went on to be important in North India, and their version of the Canon was passed on to Tibet and China, whereas the Theravada, the surviving school of Vibhajhavadins, went on to become important in South India, Sri Lanka, Burma and Thailand.

Tradition has it that there were 18 different groups in the first few centuries of Buddhism - but some scholars have suggested that it might have been more like thirty.

The Spread and Decline of Buddhism

In spite of its internal divisions, Buddhism spread very rapidly in India and beyond. By the third century BCE it was the major faith of India and had already spread successfully to Sri Lanka. A variety of reasons have been given for its success.

* Buddhist teaching was of universal application and not restricted to any tribal or cultural group, offering a skilful way of living and a hope for salvation.
* It stressed the importance of the experience of the individual and of making your own mind up, at a time when ancient traditions and authorities were being questioned.
* There were many aspects of life that the Buddha did not pronounce on, so that people were free to continue with traditional customs and gods if they liked. Buddhism was very flexible and adaptable.
* It was attractive to the growing class of travellers and merchants, detached from traditional rural beliefs, who were very important in spreading the teachings of Buddhism in their travels.

* The monastic sangha was well organised and could been seen as an example of a successful spiritual path.
* Buddhism attracted the support of leading members of society such as kings who supported its spread. One particular person who is credited with facilitating the successful spread of Buddhism in its early centuries is the Indian king, or Emperor, Ashoka.
* The teaching itself, based on wisdom and love, was very attractive. It had much to attract intellectuals in its coherent and analytical account of reality, but also offered a practical way of life for ordinary people.

However, the story is not always one of success and spread. By the 12th century CE Buddhism had almost disappeared in India, and along the silk route between India and China. It took a long time to get established in China and never replaced the other religions there. Early missions to Western countries (reputedly sent in the 3rd century BCE) were not successful.

The factors that make Buddhism attractive also make it vulnerable. The decline in India is usually attributed to two things, assimilation and military conquest. The flexibility of Buddhism means that it can become almost indistinguishable from the folk religion, and it is suggested that in India, it grew indistinguishable from Hinduism. Its otherworldly and peaceful nature make it vulnerable to military force. This happened in India and Central Asia with the Muslim invasions, and in this century in China, Tibet, Laos and Vietnam with Communism. The importance of the monastic sangha means that when this is disrupted, (eg by the destruction of monasteries in war) Buddhist teaching suffers. Buddhism has not sought to force acceptance of its teachings on people, so where missionaries met an already established sophisticated culture (eg in China) progress was slow.

Ashoka

In the political history of the centuries after the Buddha, the kingdoms of Magadha and Kosala absorbed the other tribal groups soon after the Buddha's death. By the Second Council (50-100 years after the Buddha's death) Magadha had taken over the whole area of the Buddha's ministry and was ruled by Chandragupta Maurya. His grandson, Ashoka, who came to the throne in 268 BCE, expanded the territory into a empire, covering all but the extreme south of India.

He is famous in Buddhist tradition as Buddhism's most powerful patron. We have detailed information about his reign, because archaeologists have located 32 of his edicts or decrees preserved upon rock faces or pillars throughout India. He originally came to power by slaying all other claimants to the throne, including his own brothers, and expanded his empire by military campaigns. The edicts tell us that after one particularly brutal campaign he became sickened by violence and turned to the peace of religion. He tried to set up a society based not on violence but on *Dharma* or righteousness. His decrees required people to behave morally and responsibly, obeying parents and superiors, helping the poor, being fair to servants and employees, and generous to holy men. He advised them to be merciful, truthful and pure, not to be overly concerned with material possessions, and to refrain from killing or harming living beings. He banned animal sacrifices, and may also have banned the death penalty.

He himself tried to set an example and provided many social projects such as medical and veterinary services, constructed wells and reservoirs, planted trees and provided welfare services for prisoners. He gave up hunting, the favourite sport of the Kshatriya class, and instead went on pilgrimages to the holy places connected with Buddha's life where he set up commemorative stupas. He sent out missionaries apparently as far away as Syria, Egypt, and Macedonia to spread Buddhist teachings around the world, a venture which he called 'conquest according to Dharma'. His missions were successful in Kashmir, and particularly in Sri Lanka, where the King of the Island, Tissa, was converted by Ashoka's own son. The island has remained largely Buddhist ever since. He appointed officers of Dharma to investigate how his plans were proceeding. Despite his adherence to Buddhism, he also supported teachers of other religions, and although his reign is looked back on as a golden age of Buddhism, historians have questioned quite how Buddhist he really was. For instance, Basham, in *The Wonder That was India* claims that 'in fact, the Dharma officially propagated by Ashoka was not Buddhism at all but a system of morals consistent with the tenets of most of the sects of the empire, and calculated to lead to peace and fellowship in this world and heaven in the next.'

Although Ashoka's patronage did much for the spread of Buddhism, there are disadvantages in becoming an established religion. It can be formalised and lose its inner spirit and the standard of commitment can become lower as people join for social reasons. After Ashoka's death the dynasty declined, and India split up again into a number of small kingdoms.

1.   One version of this is to be found in Conze 1959.

2.   This age is claimed in the Pali Canon (*Digna Nikaya* 16) but the passage from the *Majjihima Nikaya* 36 on page 15 may suggest a somewhat earlier age.

3.   This can also be found in Conze 1959.

4.   A version can be found in Morgan *Buddhist Stories*.

5.   *Majjhima Nikaya* 1:63

CHAPTER THREE

THERAVADA BUDDHISM

Basic Characteristics

Of the various schools which the Mahayanists refer to as 'Hinayana' (the small vehicle) the only one to survive until today is the Theravada school, 'the way of the elders'. Many English speaking scholars see Theravada as the 'real' or 'original'[1] Buddhism, as they first became familiar with the Theravada scriptures (the Pali Canon) but it is important to remember that it is only one version of the Buddhist tradition. It is conservative in nature and claims to have preserved the pure Dharma of the Buddha, unchanged since the 5th century BCE. However true that is, Theravada Buddhism today is certainly very little different from our records of it in the 5th century CE, and probably from the 1st century BCE when their scriptures were put into writing. Countries where Theravada exists today are Sri Lanka, Thailand, Burma, Cambodia and Laos.

The main beliefs which distinguish Theravada from other forms of Buddhism are as follows:[2]

1. The Buddha

In Theravada teaching the Buddha was a man, a human being like ourselves. Certainly he was the most special man who ever lived in our era because he himself, by struggling for thousands of lives, finally managed to achieve for himself the knowledge that leads to liberation. However much popular devotion ascribes special characteristics to him - such as the 32 marks of a superbeing and, his miraculous birth - it is vital not to forget that he is one of us, and we are called to achieve the state of enlightenment obtained by him. A Buddha is a very rare occurrence, and does not mean any enlightened person but only one who has achieved enlightenment for himself, and taught others. The Buddha Shakyamuni is now dead and beyond any contact with struggling beings, as are all dead enlightened ones. However, the tradition gives us everything we need to know about what he taught when he was alive.

2. God and the gods

There is nothing in Buddhism corresponding to an ultimate, personal creator. There is no divine person who made the world and watches over us, to whom one should pray for help. The Buddha is not like God because he has passed away into unimaginable nirvana and cannot be contacted. Theravadins consider that the concept of God does not stand up to the facts: there is no evidence for the existence of such a being, and the evidence points to the contrary. If there is such a loving, all-powerful being, why do innocent creatures have to suffer? However, Theravadins often believe in 'gods' - which are seen as limited beings who exist in the universe, and may be able to help with small, worldly problems. Gods are simply one of the possible life forms in samsara, more rarefied and happier than humans, but with less opportunity to progress towards nirvana. There are 26 different levels of godlike being, and the lower ones belong to the same realm - the realm of desire - as humans, and therefore may interact with humans. These gods are not immortal, and must die and be reborn again.

3. Self-reliance

Because there is no God, the Buddha is dead, and gods can only help with worldly things, it is the responsibility of each individual to sort out his or her own life. There is no saviour to cry to for help; we must all help ourselves by actually putting the eight-fold path into practice. The Buddha has given us a map of the way to *nirvana*, but we must get ourselves there. The ideal aimed at is to become an *arhat* (S) *arahat* (P), an enlightened person who has reached the knowledge of the end of all craving and ignorance. To achieve this state, total dedication is required and it is felt by most Theravadins that although the Pali Canon contains stories of enlightened lay persons, nowadays the lifestyle of monk is the most conducive to this attainment. Even monks today feel *nirvana* is a far-off goal and work instead for a better rebirth - though there may well be some *arhats*, who do not boast of their attainments. It is sometimes felt that this self-reliant religion is rather selfish, concerned only with saving oneself from suffering, but this is to misunderstand Theravada Buddhism. It is a contradiction in terms to strive to save 'yourself'. By definition, an arhat is one who has lost all sense of a 'self' separate from others, and all selfish impulses. Compassion for others, and helping them on their spiritual path, is a vital part of Theravada Buddhism. Monks teach 'for the sake of the welfare and happiness of gods and men.' Without a compassionate mind, enlightenment would never be attained.

4. Religious ritual

Theravada Buddhists do have religious rituals (to be described later see page 76ff), but this is said to be comparable to honouring a great man, and is a reminder of his teaching, rather than religious ritual as normally understood. Religious ritual in the sense of prayers and offerings which expect a favour in return are made to the gods and other supernatural beings who may be able to help you with purely worldly but not spiritual requests. Rituals are considered to be particularly appropriate for lay rather than monastic Buddhists.

5. Philosophy - *Abhidhamma* or 'Higher *dharma*'

Theravada philosophy is practical and based on analysing the factors of existence. It is put forward in the *Abhidhamma Pitaka* of the Pali Canon[3] and holds that existence can be analysed into impersonal events called *dharmas* which can be translated as atoms, elements or vibrations. There are, for practical purposes, 171 *dharmas* (S) *dhammas* (P) such as 89 different states of consciousness, 28 material qualities, 5 types of sensation. Theravada philosophy teaches that one should observe the universe as made up of a series of *dhammas* constantly leading dynamically from one to the next, without imposing false mental constructions, such as my 'self', on them. This theory of dharmas is an elaboration of the Buddha's teaching on the 5 *skandhas*. If this seems rather obscure, it should be understood as strictly practical in its aim - observing dharmas helps destroy our illusions. For example, if we observe the dharmas that make up our present state, we will observe basic elements such as a hungry feeling, a sudden fear, and see that these endlessly changing elements are the reality, and that our concept of 'my self' is an illusion. Theravada philosophy is closely bound up with psychological analysis.

6. Scriptures

The scriptures which embody the traditions of the Theravada school of Buddhism are known as the Pali Canon, as they are written in the ancient Indian dialect of Pali. They are divided into three sections **Vinaya** or disciplinary rules for the order of monks, **Sutta** or discourses of the Buddha and **Abhidhamma** or further philosophical writings.

Theravada Scriptures - the Pali Canon

The scriptures of Theravada Buddhism are known as the Pali Canon. 'Pali' is the name of an ancient Indian language and 'Canon' refers to an authoritative collection of scriptures. It consists of dialogues, stories, commentaries and monastic rules said to have been first written down in Sri Lanka in the 1st century BCE.

Buddhists believe that the content of the Canon was passed down accurately by oral tradition. Collected in book form, the complete Canon would fill several shelves of a bookcase. Originally it was written on palm leaf manuscripts which were stored in baskets - hence the alternative name *Tipitaka* (P) *Tripitaka* (S) - the 'three baskets', to refer to the three sections of the scriptures. These three sections are the *Vinaya Pitaka* or discipline section, the *Sutta Pitaka* or discourse section and the *Abhidamma Pitaka* or philosophical teaching.

I.   Vinaya Pitaka

The *Vinaya Pitaka* contains pronouncements attributed to the Buddha laying down numerous rules for the conduct of the order. With these rules, the circumstances which led to the promulgation of the rules is given, giving us interesting information about the life of the Buddha and/or the early sangha. It is divided into three sections:-

A.   *Suttavibhanga*: gives the 227 rules for monks dealing with eight classes of offences. This begins with the four rules which, if broken, entail expulsion from the order. These are sexual intercourse, theft, murder and falsely claiming supernatural powers. Following from this are 13 rules which require a meeting of the sangha to deal with them, 2 indefinite rules, 30 rules which involve penance and forfeiture, 92 rules requiring confession, 4 rules requiring only acknowledgement, 75 rules of training and 7 rules for the settlement of legal processes. After these there is a section on rules for nuns, which are similar but slightly stricter. These rules will be looked at in more detail on pages 25.

B.   *Khandhaka*: contains rules governing the organisation of the sangha rather than the conduct of individual monks. This covers topics such as admission to the order, the fortnightly *uposatha* (meeting to recite the rules), the retreat during the rainy season, the ceremony at the end of the retreat, rules about dress, furniture, medicine, food, robes, looking after the sick bhikkhus, how to deal with schisms, the procedure for reinstating suspended monks, duties of different classes of monks, ordination of nuns, plus an account of the first two Councils after the Buddha's death.

C.   A summary of all these rules arranged as a catechism for instruction and examination purposes. (In English translation, this material fills 3-6 books.)

II.   Sutta Pitaka

This section contains the discourses of the Buddha (together with a few sermons by various disciples) and is the written source of the

Buddhist Dharma. It is divided into 5 sections by length and subject matter of the sermons, rather than in any chronological order.

A. *Digha Nikaya* (collection of long dialogues): consists of 34 discourses, each of which has a name by which it can be referred to. These 34 sermons cover the following topics:- false teachings; the advantages of the homeless life; the place of caste; the true meaning of 'brahmin' (in both cases the Buddha's view that noble status is earned by behaviour rather than by birth); the evil of animal sacrifice; supernatural powers and higher states of consciousness; the relationship between life and the physical body; the evils of excessive self-mortification; the issue of the soul; a discourse by Ananda on morality, meditation and wisdom; the danger of miracles; the ethics of teaching; the stories of six previous Buddhas in earlier ages; the twelve links of causation; the parinirvana of the Buddha and his last words; the Buddha's previous life as a king; the story of a demon; another previous life story; higher types of gods; a sermon to Sakka, king of the lower gods; four types of meditation; conversion of a heretic who did not believe in life after death; why the Buddha does not work miracles or explain the origins of the universe; asceticism; the idea of a universal monarch and the prophecy about Maitreya; how caste originated historically; the faith of Sariputta; teaching, the 32 marks of a great man; the duties of a householder; protection of the 4 guardian gods of the earth; and lastly, two sermons by Sariputta. In English translation, these 34 sermons fill 3 volumes.

B. *Majjhima Nikaya* (Collection of medium length discourses): contains 152 medium length sermons, divided into 15 subsections, which together in English translation fill three volumes. It would take too long to list the subject matter of all 152 discourses - a selection will give a general idea. Discourse no.4 gives one of the Buddha's account of his Enlightenment; no.17 is about life in the forest; no.21 gives the famous simile of the saw - that one should maintain compassionate love and self control under the worst of circumstances, you should love your enemies even though they should saw you into pieces; no.26 gives the account of Buddha's renunciation, search and attainment of enlightenment; no.44 is interesting, as it is a sermon by a female disciple of the Buddha showing how women had a place in early Buddhism; no.48 recalls the occasion when the Buddha left his disciples in disgust at their quarrelling, and his teaching on avoiding quarrels; no.49 shows how the Buddha persuaded the god Brahma - thought by many to be the creator god - that he was not eternal and all-powerful after all; no.55 explains the Buddhist position on the eating of meat - a disciple should not deliberately deprive an animal of life for his food, but can accept offered meat if he knows it has not been specially killed for

him. In no.62 the Buddha advises his son, Rahula, on how to
meditate with breathing exercises, and no.63 deals with the
'undetermined questions' that the Buddha refused to answer. There
are several 'previous life' stories, the conversion of the robber chief
and a story based on the grief of a man who had lost a son, which the
Buddha used to show how all such attachments lead inevitably to
sorrow. No.112 gives the characteristics by which one can recognise
an arhat, and no.116 explains about Pratyeka-Buddhas, who are
beings who reach enlightenment by themselves, but do not go on to
teach. This is the Buddhist recognition that people in other ages and
places may have reached liberation without the teachings of
Buddhism. No.117 explains the Noble Eight-fold Path and no.129
explains about the rewards and punishments after death for good and
bad actions in life. No.141 outlines the Four Noble Truths.

C. *Samyutta Nikaya* (Collection of 'grouped' discourses or 'Kindred
Sayings'): consists of 2,889 short discourses arranged in 56 topic
groups. These 56 topic groups are organised into 5 sections. The
English translation is in 5 volumes. Examples of topics dealt with are
gods, Mara the evil one, demons, the twelve links of
paticcasamuppada, the five skandhas, the different levels of jhana or
trance, nirvana, the 37 qualities leading to enlightenment, the
Eightfold Path and the Four Noble Truths.

D. *Anguttara Nikaya* (collection of 'Gradual Sayings'): contains
short discourses arranged in numerical groups, from one to eleven, as
an aid to memory. There are 2,308 short sayings which in English
translation fill 5 volumes. Examples of such topics are the one
Buddha; the two types of Karma (ie either fulfilled in this life or after
death); the two types of gift, ie material things and the gift of the
Dharma or truth; the three good acts of generosity, renunciation and
maintenance of parents; three heretical views on the causes of our
experiences; the four types of love - loving kindness, compassion,
sympathetic joy and equanimity; the four wrong views of belief in
permanence, pleasure, self and purity where none of these exist; the
four good results of offering food to monks - long life, beauty,
happiness and strength; four sites of pilgrimage and the five mental
hindrances of lust, ill will, sloth, restlessness or worry and sceptical
doubt. There are said to be six duties for a monk - to abstain from
actions, arguments, sleep and company, and to practice humility and
association with the wise.

There are seven kinds of spiritual wealth such as modesty, eight
causes of earthquakes such as the birth of a Buddha, nine types of
person, ten contemplations including four different types of corpses,
the tenfold path and eleven ways to *nirvana*.

E. *Khuddaka Nikaya* (collection of small texts): brings together 15 originally separate works of a miscellaneous nature. Scholars believe that this section was added to the Canon later than the Four Nikayas previously mentioned, although some of the works may be themselves very ancient, with material from the time of the Buddha. The 15 works are as follows:-

1. The *Khuddakapatha* which contains nine *suttas* or sermons including the threefold refuge formula, the greatest blessings (a favourite sutta to recite in times of trouble), the offerings to be made to dead relatives and the famous *metta sutta* on loving kindness.

2. The *Dhammapada* - a poem summarising the heart of Buddhism which is a great favourite with Buddhists today.

3. The *Udana* - eighty 'solemn utterances' of the Buddha including the parable of the blind men and the elephant, the definition of *nirvana* and the story of the Buddha's last meal.

4. The *Itivuttaka* - 112 short sayings mainly on ethical topics.

5. The *Suttanipata* - a collection of 71 *suttas* some of which are considered to be very old as they refer to the life of a homeless wanderer rather than an organised monk. The *metta sutta* appears again here, and there is the description of the Buddha's temptations by Mara. There are several sermons on the futility of most philosophising and intellectual debates.

6. The *Vimanavatthu* - 85 poems about the heaven worlds where one can be reborn if one gains merit through one's deeds.

7. The *Petavatthu* - 51 poems on rebirth in the state of a *preta* or ghost, wandering and miserable as a result of demeritorious deeds.

8. *Theragatha* - 107 poems by the *theras* (senior monks) describing their feelings such as joy on achieving liberation.

9. *Therigatha* - 73 poems by the *theri* (senior nuns), again celebrating the liberation that Buddhism brought, particularly freedom from the oppressions suffered by the female sex.

10. The *Jataka* - 547 stories of previous lives of the Buddha, together with an introductory commentary on the life of the Buddha.

11. *Niddesa* - a book of commentary on certain sections of the Sutta nipata.

12. *Patisambhidamagga* - a more analytical survey of Buddhist concepts from the four main *nikayas* such as the Four Truths, *nirvana*, etc.

13. *Apadana* - verse tales of the former lives of 550 *bhikkhus* (monks) and 40 *bhikkhuni* (nuns).

14. The *Buddhavamsa* - the history of 24 previous Buddhas.

15. *Cariyapitaka* - 35 stories of Buddha's previous lives chosen to illustrate Buddhist virtues.

III. Abhidhamma Pitaka

The third main division of the Pali Canon is not the direct word of the Buddha but a more philosophical treatment of the Dharma presented in the Suttas of the Buddha. *Abhidhamma* means 'higher teaching' and is for the more advanced, scholarly Buddhist, normally an educated monk. It is considered to have been composed at the Third Council in the 3rd Century BCE when the community became concerned with maintaining the purity of doctrine and excluding heresy. It consists of seven different works:-

1. **Dammasangani** analyses existence into the 171 basic *dhammas* or 'factors' of which all other beings are made. It is considered an important exercise constantly to view the world in terms of these *dhammas* and avoid imposing false mental constructions such as my 'self' or 'my house', which can be mistaken for a real description of the universe.
2. **Vibhanga** and
3. **Dhatukatha** continue the analysis of elements and categories with particular reference to the mental elements.
4. **Puggalapannatti** categorises the different types of human personality, a knowledge of which is essential for teaching meditational techniques.
5. **Kathavatthu** discusses all the controversial points of doctrine which divided the early sects of Buddhism. In each point the Theravada view is shown to be correct. It is difficult to reconstruct the views of the other sects from this rather biased account of them.
6. **Yamaka** gives a logical analysis of Buddhist psychology.
7. **Patthana** investigates the workings of causation and the mutual inter-relationship of phenomena.

How is the Pali Canon used?

Obviously no Buddhist sits down and reads through the Pali Canon in its entirety, and the ordinary lay Buddhist will probably never actually read the Canonical material but relies on the monks to pass on the teachings. There are many different types of literature in the Pali Canon with different uses in Buddhist life. The rules and laws of the *Vinaya* are kept meticulously by the community of monks, and each monk joins in the reciting of the 227 rules every fortnight. Of the *Sutta* section, some parts are known by everybody - the parables and sayings of the Buddha being retold again and again by monks and school teachers. The story of the Buddha's life is partly based on material from the Canon and partly from later commentaries and traditions. The advice on meditation is still followed today. The Jataka stories are enjoyed by children, and are a useful way of teaching moral behaviour in an interesting and memorable form. Some parts of the Canon, such as the refuge formula, are known by heart by every Buddhist, other sections - notably the *Abhidhamma* - is mostly of interest to scholars. Sometimes Theravada Buddhists recite certain sections of the scriptures as a form of semi-magical protection in times of trouble - these recitals are known as *paritta* or *pirit*. The *metta sutta* on universal love, and the *mangala sutta* on the blessings of life are used to promote welfare. The *Angulimala sutta* is recited to protect women in childbirth. Among Theravada monks, even in these days of printed books, it is still considered meritorious to learn sections of the scriptures by heart, as was originally intended. The *Dhammapada* is a great favourite with modern lay Buddhists, and the most likely portion of the Buddhist scriptures to be found in a layperson's home. Selections from the Canon are used in the morning and evening chanting of Theravada monastic communities.

Copies of sections of the Canon are treated with great reverence. Ancient scriptures are considered to be relics of the Buddha, and are to be found buried in stupas.

The Theravada Way - Morality

'Cease to do evil, learn to do good, purify the mind, this is the teaching of all the Buddhas.' (Dhammapada 184) This famous quotation from the Pali Canon demonstrates the centrality of ethical behaviour in the Buddhist Way, and also the teaching that conduct, good or bad, stems ultimately not from the body but from the mind. Especially for lay people, living a moral life could said to be the heart of Buddhism - the Buddha's teaching for laypeople always centred on 'giving, morality, heavens and detachment'.

Lay Morality

When you become a Buddhist you recite three times the threefold refuge formula, taking refuge in the three jewels of the *Buddha*, the

Dharma (his teaching) and the *Sangha* (community of monks).

Buddham saranam gacchami	I go for refuge to the Buddha
Dhammam saranam gacchami	I go for refuge to the Dhamma
Sangham saranam gacchami	I go for refuge to the Sangha

(This is repeated a second and third time.)

You also undertake to keep the 5 precepts of morality definitive of Buddhism:

'I undertake to abstain from killing
I undertake to abstain from taking what is not given
I undertake to abstain from misuse of sensual pleasures
I undertake to abstain from false speech
I undertake to abstain from drugs and alcohol as they tend to cloud the mind.'

These rules are fairly self-explanatory. **Killing** includes taking the life not just of humans but of any 'sentient being' which includes animals but not plants. Some Buddhists eat meat, but will never kill the animal themselves, leaving the job to a butcher of another religion. **Taking what is not given** includes stealing in all its forms such as wasting your employer's time, etc. Many Buddhists see gambling as prohibited by this precept. The **misuse of sensual pleasures** mainly refers to sexual misconduct, which is partly determined by social custom. It is generally interpreted as forbidding adultery, incest, and the use of prostitutes or slaves. Some modern Buddhist teachers prefer to extend its meaning to cover selfish indulgence in any sense pleasure, such as overeating. **False speech** includes not only lying, but gossiping, spreading rumours, speaking harshly and cruelly and causing quarrels. **Drugs and alcohol** are given up not for some illogical taboo, but simply because Buddhism aims to get more control over one's mind and behaviour, and drugs and alcohol have the opposite effect. Buddhists have a commonsense attitude to this and are not shocked by drinking a sociable sherry, but consider the use of alcohol as pointless and potentially morally dangerous.

Pious Buddhists may take upon themselves three extra precepts, often on a holy day: abstention from a luxurious bed (sleeping on a mat), abstention from food after midday and abstention from amusements and adornments (jewellery, fancy clothes, dancing, shows, etc). This is a particularly popular practice with older people, who may spend the whole day at the temple, meditating and listening to sermons.

As well as rules about what not to do, Buddhism encourages positive virtues - to be content with a simple life, detachment from materialistic concerns, love and compassion for all beings, self discipline and tolerance. Each person should fulfil his or her duties for a lay person, this could involve looking after family and relations, earning a livelihood and being sensible with money. The following is a summary (from the Pali Canon) of the Buddha's advice to a young man called Sigala, about the responsibilities of a householder (*Digha Nikaya* 3.185-191)

1. It is important to take care of your family. You must respect, listen to and obey your parents when you are young and look after them when they get old. You must look after your children, not just materially but you must teach them how to be good, see that they are educated and help them to make sensible choices about a career and marriage.

2. It is important to make a success of your marriage. You must be loving and faithful to your partner and work hard at your side of the partnership whether it involves going out to work or looking after the house. Husbands and wives should be fair to each other, trust each other and not waste the joint money. They should also enjoy themselves together, for example, the Buddha suggests a husband should buy his wife presents or clothes and jewellery!

3. It is important to choose the right friends. You should keep away from those who will have a bad influence on you and choose friends who are, if anything, better people than yourself. Friends are perhaps the biggest influence we have, especially when we are young. You should always be kind to your friends, keep promises, help them in times of trouble, advise them about their problems, tell them if you think they are doing wrong (gently!) and help them to look after their family and possessions.

4. It is important to have good relationships between teachers and pupils. You should respect your teachers, appreciate that they are helping you to learn, be polite to them and work hard. If you are a teacher you should respect your pupils, try to give them the best possible education and help them to be good people as well as people that know a lot.

5. It is important to have good relationships between employers and employees, or workers and management. Employers must care for their workers, give them decent wages and conditions to work in, sickness benefits and holidays that are fair. If you work for someone else, you should respect your employer, work hard and not waste time that you are being paid for, not be always greedily asking for more pay etc. Employers and employees should do their best to work together and not be always complaining about each other, but praising each other.

6. It is important to earn a living in a good way, and choose a good career, money is not bad in itself, you need money to look after your family and friends. Money should not be wasted, nor should you be a miser. You should use money sensibly to keep your family and friends happy, your business going and to help others in need. In the Eightfold Path, the Buddha listed 'Right Livelihood' as one of the important areas of morality. We ought to choose a career which does no harm to living beings or breaks the precepts.

The Buddha's advice is very down to earth and practical, as is seen in the following paraphrase of some more of advice to Sigala (*Digha Nikaya* 3.181)

Remember there are six main ways of wasting time and money. Drinking, wandering the streets late at night, going to fairs and festivals, gambling, mixing with a bad crowd and being lazy.

There are six reasons why drinking is bad. It wastes money, it leads to quarrels and fights, makes you ill, gives you a bad reputation, leads you to do immoral things you will regret and weakens the brain.

There are six reasons why roaming the streets late at night is bad. You are most likely to be mugged, your family at home are without your protection, your property is more likely to be burgled, you will be suspected of crimes by the police, rumours about you will be believed and you will be exposed to all sorts of trouble.

Going to fairs and festivals means you will spend your time thinking about music, instruments, dancing and all the other entertainments and forget the important things.

Gambling is bad, because if you lose you lose money, if you win you make enemies, no-one trusts you, friends despise you and no one will want to be married to you.

Mixing with a bad crowd, means that your friends are hooligans, drunkards, drug addicts, cheats and criminals and you are bound to be led astray by them.

Being idle is bad, because you waste your life getting nothing achieved, no money earned. The idle person can always find an excuse for not working, 'it is too hot', 'it is too cold', 'it is too early', 'it is too late', 'I'm too hungry', 'I'm too full'.

Sermons on morality for laypeople tend to lay great stress on *karma*, and the fear of a bad rebirth and hope for a good rebirth. When the Buddha spoke to lay people he always concentrated on the topics of 'morality, giving, heavens and detachment', as most lay people are content to hope for a better rebirth rather than make any serious attempt at attaining nirvana. The Buddhist scriptures contain frightening pictures of the sufferings of the various hell worlds, and life as a miserable ghost. Bad *karma* has a twofold effect - you will be miserable in this life as you lose friends or suffer from guilt, and you will be reborn in some miserable condition. Good *karma* leads to peace, calm, untroubled sleep, love of friends and good health in this life, and a good rebirth after death - perhaps a sojourn in one of the heaven worlds where life is like a paradise.

However, people who are more spiritual realise that Buddhism is not really about seeking heavenly rewards for good deeds; the Buddhist way is to do good deeds for the sake of helping others, reducing your craving and reaching the total unselfishness of nirvana. Although the moral teachings of Buddhism look more or less the same as those of other faiths (eg not to kill, steal, lie) the motivation behind them is different. They are not commandments from a divine being who has to be obeyed, but guidelines for making spiritual progress. Therefore Buddhists do not follow the precepts slavishly, but judge the circumstances. Normally it is wrong to lie, but occasionally it might seem to be the most loving and helpful thing to do. (This judging of circumstances is called *upaya kausalya* ,'skilful means', in Mahayana Buddhism. An enlightened person is said to have the ability to know what is the right thing to do or say in all circumstances - the unenlightened are usually safer keeping to the guidelines.)

Whether keeping to the guidelines or not, the important thing is your intention - whether your action springs from selfish or unselfish motives. Right intention is one of the eight aspects of the Noble Path. It is not so much what you do as why you do it that is important for your spiritual progress. It is also important that the mind is purified through meditation and mental training, because it is easy to be confused about one's real motives for actions.

Monastic Morality

The moral rules for monks are far more detailed, and outline a far stricter lifestyle. When one is ordained as a monk or even a novice, after taking the three refuges one takes the basic five precepts plus another five as follows:
To abstain from food after midday;
To abstain from a luxurious bed, ie to sleep on a mat;
To abstain from frivolous amusements, eg music, dancing, shows;

To abstain from personal adornments, ie no jewellery, and to wear
only the basic robe;
To touch no silver or gold, ie to have nothing to do with money.

Most Theravada monks keep these rules strictly, not only for their
own training, but also because the lay people would lose all respect
for them if they are seen to break the rules and possibly lose faith in
the Buddhist way. They have a duty to show a good example.

As well as these ten precepts, Buddhist monks have to keep the 227
rules of the Vinaya discipline, (see p48) which are a mixture of moral
rules and rules of etiquette and organisation. The first four rules are
serious moral issues, which lead to expulsion from the order if they
are broken:
1. No sexual intercourse of any kind whether heterosexual or
    homosexual;
2. Serious theft;
3. Murder or subtle forms of murder such as encouragement to
    suicide;
4. Deliberately and intentionally to make false claims to supernormal
    powers.

These four lead to total expulsion as they make a mockery of the
Buddhist life. Thirteen offences lead to temporary suspension and
involve serious proceedings by a whole monastic community and a
special ceremony of reinstatement. These include lesser sexual
offences such as masturbation, caressing a woman, attempting to
persuade a woman to sexual intercourse, etc, offences which misuse
the position of a monk such as acting as a go-between or demanding
special treatment, causing quarrels in the community and making
false accusations about other monks, building a separate private
dwelling and refusing to move if his behaviour is causing a scandal.

Lesser offences involve penances such as forfeiting the right to certain
communal possessions, or are left to *karma* and bad rebirth - although
the effects of this can be lessened by sincere repentance and
confession. Examples of lesser offences are accepting money and
being involved in trade, preaching to a woman alone, teaching the
Pali Canon word for word to laymen, boasting of supernormal
achievement to a layman, gossiping about other monks, destroying
animal or plant life, engaging in agriculture, drinking alcohol, sleeping
for more than two nights in the same room as a lay person, and even
looking at an army.

Other rules in the Vinaya are practical ones such as the obligation to
care for sick monks, illustrated by Buddha himself, and the rule
forbidding footwear other than soft sandals, because of an occasion

when monks wearing clogs disturbed their fellow monks' meditation and destroyed insect life unnecessarily.

The 227 rules of the Vinaya are recited once a fortnight in the community. They are known as the *Patimokka* (P) or *Pratimoksha* (S) rules and the recitation ceremony is called the *Uposatha*. Monks who have infringed the rules are expected to confess. There are even more rules for nuns (when nuns existed) which seek to establish the superior authority of the male bhikkhu. Nuns must keep eight important rules:

1. To respect as a senior any monk no matter how young
2. To keep the rains retreat only where monks are present
3. To wait for the monks to appoint the uposatha day and preach the patimokka sermon
4. The ceremony at the end of the retreat can only be undertaken in the presence of monks
5. Penance for lesser offences must be given by both orders
6. Full ordination can only be given by the presence of monks as well as nuns
7. No nun can criticise a monk
8. No nun can officially admonish a monk

Many of the rules for monks are genuinely concerned with promoting the reduction of craving and the path to nirvana; however, many other rules are simply practical and others seem to uphold the good image of the sangha in the eyes of the public.

For instance, it is not enough not to touch a woman, but one must avoid any possibility of being suspected of such a thing by never sitting alone with a woman. The good image of the sangha is considered necessary to fulfil its role as an example to the people. For more on the monastic lifestyle, ordination customs etc, see p72.

The Theravada Way - Meditation

Meditation is central in Buddhism because only through deliberate training of the citta (mind-and-heart) can one begin to purify the mind of false views, cravings, hatreds, and follow the path which leads to nirvana. It was as a direct result of meditation that the Buddha himself attained enlightenment, and it was in a state of deep meditation that he finally died.

Meditation involves one-third of the Noble Eightfold Path - right effort, right mindfulness and right concentration. **Right effort** is the deliberate cultivation of the good aspects of one's personality and the deliberate suppression of undesirable aspects. One must also cultivate new virtues and avoid gaining any new vices. These are called the 'Four Right Efforts'. **Right mindfulness** is the development of awareness and **right concentration** refers to the deliberate cultivation of higher states of consciousness through meditation.

Meditation is in many ways personal and practical and cannot properly be described in words, only experienced. Ideally one should have an individual teacher who can guide you as appropriate for your own problems; inappropriate meditation can lead to dangerous results as was found in the Buddha's lifetime when several monks committed suicide when concentrating too much on disgust for the body. Meditation can become disturbing if the mind reaches different states of consciousness or uncovers fears long hidden in the unconscious. As the goal of meditation is to reveal 'the truth about the way things are' (*dhamma*), it might cause trauma before calm.

It is important to have the correct situation to meditate in. The early followers of the Buddha often chose the lonely forest; modern practitioners might choose a quiet room. It helps to have a regular time set aside every day when one is neither too hungry, full or sleepy. A Buddha statue and a candle might help to create the right atmosphere. The traditional posture is the crosslegged lotus position, ie with the soles of the feet on the opposite thigh, this position is said to keep the mind alert. An alternative is to sit upright in a chair with the feet together, the back straight and the hands folded in the lap palms upwards. Traditionally the right hand rests on the left.

There are two basic types of meditation - *samatha* (leading to calmness and control of the mind) and *vipassana* (leading to insight into the nature of reality).

Samatha meditation

Samatha meditation usually starts with the cultivation of **mindfulness** - the awareness of oneself and the various states one is in. There are four main types of mindfulness - being mindful of the body, feelings, mind and mental states, in other words becoming aware of the current state of the five *skandhas* of body, sensations, perceptions, impulses and consciousness - simply observing what is there and how one state succeeds another, as a preliminary to further control over oneself. Mindfulness tends to lead to a calming of physical and mental states, which is not only useful in itself but indispensable for further meditation. It is usual to start with mindfulness of the body which in practice means observation of some bodily process like breathing or walking. Breathing meditation is usually taught to beginners. The idea is to attempt to concentrate solely on breathing, letting all distracting thoughts and feelings fade away. It helps to count the breaths - up to about one hundred - and to try to feel the air entering and leaving through the nose.

Samatha meditation involves the gradual attainment of higher states of consciousness through becoming totally detached from the external world of sense perception and from the normal run of thoughts and feelings. The states which can be reached in *samatha* are very difficult to describe, but the Buddhist scriptures speak of four levels of *jhana* (P) or *dhyana* (S) in which the mind is increasingly detached from normal consciousness, and passes beyond the realm of sense-desire into that of pure form. Beyond the fourth level it is claimed that one can go on to increasingly rarefied states of consciousness known as the 'Four Formless *Jhanas*' or on to the six 'superknowledges' of psychic powers, supernatural hearing, the ability to read minds, ability to see into the past, clairvoyance and the final knowledge that all the outflows of desire, hatred, becoming and wrong views have been destroyed (which is equivalent to reaching nirvana).

The 'formless *jhanas*' and 'superknowledges' become increasingly difficult to imagine but the first four jhanas are often described, and are particularly important as the Buddha passed into *parinirvana* (S) at the fourth *jhana*. They are described in the Buddhist scriptures as follows: **The first level of *jhana*** is a state of detachment like that achieved by the *bodhisattva* as a boy under the tree at ploughing time. Filled with a sense of rapture and joy, one is still thinking in the ordinary, discursive type of way, but with a high degree of clarity and concentration. **The second level of *jhana*** is reached when one learns to quieten the endless chatter of the mind and can dwell in a state of stilled consciousness, concentrated, rapturous and joyful. **The third level of *jhana*** is reached when the excitement of rapture fades away leaving a more spiritual and rarefied joy. **The fourth level of *jhana*** passes beyond even joy to a state of clear, calm, pure consciousness, totally peaceful and undisturbed. This state is sometimes referred to as *samadhi* (concentration) and is described in the same words that are used to attempt to describe *nirvana* - cessation, peace, purity, etc..

The fourth *jhana* sounds, to the ordinary person, like the highest state of consciousness one can possibly imagine achieving, but Buddhist texts talk of a further four 'formless states' described as 'endless space', 'endless consciousness', 'nothing whatsoever' and 'neither perception nor non-perception'. Perhaps these are not meant to be 'higher' states of consciousness than the fourth *jhana* but descriptions of 'deeper' states of consciousness that the fully trained mind can explore. These states are not mentioned in the Buddha's enlightenment and so are perhaps not vital for liberation.

The meditation on love is a down to earth type of meditation which can be safely recommended to beginners and non-Buddhists. This involves the conjuring up of loving feelings which are then sent out to all beings in the universe. There are four types of loving feeling, known as the *Brahma-viharas* or 'Godlike states' as they resemble the sort of total and unconditional love attributed to God.

The first is *metta* (friendliness or loving kindness), the feeling of wishing well to all beings 'may all beings be happy and at their ease, may they be joyful and live in safety'. In the actual practice of this meditation one is advised to begin by feeling the love for oneself especially if your sense of self esteem is low, and then extending this feeling in ever-increasing circles to a friend of the same sex, a fairly neutral person and finally an enemy. The love should finally embrace the whole universe down to the last insect. This type of meditation is meant to spill out into your daily behaviour and help you become a more loving person in practice; but even just thinking loving thoughts helps to purify your mind, and may actually have some kind of effect on the world.

The second type of love is *karuna* (compassion}, the sincere sorrow over all the sufferings undergone by beings in this world and the wish that they could be freed from suffering, with the resolution that you will do everything you can to help them.

The third type of love is *mudita* (sympathetic joy), the sincere rejoicing in the happiness of others, a genuine gladness over the times when things go well for others, both physically and spiritually - for some a harder thing to feel than compassion which can contain elements of condescending pity.

The fourth type of love is *upekkha* (even-mindedness), the loving of all beings equally, not being selectively attached to family or friends, but feeling the kind of love a mother has for her child for all beings without exception. Even-mindedness also means not getting too carried away with these feelings emotionally, but having a clear and genuine goodwill to all.

Vipassana meditation

Vipassana meditation is a more intellectual process and involves analytical thinking. It resembles a deeper type of mindfulness where the meditator analyses the real makeup of his own physical and mental states, and the environment he lives in. It involves deep contemplation of the truths of Buddhism, such as the Four Noble Truths, impermanence, and 'no-self', until these are seen to be true in one's own experience - one can then be said to have gained *vipassana* (insight) into oneself and the world, and to have increased in wisdom.

Some Buddhists stress the importance of *samatha* and others *vipassana*. What is clear is that both calm and insight are needed to penetrate 'the truth of the way things really are'.

The actual topics for meditation, especially of the more thinking kind, are endless, but there is a list of forty traditional topics which have been found useful for the different types of person. The 5th century CE Theravadin writer, Buddhaghosa, divides people into six basic types and recommends certain practices for each type. The extrovert person, inclined to **greed** and too attached to the material world, should meditate on the ten different types of decomposing corpses to help to dislodge his attachment to worldly pleasures. Sometimes meditators even went into cremation grounds to bring this lesson home. Another useful topic is to analyse what the human body is really made up of under the skin, which should help induce disgust for it. This is not appropriate for introverted or depressed people however but those whose zest for life is too strong. The cheerful type of person with a simple, sunny nature inclined to **faith** should concentrate on the happy and faith inspiring aspects of Buddhism, such as the recollection of the Buddha and his good qualities, the wonders of the *Dharma*, the shining example of the *Sangha*. He should think about morality and generosity to inspire himself to positive action, and about the gods and heavens.

The negative type of person inclined to **hatred** should cultivate the four *brahma-viharas* or types of love, and try to relax by concentrating on discs of pure colour - blue, yellow, red or white. The two confused types, ruled by either **delusion** or too much **discursive** thinking should try to gather themselves together by mindful breathing and by concentrating on one object.

The type of person ruled by **intelligence** and therefore the least far from the Buddhist goal, can advance best by meditating on the truths of death, peace, analysing the body into the four elements, and perceiving the disgusting aspects of the process of food.

Useful for any type of person at any time are the final ten topics - concentration on a *kasina* (device) such as earth, water, fire, air, light, or an enclosed space eg a circle or square. If they can be achieved the formless *jhanas* of endless space, endless consciousness, nothing whatsoever and neither perception nor non-perception are recommended for all personality types.

In actual practice people will develop their own combination - a common pattern would be to start with mindfulness of breathing, pass on to concentration on one object, then thinking about some aspect of Buddhism, then finally sending out thoughts of love.

Magical Powers

It is often said that supernormal powers can be gained by having a mind made powerful through meditation. The Buddha himself is attributed with supernormal powers as are some of his disciples, notably Moggallana. However, these are very underplayed in Buddhism, the Buddha often forbids his monks to display these powers, and it is against the *Vinaya* rules to display magical powers to laymen. It is considered that they can be a distraction from the path to *nirvana* (they can be achieved by non-Buddhists), they are not essential, but can occasionally come in useful for teaching purposes. The five mundane superknowledges (as opposed to the sixth superknowledge which is supermundane and equivalent to *nirvana*) that are said to be achievable by the mind made supple by *jhana* meditation are magical powers, supernatural hearing, the knowledge of others' thoughts, the recollection of former lives and clairvoyant knowledge of the situation of all beings and the *karma* that caused it. Two of these powers feature in the Buddha's enlightenment experience, and he is seen exercising the others in the Pali Canon. The magical powers are said to include the ability to create magical doubles of oneself, the power to become invisible, to pass through walls or other solid bodies, to dive in and out of the earth as if it were water, to walk on water as if it were earth, to fly through the air, to touch the moon or sun, to travel either in person or in a magical 'mind made' double to other worlds and planets, including the realms of the gods, the ability to turn a little food into much, or ordinary food into delicious food and the ability to appear in other forms, ie as a different person, or an animal.

As these powers are kept quiet by accomplished meditators, it is difficult to comment. Although much of this seems quite unbelievable in the modern scientific age it is perhaps not totally mythological. It is interesting that similar powers are attributed to holy men in other religions, such as Jesus. Possibly they are meant to be taken in a symbolic way, but some people do claim to have witnessed such marvels.

The Theravada Way - Wisdom

The meaning of 'wisdom' in Theravada Buddhism is complete insight into things as they really are. At its highest level it is another word for enlightenment. For lesser beings it means some level of understanding the truth that was discovered by the Buddha. In Indian philosophy 'understanding the truth' is never a merely intellectual affair; but affects one's whole life - a person is not considered wise unless his or her knowledge is reflected in moral behaviour, mental and emotional states. Thus, the Buddha not only discovered how to overcome craving and ignorance and escape from samsara, but actually achieved this escape. To gain wisdom then, is to see the truth of the Buddha's discovery, the Four Holy Truths, the chain of causation, the impermanence, unsatisfactoriness and lack of essence in life, and the reality of nirvana. This is referred to in the eightfold path as having the right 'view' and the right 'attitude' (ie the practical application of wisdom). At first, the Buddhist provisionally accepts these truths with faith, trusting the authority of the Buddha. However, with sustained effort at analytical thought and deep meditation one should penetrate into the truths for yourself, to reach the state where you no longer have to believe but actually **know**. Some aspects of Buddhist wisdom require more faith than others; it is fairly easy with some serious reflection to accept the truth of *dukkha* (suffering), rather more difficult to accept the truth of *anatta* (no-self), and one could not be said to have personally verified the truth of rebirth until one gained the ability to remember past lives, which is a rare occurrence.

The method of gaining wisdom in Buddhism is a combination of study and deep meditation. A gifted teacher is an invaluable help, and there has long been a tradition in Indian religion of having a personal religious counsellor who guides your progress at the appropriate rate. An example of a gifted Buddhist teacher is the 2nd century BCE monk and philosopher Nagasena who explained the main concepts of Buddhism to a king of Greek origin and managed to convert him to Buddhism. Their conversations are recorded in *The Questions of King Milinda*, a book not actually in the Pali Canon but widely respected as scriptural in the Theravada world.[4]

King Milinda has been identified as a real historical figure, who ruled over an area in the extreme North West of India, which had been conquered by settlers from Central Asia which was then part of the Greek Empire. Milinda is the Indian version of the Greek name Menander. As a good ruler, Milinda was interested in the religious beliefs of his subjects and kept up the customary rites of the Brahmin priests. As an example, we will look at Nagasena's explanation of two difficult Buddhist concepts, no-self and *nirvana*.

Anatta (no-self)

Nagasena very cleverly introduces the concept of no-self when first presented to the King. When asked his name, instead of the polite reply expected, Nagasena answers that although he was named Nagasena this is a mere label as are all names, and does not actually imply that there is a corresponding entity in reality 'no real person can be apprehended.' Nagasena is really denying the idea of the *atman* but the King initially imagines that Nagasena is denying the existence of the psychophysical organism that the King sees standing before him, which is totally absurd. Who would then be doing the denying? The King tries to bring out this absurdity by arguing that if there are no real persons, it makes nonsense even of Buddhism. Who then gives to the monks, commits evil actions, follows the Buddhist path, meditates, etc? However, the King has misunderstood. Nagasena is not claiming that he does not exist in a conventional sense but that he does not exist as a permanent, separate, independent entity - the *atman* believed in by the Hindus. A person merely exists as a collection of impermanent factors temporarily combined in a certain way, interdependent with his environment and conditioned by external factors. We call this 'myself' for convenience, but this use of words is misleading - we can start thinking there is an eternal separate independent reality called 'me'. The antidote to this danger is an analysis of the human being, of the kind used in Buddhist meditation. Nagasena does not preach 'the truth of no-self' but challenges the King to analyse the human being and see if he can find a 'self'.

The King proceeds to do this and lists the thirty-two physical parts of the body recognised by Buddhists - nails, bones, heart, lungs, blood, bile, urine, etc. (An analytical form of meditation recommended to those who want to overcome sexual desire). None of these deserve to be viewed as the 'real me'. Nor do any of the five *skandhas* which make up a human being - your physical form, your feelings, your perceptions, your impulses or your consciousness. None of these can be said to be the 'real you', as they are always changing without you claiming to be another person. They are outside your full control. What applies to the *skandhas* separately, applies to them when taken together; yet, other than the skandhas, no 'you' can be discovered. A 'self' (as an entity rather than a word) just cannot be found by analysis.

To make this clearer Nagasena compares the label 'self' to the label 'chariot'. One uses the word chariot without any problems in everyday speech, yet if the same technique of analysis is applied, one cannot actually find an entity to which the word chariot applies. The word does not refer to any of the component parts of a chariot such as axle or wheel, nor to a combination of such parts which could equally easily be a cart, or heap of spare parts; nor is 'chariot' some mysterious invisible entity separate from the parts and dwelling within them. The word chariot is merely a label to describe a collection of parts put together in a certain way for a certain use. This does not mean that chariots or people do not exist in the ordinary sense of the word; it is appropriate to use the word when the required parts are present in the correct combination. However, it does mean that chariots and people do not exist on the level of ultimate reality, the eternal, unconditioned level of being. The word 'self', then, does not mean the *atman*, an eternal, unconditioned ultimately real entity, but is simply a convenient label for a collection of atoms and mental processes, temporary, impermanent and dependent on conditions, viewed in a certain way.

Rebirth

If there is no *atman* or soul-self, rebirth cannot be understood as in the Greek or Hindu idea of eternal soul changing bodies like discarding worn out clothes for new. If no soul passes on, how can there be continuity between one life and the next? King Milinda asks Nagasena whether the person in one life can be said to be the same as the person in the next life, or whether the two are really two different persons. Nagasena replies that the two are neither identical nor completely different. The relationship is one of cause and effect; you in your next life are related to you in your past life because the two are joined in a series of continuous cause and effect. The situation is only the same as that we observe happening during the course of one life; the relationship between 'you' as a baby and 'you' as an adult is not one of identity nor complete difference, but the adult is a direct result of the child together with everything that has happened to it in between. A person is a series of events, one arising from the one before, conditioned by it. This happens from one moment to the next as one *dharma* succeeds another, from one day to the next, one year to the next, one decade to the next, one life to the next. Nagasena makes other comparisons which might help; the flame in a lamp burning at the end of night is not the identical flame that was burning at the beginning of the night, but is a direct result of it. Milk, curds, butter, and ghee (clarified butter used in Indian cooking) are not identical but are a direct result of each other being subjected to certain conditions.

Because each life is a direct result of the one before, the process of *karma* can operate; what 'you' are in your next life will be a direct consequence of what 'you' are doing in this one, just as a person malnourished in childhood may suffer illness as an adult. Nagasena compares the process of *karma* to planting seeds. If a thief steals mangoes from a tree, he is not actually stealing the identical mangoes planted in the ground by the farmer, but as the mangoes on the tree were a direct result of the mangoes planted in the ground, he will still be punished for taking the farmer's property. Similarly, deeds done in one life lead to consequences in the next.

Nirvana

Nirvana is notoriously difficult to talk about, yet unless suffering beings are given some notion of what it is, they will not be inspired to strive to gain it. Nagasena manages to give King Milinda sufficient idea of nirvana to inspire him to become a Buddhist, through discussion and comparisons. Much of what he says is in response to the King's questions and therefore appropriate to the King's thinking.

Nirvana is first of all cessation; it is the complete stopping of the miserable cycle of life called *samsara* and therefore the end of all misery. It is not an automatic achievement but can only be gained by those who make a personal effort. We may not be able to imagine it, but can know that it is supremely worthwhile from the example of those who have achieved it, in the same way as we do not have to have our own hands cut off before we believe it would hurt. *Nirvana* in itself is ineffable, indescribable, but some of its qualities can be hinted at by comparisons. It is ease, peace. It is like cool water removing the heat and thirst of our desires. It is like medicine curing our suffering and leaving us in secure health. It is like space in that it is immeasurable and infinite, never came into being nor will ever pass away, cannot be grasped or stolen, is not dependent on anything else, and provides an environment for enlightened beings, as the sky does for birds. Like the magic wishing jewel of Indian folklore, it grants all the heart's desires and brings great joy. Like a rocky mountain peak it is inaccessible to the dreary passions of *samsara* and just **is**, without any reference to human desires and reasons.

Nirvana is not the result of a causal process. It is not affected or conditioned by any external factors. It is a misuse of words to claim that nirvana is 'caused' by the eightfold path - the path does not cause nirvana, rather it enables one to realise nirvana, which has always been there. This is compared to the way a man can travel to see the Himalayan mountains but cannot cause them to come to him or cause their existence; or the way a man can travel to a distant shore, but cannot cause the shore to come to him, and did not cause its existence. Just as the Himalayas are unaffected by the man, *nirvana* is unaffected by any external conditions.

As *nirvana* is described as unconditional, not made, not produced, not existing in time either past, present or future, not detectable by senses, it is very easy to get the impression that nirvana is something negative. However, it is 'something which is' because it can actually be experienced by the purified mind of an enlightened person. Like the wind, you cannot point it out or grasp hold of it, but it can be known from its effects.

When a person achieves nirvana but is still living a human life, he still feels physical pain like anyone else (as the nerves etc are still present) but he is free from all mental pain and confusion and can more easily cope with the physical pain. An arhat does not commit suicide, because he is content to let the cycle of his life run down to its end, having passed beyond all selfish desires. He may still enjoy physical pleasures such as eating good food, but he does this without any attachments or cravings. He will look after the body and give it its requirements, but not out of greed for pleasure but simply to stay alive and healthy in order that his body and mind may function as they should.

Nagasena's explanations of *anatta*, rebirth and *nirvana* are helpful even today, as we might ask similar questions to those of a Greek King of the 2nd century BCE. He is an excellent example of a wise teacher with the gift of *upaya* or knowing the right thing to say. He works at the King's level of knowledge and understanding, responding to questions initiated by the King. He is not contemptuous of the King's ideas, but lets him work them through for himself. Instead of preaching at the King, he leads him to work out the answers for himself, by encouraging analytical thought; yet he does not leave the King without help, guiding and controlling the discussion from the very beginning -Nagasena is really in control of the direction of the discussion, yet the King is made to feel he is.

Finally, we are told that Nagasena did not just talk about Buddhism, but actually lived it, teaching the Dharma by example. Without this, he would be a clever intellectual, but not what Buddhists would call a man of wisdom.

Theravada countries - Sri Lanka

Countries which practice Theravada Buddhism today include Sri
Lanka, Burma, Thailand, Laos and Cambodia. The first three see
themselves as strongholds of the Theravada tradition, Sri Lanka
claiming expertise in the *Sutta* section of the scriptures, Thailand in
the *Vinaya* section and Burma in the *Abhidhamma* section.

History

Sri Lanka was the first country beyond the Indian mainland to which
Buddhism spread, and the Sri Lankan Buddhists are very proud of
their 2,300-year-old tradition of Buddhism. The people of Sri Lanka
are 80% from the Sinhalese race, most of whom are Buddhists. Others
are Hindu Tamils, with some Muslims and Christians. The Sinhalese
people are thought to have originated in North East India and to have
invaded Sri Lanka in the 5th century BCE. Tamils from South India
also settled in the North and East of the island.

The Sinhalese capital was established at Anuradhapura. In the 3rd
century BCE King Asoka of India sent his son, a monk called
Mahinda, with four other monks, to preach Buddhism to King Tissa.
The King was successfully converted, a *sangha* and monastery
founded, and holy relics brought from India. King Tissa tried, like
Ashoka, to establish a civilisation based on Buddhist precepts and
built many reservoirs to help his people. Anuradhapura remained the
capital and centre of Buddhism until the 11th century CE. Many
ancient monuments and relics from this time can still be seen today.
Perhaps the holiest is the Sacred Bo-tree said to have been grown from
a cutting of the original Bo-tree (the tree under which the Buddha was
enlightened) brought from India by Asoka's daughter, a nun called
Sanghamitta. Many huge stupas (or dagobas as they are called in Sri
Lanka) can be seen, dating back to the 3rd and 2nd centuries BCE.
One is said to contain a relic of the Buddha's collarbone. This early
history was not without troubles. During the 2nd century BCE Tamil
invaders ruled over the Sinhalese, leading to the famous struggle by
the Sinhalese hero Dutthagamani in the 1st century BCE. The
Sinhalese regained Anuradhapura at the cost of much bloodshed, in a
war fought in the name of Buddhism. Even monks disrobed and
joined in the fighting, on the grounds that violence was justified to
protect their Buddhist tradition. In the two thousand years since then,
Buddhism has always been closely tied in with Sinhalese nationalism.
It was in these troubled times that the Pali Canon was put into writing
for the fear that the Buddhist tradition would be lost.

In the early centuries CE several monasteries were founded following different Buddhist sects, including some of Mahayana influence. In spite of upheavals, Buddhism seems to have flourished and much care spent on building stupas and statues, such as the beautiful 4th century statue of the Buddha meditating. In the 11th century a dynasty of Tamil Kings ruled and Buddhism declined. Many monasteries were sacked. When Buddhism was revived in 1065 the order of monks had to be reintroduced from Burma, and the order of nuns had died out completely. The 12th century King Parakramabahu defeated the Tamils and built many stupas, monasteries and statues in the new capital of Polonnaruwa. Again the remains of these can still be seen today. A particularly beautiful monument is the huge carving of the Buddha meditating and the Buddha's *parinirvana*, hewn out of rock. The Kings at this period were honoured as *bodhisattvas* or future Buddhas. Polonnaruwa fell in the 13th century and the island was divided into smaller kingdoms, some Tamil-ruled. At the same time contact was established with the outside world through Arab traders whose Muslim descendants still live in Sri Lanka today and among other trades come in very useful as butchers. In the 15th century the Chinese invaded, which was probably the island's last contact with Mahayana Buddhism. In 1505, the Portuguese invaded and took over the coastal kingdom around Colombo. Some people were converted to Catholicism and many adopted Portuguese names.

The central mountain kingdom of Kandy remained independent, but at times was ruled by Kings who favoured Hindu Shiva-worship. Buddhism in the 16th and 17th centuries was very weak. There was not even the quorum of five monks needed for ordination ceremonies, which meant the King had to send for Burmese monks to perform these. Pali scholarship was at an all-time low and the ordinary people were drifting back into superstitions.

In 1658 the Dutch invaded, originally invited to help evict the Portuguese. They began the colonial system of growing cash crops like sugar, tobacco and coffee, and attempted to convert people to Protestant Christianity. This was less successful as it lacked the appeal of the more colourful Catholicism.

In the early 18th century there was a revival of Buddhism under a Kandyan King who was actually a Tamil. This time monks from Thailand were brought to the island and established an order of monks which still today is known as the Siamese Order, divided into two chapters, based in two very influential monasteries in Kandy. A separate order was introduced in 1802 from Burmese tradition, and a third in 1864 for lower-caste monks, excluded from the Siamese order.

In 1796 the island became part of the British Empire and the fiercely independent Kingdom of Kandy finally fell in 1815. The British continued the cash-crop policy and concentrated on growing tea, rubber and coconut, which have dominated the Sri Lankan economy up to today. They also brought in Tamil labourers for plantation work, which increased the racial problem causing such violence in the 1970s and 1980s.

The presence of the British caused some loosening of faith in the traditional Buddhism, especially in the face of Western scientific advances. However, other Westerners were attracted by Buddhism and actually helped in its revival. The late 19th century and early 20th century Theosophical Society was very influential here (see p156). Colonel Olcott, one of the founders of Theosophy started up the Young Men's Buddhist Association to counteract the attractions of the YMCA and pioneered Buddhist Sunday Schools. He designed the Buddhist flag, still in use today. Olcott also encouraged Dharmapala, a Sinhalese man who started the Anagarika Movement. This was a way of life half-way between that of a monk and a layman. Anagarikas wear white and combine the spirituality of a monk with a more practical living in the world of a layperson. Dharmapala was involved in the establishment of a the Mahabodhi Society which aimed to unite Buddhism internationally and reclaimed the sacred sites in India from Hindu ownership. Dharmapala visited England in 1925 and formed the British Mahabodhi Society, which still continues today. It is ironic that many of the intellectual Buddhists of this century in Sri Lanka learned about Buddhism from books written by Western scholars, and follow a kind of 'reformed', rationalised Buddhism, rather different from the traditional practice of 2,300 years.

Politically, Sri Lanka gained independence in 1948 and established a democratic government on British lines. The power has alternated between a conservative and socialist/nationalist party. Both parties have favoured the promotion of Buddhism, partly as a statement of national identity in opposition to the Christianity of the British Empire. This has pleased the Sinhalese Buddhist majority and has had the backing of the politically powerful Buddhist orders. This pro-Buddhist attitude has alienated many in the Tamil Hindu minority, who fear discrimination against their language and culture. This has led to the current campaign for a separate Tamil state in the Northern half of Sri Lanka.

The Monastic Sangha

The *sangha* (community of monks) is the centre of Buddhist life; wherever the sangha flourishes, the faith of the people follows. The original *bhikkhus* who followed the Buddha were homeless wanderers dressed in scrapheap rags, sleeping under trees, but today's monk will more likely live in a monastery and wear robes donated by the lay folk, a tendency that had already started during the lifetime of the Buddha. In Sri Lanka today there are approximately 15,000 monks who still command great respect from the community.

In Sri Lanka, though not in other Theravada countries, a boy tends to become a monk for life, although it is no shame to leave the monastery if this seems desirable, as all things are impermanent. One can become a novice monk at any age; many join in boyhood - over the age of seven, others as youths searching for meaning in life, and still others upon retirement.

The ceremony of ordination follows traditional instructions going back to the time of the Buddha. There are two levels of ordination - ordination as a *samanera* (novice) and full ordination as a *bhikkhu* (monk), for which one must be at least twenty years old. If a boy joins the order as a novice at a young age he usually attends *pirivena*, the monastic school or seminary.

The candidate for ordination has his head and beard shaved off, during which time he should meditate upon his departing hair as a lesson in impermanence and humility. He is bathed with water as a symbol of purification, and has the requirements of his monastic life prepared, such as robe, bowl, sandals, umbrella. These are usually donated by his family. If the ordination is to full monkhood, the candidate will have previously been examined in his knowledge of the Buddha's teaching and the monastic rules. The ordination requires the presence of at least five monks of good standing, and takes place within the *sima* (boundaries of the monastery), marked out in a special ceremony. The candidate is usually presented for ordination by his tutor as sponsor. He kneels in front of the presiding monk wearing the white of a layman and carrying his yellow robe. He asks permission to be allowed to wear the yellow robes and become ordained. The presiding monk ties the sash of the robe around the candidate's neck, while he recites a formula of meditation on the perishable nature of the body. The candidate then puts on his robe with special words expressing the purpose of the robe as necessary covering only, and not for ornamental use. He then begs forgiveness for faults and asks to be administered the three refuges and the ten precepts of a monk. The threefold refuge formula is recited three times and the ten precepts recited after his tutor. If the ceremony is an *Upasampada* (full ordination), further rituals are involved. His alms bowl is solemnly strapped to his back and he is examined on certain traditional points as to his suitability to join the order. This involves a solemn asserting of his real name, his tutor's name, his possession of the material requisites such as robe and bowl. He must then swear that he does not suffer from any disqualifying disease, that he is human and a male, free from slavery, debt or military service; that he has the permission of his parents, and is twenty years of age. If the assembly is satisfied, and the lack of objection is shown by silence, the candidate is accepted as a *bhikkhu*.

A monk who has been ordained for ten years is given the title *thera* (elder), and one who has been ordained for twenty years *mahathera* (senior elder). He may live in various types of monastery. It might be in one of the large monastic foundations which include a school or even an institute of higher education; it might be in a small establishment of one or two monks who function as a type of parish priest to a village community; or it might be the life of a forest dwelling or hermit monk, living completely away from society in a life dedicated to meditation. The name for a monastery is a *vihara*. It consists typically of the *pansala* (monk's living quarters), a temple or shrine with a statue of the Buddha, a preaching hall, a *stupa* (relic monument) and a bo-tree, surrounded by a protective parapet.

The lifestyle of the monk is strict, according to the 227 moral precepts and other rules of the vinaya. The organisation of the community is democratic, and the position of abbot is an elected one. Respect is shown for seniority in the order, calculated on how long one has been ordained. Monks have few personal possessions in order that they are as detached as possible from worldly concerns. Normal personal requisites would include two sets of robes, a bowl, sewing equipment for mending one's robe, a razor, fan, umbrella, sandals and prayer beads. The sleeping mat and other bedding is often donated by the parents. Monks' robes are shades of bright orange in Sri Lanka. The original idea was to sew together rags which were then dyed with natural pigment in the earth - producing an ochre colour. Nowadays the robes are donated by the lay people once a year or more.

Monks are not allowed to work for money and rely on lay people for support. This may be given in the traditional alms-round, where monks travel through the villages and people give food. Monks may be invited to certain families' houses for meals on a rota system or lay people may bring food to the monasteries. Some monks prefer to practice the traditional alms round as they feel it is more dignified, a useful form of self-discipline and an exercise in humility. It should also be an occasion for mindful meditation. Despite theoretical poverty, some of the large monasteries have become wealthy landowners through donations and have considerable worldly influence. Individual monks however still have the bare minimum.

Monks also renounce family life and remain celibate. A wife and children bind you fast to worldly concerns, worries and joys, and sexual desire is considered one of the most powerful of the selfish cravings tying you down to *samsara*.

The typical day of a monk includes an early rising, two meals, breakfast and lunch with only tea allowed after midday. Periods of the day will be set aside for meditation, study of Buddhist texts, and services to the lay people. These involve performing ceremonies, preaching sermons, administering the precepts and counselling. The hermit monks spend much time in meditation, other monks may be teachers with little spare time for meditation. Once a year they must keep the *vassa* (rainy season retreat) during which their movements are more restricted and religious practice intensifies. At the end of the retreat is a ceremony involving the lay people (Kathina).

There have been no fully ordained *bhikkhunis* (nuns) in the Theravada tradition since the line of ordination died out in the 11th century. However, there are women who shave their heads and wear the orange robes. They keep all the ten precepts of a monk and are referred to as 'ten precept mothers'. However, they are technically only lay sisters or *upasikas* and do not have the same social status as monks. They tend to have more difficulty obtaining donations and may have to do their own shopping and cooking. This may be something that will change with social changes.

The Lay Buddhist

In Theravada countries lay Buddhists are seen as inferior in religious status to monks. Their religion can only be a part of a life that has many other concerns, such as earning a living and family life. Traditionally, monks had superior religious education and lay people would have been taught their religion by them. Today, however, there are lay professors of Buddhist studies, and, as in other religions, the relationship between monks and householders is undergoing some changes. Lay Buddhists have different levels of involvement in the religion. Some are nominal or 'social' Buddhists at times like funerals, others are very pious in religious observance, and others will investigate the philosophy and doctrines of the religion, practice meditation and become as learned in the religion as many monks.

The typical ordinary lay Buddhist in Sri Lanka does not aim for nirvana as an immediate goal. His idea of nirvana may be very hazy, but he will recognise it as an ultimate goal for some other lifetime. Meanwhile, his or her main religious task is to amass *punya* (merit) or good *karma* to ensure that his or her next life will be a good one.

Buddhist lay people have a strong belief in rebirth and *karma*. This tends to give them an attitude of acceptance of their present circumstances; if one is in a poor situation and others have riches, this must be accepted as it is probably due to the *karma* from one's past existences. However, not all misfortunes are attributed to bad *karma*. Some events have obvious physical causes, or may be caused by supernatural beings such as gods or demons. Although belief in *karma* leads to acceptance of the present situation, it also means one can do something about one's future by collecting merit. Merit can be gained in three main ways - by moral behaviour, by taking part in religious ceremonies and by supporting the *sangha*. The path of the lay Buddhist is not so much morality, meditation and wisdom as morality, generosity and piety.

The main moral precepts kept by Buddhist laypeople have been described in the chapter on morality (see p 53ff). Most people respect the precepts even if at times they may be broken or bent. Killing living beings is deplored, but many Sri Lankans will eat meat, if they can afford it, and especially fish. This is a compromise with reality, as the island cannot afford to ignore the source of protein on its shores and lakes. Those who eat meat generally excuse themselves by not killing the animal themselves, even if they reared it for eating. As a result of this bad conscience of Sinhalese Buddhists, most butchers seem to be Muslims. Alcohol is legal and readily available, but drinking is frowned on by the respectable and banned in the holy city of Anuradhapura out of respect for the Buddha. Materialistic greed is considered very un-Buddhist and frowned upon, although here Buddhism has to compete with the pressures of modern advertising of Western-style consumer products. As well as following the precepts, there are ten good deeds traditional (though not canonical) in Sinhalese Buddhism. Meritorious deeds include generosity, morality, meditating, rejoicing in another person's merit, giving away merit, serving others, showing respect to one's seniors, preaching Buddhism, listening to preaching and right beliefs.

Worship, festivals and ceremonies

Merit can be obtained by visiting the temple to perform *puja* (worship), taking part in festivals, going on pilgrimages and taking part in special ceremonies. Compared with the personal insight expected of the monk, the average lay person's Buddhism is more a matter of faith in the Buddha and that his teaching and his *sangha* are correct, whether or not they have fully understood it in the way the Buddha originally intended. This faith is expressed by frequent recitations of the formula of 'going for refuge' to the *Buddha*, the *Dharma* and the *Sangha* (see p53f), together with the renewed

undertaking of the five precepts. This may be done formally as a kind
of daily prayer in front of a small shrine of the Buddha in the home.
Many modern homes have at least a statue of the Buddha before
which are candles and flowers; however, this is relatively recent, since
cheap mass produced plaster statues became available. At any time of
the day or week, the pious layperson can visit the temple and make an
offering to the Buddha statue, *stupa* or bo-tree. This is particularly
popular on *poya* days, the holy days that occur four times a month at
the main phases of the moon, full moon being particularly holy.
Modern temples tend to be very bright and colourful, with three main
features. There will be a shrine room with a main Buddha image and
many other images, either statues or wall paintings telling the story of
Buddha's life, his previous existences, or depicting the future Buddha
Maitreya, Buddhas of past ages, arhats, or attendant gods. The statues
of the Buddha may be sitting crosslegged, standing, or lying (either
resting or depicting the parinirvana). There is a tendency to make the
statues very large, so that even the most uneducated person or small
child will be aware of the importance of this man. The temple thus
functions as an educational visual aid, as stained glass windows used
to do in English churches. People make offerings before the Buddha
image of the kinds of things offered to gods in India - foods, flowers,
lights, incense, and water. On *poya* days at the temples food is offered
twice a day, together with drumming. Although it looks very much
like the worship of a god, Buddhist *puja* is interpreted as showing
respect to a great man. It is not giving a gift to a supernatural being in
the hope of a supernatural reward but an act of dedication to the
Buddha's way, and a way of reminding yourself about his teaching. It
brings merit and purifies the mind. This interpretation is seen in the
Pali verses which are recited while offerings are made. When offering
flowers, one is reminding oneself of the truth of impermanence. While
offering incense, one should meditate on the infinite virtues of the
Buddha which is the true perfume. The offering of light is a symbol of
the enlightenment which Buddha's teaching brings:

In this way, traditional religious ritual has changed its meaning, and
become almost a form of meditation. The offerings which ordinary
people make have taken on a symbolic meaning, geared to the
spreading of the Buddhist message. Some of the rituals engaged in by
the lay people seem to have overtones which go against strict
Theravada doctrine, but this seems to have been tolerated in the case
of ordinary people since the time of the Buddha himself; people have
got to progress at their own pace. Thus in describing Sinhalese
Buddhist practice, Richard Gombrich suggests that although the
ordinary Buddhist understands that the Buddha is dead and cannot
help you, emotionally, in his heart, he wants a relationship with a
being who can help. For example, the offering of food is accompanied

by the words 'May the Lord accept this food from us, taking compassion on us.' Gombrich expresses this rather well in his comment that, for the ordinary Sinhalese, the Buddha is 'cognitively human but affectively divine'.[5] Another ceremony with supernatural overtones is the special ceremony needed for painting in the eyes of a Buddha image, after which it is somehow 'sacred' and 'alive'. Some practices seem left over from earlier customs - Buddhists will decorate the sacred bo-tree with brightly-coloured Buddhist flags (blue, yellow, red, white and orange stripes) which may be a survival from worship of tree spirits. Another meritorious practice is to circumambulate a *stupa* in a clockwise direction. A stupa is a dome-shaped monument built to house relics of the Buddha, or other holy people. In Sri Lanka they are usually painted brilliant white.

Particularly pious lay people - referred to as *upasakas* (if male) or *upasikas* (if female) - may spend the whole poya day at the temple, making offerings, listening to preaching and observing the eight precepts, which are formally administered and later absolved by a monk. They wear white and refrain from eating after midday, using comfortable chairs and beds, personal adornments and amusements. This is usually confined to older people, especially women.

Lay Buddhists enjoy colourful religious festivals. In Sri Lanka the main festivals are Wesak, Poson, Asala, the Perahera, and the ceremony at the end of the monk's rain retreat (Kathina).

Wesak occurs on the full moon of May and celebrates the Buddha's birth, enlightenment and death. More people than usual attend the temple, cards and gifts are given to friends and relations, processions are made, houses are decorated.

Poson on the full moon in June is peculiar to Sri Lanka as it celebrates the first arrival of Buddhism in the island when Asoka's son converted King Tissa.

Asala on the full moon in July celebrates the Buddha's conception, renunciation and First Sermon.

The Perahera (procession) is a festival which takes place in Kandy in the centre of the island, around the temple where the Buddha's tooth is kept. It occurs over 15 nights leading up to the full moon in August. There are colourful processions of decorated elephants, dancers, drummers and musicians. The festival honours the relic of the Buddha's tooth, and a replica of the golden casket in which it is kept is carried in the position of honour on the back of an elephant.

At the end of the rain retreat for the monks, there is a joyful ceremony

(Kathina) where the lay people give the monks new robes and other presents, and cook extra special food for them.

Pilgrimages are a popular way of earning merit, as they combine religious duty with a sense of holiday and of a goal in life. There are sixteen places of pilgrimage in Sri Lanka, which are associated with a legendary visit by Shakyamuni Buddha himself during his lifetime. A favourite pilgrimage is to climb the mountain known as Siripada, or Adam's Peak, which is said to bear the mark of the Buddha's footprint. Another would be to visit the sacred bo-tree and other ancient and holy sites in Anuradhapura.

The only 'lifecycle' ceremonies performed in Buddhism are the ordination ceremony and funeral ceremonies. There is no religious ceremony for birth or marriage which are considered purely worldly events and nothing to celebrate as far as Buddhism is concerned. The funeral ceremony prior to cremation does involve the monks, as death is significant in Buddhist thought. It is a good occasion to cause the living to reflect on the Buddhist truths of suffering and impermanence and monks will preach a sermon on those themes. Actions are also performed which are considered to aid the dead person. The corpse covering is given to the monks, the three refuges and five precepts are recited and the merit of the ceremony is transferred to the dead person by the symbolic act of pouring water. The funeral pyre may be covered with a paper *stupa* which is then set alight. People in mourning wear white, and white flags decorate the bereaved household and surrounding area. At fixed intervals after the funeral - one week, three months and on the anniversary - the bereaved offer meals to the monks to transfer the merit to the dead person by the water pouring ceremony.

This sharing of merit with a dead person is intended to improve their rebirth, but seems to go against a strict doctrinal interpretation of an individual's fate depending on his own *karma*. However, sharing of merit is a very old tradition in Buddhism. One is encouraged to share one's merit with the gods and *pretas* who cannot make their own, even in the Pali Canon. In defending this practice, Sinhalese Buddhists may say that what is really happening is that you are giving the dead person a chance to rejoice in your merit-making ceremony, and thus create his own merit. Or they may refer to the truth of *Anatta* as showing that we are not separate selves, completely on our own and uninfluenced by other people. It may be interpreted as merely a psychological consolation for the living who need to feel they are doing something for their dead relatives. However, whether or not sharing merit actually 'works', it seems a highly Buddhist attitude to want to share one's good *karma* with other beings, an attitude developed further in Mahayana Buddhism. Even in the Pali Canon the Buddha advised making food offerings for the *pretas* (hungry ghosts), though this may have been simply a survival of ancient ceremonies to placate dead spirits.

Another Buddhist ceremony which seems to seek supernatural aid against strict Theravada teaching is the ceremony of *pirit*, or reciting Buddhist texts as a protection against evil. As mentioned previously, certain texts from the Pali Canon are ritually recited by the monks for protection, which would make sense if a god were being asked for help, but not if one's fate is all one's own making. The *pirit* ceremony is undertaken at times of sickness, dedicating a new house, or particular troubles. A reel of thread is held by the monks and passed around the lay people involved. Texts are recited and water sprinkled. Some people explain the recitals as an attempt to convert evil spirits to more kind, Buddhist behaviour, but it represents an attempt to harness the power of Buddhism to a more worldly end. Some Buddhists say that it is not anything supernatural but the power of your own faith that protects you, thus reconciling the ceremony with orthodox doctrine.

Such practices reveal a gap in Theravada Buddhism, for it is that a religion that does not offer supernatural solutions to worldly problems, which is a function many people seek in religion. This gap is filled in Sri Lanka by turning to the gods, whose existence not even the Buddha denied. Gods may have the power to help with worldly problems, although it is clearly realised that they are impermanent beings and cannot help you spiritually. Thus, worship of the gods is hardly religion at all to Sri Lankans, more a matter of worldly pragmatism. The gods worshipped are often Hindu gods, who may have their own temple or *devale* or may even share a temple with the Buddha. Favourite gods are the Hindu gods Vishnu and Skandha or Kataragama.

As well as Hindu gods, local divinities, who may be ancient nature spirits, or deified saintly people from long ago, also receive requests for help. One such god is Dadimunda who is associated with exorcisms of women possessed by spirits. The ceremonies surrounding his worship are more exciting and emotional than the tranquil Buddhist ones. There may be dancing, and oracular statements delivered by people temporarily possessed. Sri Lankans may also believe in demons or evil spirits and there are various ceremonies to ward off their evil influence. This, however, has very little to do with Buddhism. The Buddhist orthodoxy tends to have an attitude of tolerance to such practices, just as the Buddha had with the folk beliefs of his day.

In conclusion, monks and lay Buddhists in Sri Lanka have different but mutually inter-dependent roles. The lay people are involved in practising morality, piety and generosity, supporting the monks with food, robes, other material needs, and with sons to keep the sangha going. The monks concentrate on morality, meditation and wisdom and seek to conserve and spread the teachings of the Buddha. They do this by preaching, teaching in Sunday Schools, performing religious ceremonies for the people and by example; which is why it is very important that they keep strictly to the Buddha's way.

Theravada Countries - Thailand

Thailand today is, at least on paper, one of the most Buddhist countries in the world, with 94% of its population adhering to the faith, a King who is constitutionally stipulated to be a Buddhist, and government supervised organisation of the sangha.

History

The history of Buddhism in Thailand is rather difficult to trace, as the country has only existed in its present form since the 18th century. Scholars differ over the question of when Buddhism first arrived in Thailand. Tradition claims that Ashoka's missionaries brought Theravada Buddhism to Thailand in the 3rd century BCE, which is the earliest possible date.

The Thai people arrived in the area around the 12th to 13th century CE, having originally come from China. Thai monks travelled to Sri Lanka to obtain ordination in the Ceylonese tradition. This Theravada of the Sri Lanka tradition soon superseded the other forms of Buddhism in Thailand. It was officially supported by the King, a tradition which has continued ever since. The country, unlike Sri Lanka, Burma, or Laos, was never colonised by European powers, which helped the survival of traditional ways; however, the country has been very influenced by America since the Second World War, especially during the Vietnam War when Thailand was the centre for soldiers on leave.

The Monastic *Sangha*

Since the 13th/14th century CE, Thailand has followed the Theravada tradition of Sri Lankan Buddhism, so the way of life of the monks is very similar to that of a Sri Lankan monk. However, there are some differences. One of these is that it is a custom in Thailand for every young man to spend some time as a monk. Thus the meaning of monkhood and its relation to lay life is somewhat altered. Boys will be ordained as a novice usually between twelve and eighteen, or more popularly as a *bhikkhu*, at the age of 20.

The ordination ceremony is more elaborate than in Sri Lanka and made into more of a social occasion. The basic ordination, receiving of robes, etc, is the same, but can last for two days. Generally seven days are spent in the monastery in preparation for the ceremony, learning the appropriate Pali phrases. On the first day of the ordination, the candidate is shaved at home and dressed in beautiful clothes resembling those of Prince Siddhartha. Then the monks come to his home to perform a pirit-type ceremony of chanting, holding cotton thread and sprinkling water in order to give strength to the candidate. After the monks depart, there is a lay ceremony, intended to strengthen the boy's *khwan* (vitality). This involves offerings arranged on a conical structure resembling a tree, reminders of everything the boy's parents have done for him, waving candles, anointing of the boy, and the tying of his wrists which symbolises the firm attachment of the boy's 'spirit' to him. People feast, sing and dance throughout most of the night, although the candidate is not involved. In the morning he is led in procession to the monastery with musicians, dancers and girls carrying gifts for the monks. The parents or sponsors bring the robes and other requisites. The ordination proper occurs in the traditional way, and the ceremony ends with a blessing and the pouring of water to share the merit with ancestors.

Ordinations usually take place in June, one month before the rains retreat is due to start. Many boys will only stay until the end of the rains retreat, a period of four months, in which they will learn some of the basics of Buddhism, a few Pali chants and some self-discipline. It is considered to be a useful experience, and functions socially as a kind of rite-of-passage into adult life. This is seen in the way many young men spend their time in the monastery immediately before getting married. Sometimes younger boys become monks to make merit if, for example, a grandparent has died. There is also a special ceremony of disrobing and leaving the order where the boy takes the five precepts of a layman again. It is traditional for him to be met at the monastery gate by a young girl, often his girlfriend.

As a result of this institution of temporary monkhood the number of monks in Thailand varies. Normally there are about 150,000 but in the rains retreat season the number swells to 300,000. Some monks may remain for longer than four months, perhaps a year or two. Others are monks for life. These monks will have a much greater knowledge of Buddhism and study Pali, practice meditation, preach and in various ways give their life to the *Dhamma*. There is a well-developed system of education for monks involving nine grades of examination. There are also special monastic universities where monks can learn secular subjects as well as Buddhism in order to be fully prepared to guide the modern, educated Buddhist layman.

The *sangha* is organised bureaucratically into provinces, districts, communes and individual temples or *wats*; and administered by a committee headed by a *sangharaja* (chief monk) who is employed by the government. There are two different orders, the smaller being a reformist group from the 19th century. There have been attempts to make sure Buddhist monks are relevant to 20th century life. They may teach in state schools, supervise development projects such as building of wells and roads in rural areas, preach on radio and television and involve themselves in various services for the people.

Traditionally, monks have been close to the people, the wat being the centre of village life and used as school house and community centre. Monks have always provided traditional herbal medicine, storage facilities for treasures or documents, or a place to sleep for the night. There are pockets of great poverty in both rural and urban areas and some monks feel their role is in social work; one example is the Wat Tam Krabok, a monastery devoted to helping heroin addicts, with a good success rate in a country where addiction is a major problem.

Some monks do not take part in political or social activities, but keep to the strict lifestyle of the forest monasteries. These (found in Sri Lanka as well as Thailand) consist of very simple dwellings. There may be a central meeting hall, and the monks themselves live in *kutis* (huts) or even caves. The monks specialise in meditation, rather than study or advising lay people. They keep strictly to the *vinaya* rules, and may add some extra *dhutangas* (austere practices), such as living only off alms food, eating only from the alms bowl, only one meal a day, living away from people, sleeping outside. Thirteen of these were allowed by the Buddha. Sometimes these 'austere practices' are undertaken while on a pilgrimage or journey. The forest dwelling monks are admired for keeping the lifestyle of the early *sangha*.

Thai Lay Buddhists

Lay Buddhists in Thailand devote themselves to morality, generosity and piety in the same way as their Sri Lankan counterparts, although some ceremonies and festivals, are different. Moral rules and attitudes are identical, and giving to the monks is much encouraged, especially at the daily alms round, which still occurs in the traditional way. Other popular ways of earning merit are building temples, sponsoring ordination, putting gold leaf on statues and releasing caged birds. Temples are visited and the usual offerings made, especially on the holy days. The design and contents of the temple are of the same basic plan as in Sri Lanka, but with a characteristically Thai style. This can be seen in the Thai temple in Wimbledon. *Stupas* are more bell-shaped or pointed than the round Sri Lankan monuments. Buddha images have a more pointed headpiece. Lay Buddhists are becoming increasingly interested in meditation.

The festivals of Wesak and Kathina are similar, but the latter may be accompanied by fireworks and an autumn fair. There is also a ceremony at the start of the retreat season when monks are given clothes in a candlelit procession. Other Thai festivals are Songkran, the Ploughing Festival, Loy Krathong, and the elephant festival.

Songkran is the Thai New Year and lasts three days in the middle of April, the hot season. The first day involves visiting the temple, rescuing fish from drying ponds and freeing them into the river, freeing caged birds and visiting relations. Large family meals are prepared and in the afternoon water is thrown over everyone and boats are raced. The statue of the Buddha is also sprinkled with water. This may originate in a fertility festival designed to remind the rains to come. The second day of Songkran is celebrated with the flying of kites and elaborate fireworks. The third day is usually devoted to traditional dancing, plays and shadow puppets. At midnight the temple bell is struck to mark the end of the festival.

In November, Loy Krathong is celebrated at full moon. The custom is to float lighted candles in little leaf cups upon the river. This is said to symbolise our journey toward the 'other shore' of nirvana. Also in November is the elephant festival, with races and processions. Elephants featured in many of the parables of the Buddha, especially as a symbol for the necessity of training.

Thai people may also believe in the gods derived from Hinduism, local gods and spirits for which there are various ceremonies. These might be connected with growing crops, pregnancy, marriage or worldly troubles - all the areas of life for which there is no particular Buddhist ceremony.

---

1. John Snelling 1987 p85
2. This list should be taken in the spirit of the 'raft' - a summary by the author, meant to be helpful but not ultimate.
3. see p53
4. For selections from this book, see *Buddhist Scriptures*, tr Conze, 1959
5. Gombrich 1971

CHAPTER FOUR

MAHAYANA BUDDHISM

Most Buddhists from China, Japan, Tibet, Korea, Mongolia, Vietnam and the Himalayan kingdoms of Nepal, Sikkim and Bhutan refer to themselves as 'Mahayana' Buddhists, Buddhists of 'the Great Vehicle', as opposed to that which they refer to as 'Hinayana' or 'Small Vehicle' Buddhism, represented nowadays only by the Theravada tradition. The name Mahayana suggests a superior path, or one with more room for more types of people, both of which Mahayana would claim. From a Mahayana viewpoint, 'Hinayana' Buddhism has its limitations, but from a Theravada viewpoint, their tradition is not a 'small vehicle', but the original, pure teaching of the Buddha, with which Mahayana Buddhists have tampered. There has however been little animosity between the two wings of Buddhism. Buddhism has always been tolerant of diversity, and in the heyday of Buddhism in India, Mahayana and non-Mahayana monks lived side by side in the same monasteries. In the historical development of Buddhism, Mahayana and Theravada Buddhism have flourished independently in different parts of the world.

Mahayana is not a unitary phenomenon, but really just a useful label to describe a vast variety of Buddhist traditions, which have in common their acceptance of one or more *sutras* (S) or scriptures not found in the canon of Theravadins, and which are followed in the Northern and Far-Eastern countries mentioned above. In addition, Mahayana Buddhists share new - but differing - ideas about the goal of Buddhism, the Buddha(s), beings called *bodhisattvas*, and analyses of the nature of human consciousness and the universe. Mahayana is not so much a sect, denomination or school of thought, but a much vaguer 'movement', which would identify its key concepts as wisdom and compassion, and its goal as the aspiration towards Buddhahood for the benefit of all beings.

Although it seems to have originated about the last century BCE, it was not a widespread movement until several centuries later. It is not clear how this new movement began. It has been suggested that it developed from the Mahasanghika school, but there is no real evidence for this. Others have seen it as a lay protest against arrogant monks - but the evidence is that developments in Buddhist thought tend to come from those who specialise in it in the monasteries. A further suggestion is that it was influenced by developing Hinduism - but although similarities can be found, it is hard to know which way round the influence worked. It seems safest to agree with Paul Williams that 'the origins of the Mahayana are obscure in the extreme'.[1]

The Mahayana Sutras are accepted as scripture and as the word of the Buddha by Mahayana Buddhists only. Historically, the earliest of these seem to date from the 1st century BCE, and others many centuries later, but Mahayana tradition is clear that these are the genuine teaching of the Buddha. In what sense? The answer to this is varied. Some claim that the Mahayana sutras were taught by the historical Buddha Shakyamuni while he was on earth, that Mahayana and non-Mahayana teachings were delivered to different groups of listeners according to their capacity to understand. There is a tradition that at the same time as the Council of the *arhats* met to recite the Pali Canon, there was a Council of *bodhisattvas* gathering to recite the Mahayana scriptures. When queried as to why these scriptures did not come to public notice until centuries later, one explanation is that they were given into the keeping of the Naga-spirits until the time was ripe. Another suggestion is that the sutras were not revealed by the historical earthly Buddha, but by the Buddha conceived of by Mahayana Buddhists as still present either as a heavenly being or spiritual reality. This could either be Shakyamuni in his heavenly form, or another Buddha altogether, seen in visions that come in deep meditation. Another approach is to say that, even in the Pali Canon, the word of the Buddha is not just that literally spoken by Shakyamuni, but also words spoken by others that he approved of. Thus anyone who speaks from the complete insight into reality, known in Mahayana Buddhism as perfect wisdom, is speaking the word of the Buddha. This has to be taken in the context of the sayings even in the Pali Canon that whatever leads to spiritual progress 'dispassion, detachment, decrease of materialism, simplicity, content, solitude, delight in good', 'this is the master's message' (*Vinaya* 2.10); and also the remembrance that all teaching is like a raft, a means to an end rather than the end itself.

Some Characteristics of Mahayana

Before plunging into the diversity of Mahayana scriptures, teachings and practices, it might be useful to have a brief summary of the general characteristics of Mahayana Buddhism by which it is distinguished from Theravada (and other non-Mahayana) Buddhism.

The following is to be taken as a provisional guideline to give an orientation for beginners, a raft to throw away, and in the light of what was said above about the diversity of Mahayana.

1. Mahayana Buddhists accept one or more of the Mahayana scriptures as the word of the Buddha. There are two main collections of these scriptures, together with versions of the material in the Pali Canon, and other commentaries etc - the Tibetan and the Chinese.

2. The goal for most Mahayana Buddhists is no longer to become an *arhat*(enlightened person) and reach *Nirvana*, but to become a *bodhisattva* - and eventually a Buddha - in order to save others as well as oneself. Those who aspire to do this are on the path of the *bodhisattvas* (beings of enlightenment), who seek enlightenment not for their own sake but for the sake of all others.

3. It is therefore possible that help can be gained from beings further advanced on this path. Mahayana Buddhists speak of *bodhisattvas* as heavenly beings with the power to help those who call on them. These *bodhisattvas* have their own names, characteristics and iconography and may appear in visions or be the focus of meditation. Some of the more well-known are Avalokitesvara, Manjusri, Maitreya, Kshitigarbha and Tara.

4. The Mahayana universe - or multiverse - is even larger than the cosmology of the Theravada Buddhists. In addition to this world-system, with its three realms of sense-desire, form and formlessness, there are other world-systems, in which may dwell other Buddhas than the Shakyamuni Buddha of this world system. Among the more well-known of these Buddhas are Amitabha, Akshobya, and Vairocana. Like the *bodhisattvas*, some of whom share their worlds, the cosmic Buddhas may appear in visions, be the focus of meditations, or be asked for help.

5. According to some Mahayana scriptures Shakyamuni Buddha, the Buddha of our world system, is available in a glorious, heavenly or spiritual form, like the other Buddhas and **bodhisattvas**.

6. For some Mahayana Buddhists, especially in Chinese and Japanese traditions, the word Buddha no longer refers to particular beings, whether earthly or heavenly, but to the ultimate reality underlying the whole universe, everywhere and in everyone.

7. Mahayana Buddhism developed several different philosophical approaches. The most influential of these are the philosophical schools of the Madhyamaka and the Yogacara/Cittamatra. In

addition to these, there are concepts particularly important to the development of Far-Eastern Buddhism, such as the concept of the *tathagatagarbha* (Buddha-nature) and the 'interpenetration of all things' taught by the Hua-yen tradition.

8. It is sometimes claimed that Mahayana is more lay-oriented than Theravada, in that both lay and monastic followers are called to the *bodhisattva* goal. Yet it is hard to uphold this, as the monastic *sangha* has remained central in most forms of Mahayana Buddhism, notably in Tibet, and from the beginning (in both Theravada and Mahayana) the Buddhist community is referred to as the fourfold *sangha* - monks, nuns, laymen and laywomen.

9. Mahayana monks (and nuns where they exist) follow the *Vinaya* rules as passed down by non-Mahayana traditions. It happens that the Tibetans received the *vinaya* of the Mulasarvastivadins and the Chinese those of the Sarvastivadins and the Dharmaguptaka tradition. These are very similar to the Theravadin *vinaya*, with slightly differing numbers of rules. Whereas the Theravada have 227, the Mulasarvastvadin have 258 and the Dharmaguptaka 350. It is somewhat more likely to find Mahayana than Theravada monks adapting the *vinaya* to suit the circumstances (eg Zen). Tibetan monks may cook their own food; Zen monks will even grow it. This is one aspect of the Mahayana concept of *upaya kausalya* (skilful means) whereby teachings and practices are skilfully adapted to the circumstances in order to best help beings make spiritual progress.

10. Finally, Mahayana is characterised by its diversity. It is not a single school of Buddhism in the sense that Theravada is, or the Sarvativada was, but a convenient label for a whole variety of teachings and practices, suitable for different sorts of people in different cultures and at different levels of spiritual development. This is one of the senses in which it is the 'great vehicle'.

Some Mahayana scriptures

There are many Mahayana *sutras* (S) or scriptures, existing in different languages, teaching somewhat different doctrines, but all portrayed as the genuine word of the Buddha. There are two full collections, in Tibetan and Chinese, and in addition individual *sutras* or sections thereof exist in Sanskrit or other Indian or Central Asian languages. It is thought that most, but not all, of the sutras originated in India, and were then translated into languages like Tibetan and Chinese. It is very difficult to be sure about the dates and provenance of the originals of the *sutras*.

The Chinese and Tibetans placed immense value on these *sutras*, and there are many stories of individuals from both areas setting out on lengthy and dangerous journeys to India in order to obtain these precious texts. The well-known tales of 'Monkey' have a historical basis in the travels of a 7th century Chinese monk, Hsuan-tsang, on such a quest. It is difficult in these days of throw-away paperbacks to appreciate the precious nature of books, let alone scriptures, to people in earlier ages. Tibetan Buddhists today keep the *sutras* carefully wrapped and stored in the highest places of honour on their shrines, above even the images of Buddhas. The Chinese invented printing, in the eighth century, and its first uses were to reproduce Buddhist images, chants and texts.

The Chinese collecting of scriptures began around the first century CE, with important translations being made in the fourth century and the first printed collection in the tenth century. The Tibetans began collecting scriptures from possibly as early as the seventh century, but particularly in the eleventh century 'the age of translators'. The Tibetan canon was completed in the fourteenth century. Useful summaries of the contents of these canons can be found in Robinson (1982). The modern Chinese canon contains 2184 texts including the *Vinayas* (monastic disciplines) of several different schools other than the Theravada; equivalent material to the *Sutta* (P) section of the Pali Canon; *Abhidharma* material (see page 52) from several non-Mahayana schools other than the Theravada; many Mahayana *sutras*; *tantras* (see page 97); *shastras* (S), or writings from the main Mahayana philosophical schools; commentaries; history; material from non-Buddhist traditions; and dictionaries and catalogues. The Tibetan canon is divided into two sections, the Kanjur or word of the Buddha, and Tenjur or Teachings. The Kanjur includes monastic *Vinaya*, Mahayana and non-Mahayana *sutras*, and *tantras*. The Tenjur includes commentaries and writings of the important Mahayana philosophical schools, non-Mahayana Abhidharma, and scholarly works on subjects like medicine and grammar. Obviously, with such huge collections of material, very few people will have read it at all at first hand. In addition, the different *sutras* and philosophical schools say somewhat different things. Chinese Buddhists tend to one of two strategies. Several forms of Chinese Buddhism concentrate on just one Mahayana *sutra*, which is seen as the final, most important or most relevant teaching of the Buddha. Other forms accept the collection of sutras, but rank them in order of fullness of revelation. For example, the non-Mahayana material could be seen as preliminary teaching, some Mahayana *sutras* as intermediate teaching, and their favourite

Mahayana *sutra* as the most advanced and full form of the Buddha's word. The Tibetan attitude tended to be to treasure all the material, but to study Buddhism, not directly through the *sutras* and *tantras*, which can seem difficult and confusing, but initially through the commentaries and teachings of the philosophical schools, both the ancient writers contained in the Tenjur and modern living teachers, after which the scriptures can be approached. It is important to add that sutras were not texts for idle reading, but to be put to use in the context of ritual and meditation, and with the guidance and explanations of a personal teacher.

The Prajnaparamita Literature

Both Chinese and Tibetan canons contain sections of sutras known as *Prajnaparamita* (Perfect Wisdom). There are several texts in this category, of varying lengths. It is very difficult to date these texts, but scholars have suggested that the earliest text is the 8000 verse *Prajnaparamita*, around 1st century BCE to the 1st century CE. This was then expanded into longer texts (100,000, 25,000 and 18,000 verses) up to 300 CE, then restated in brief versions, the *Diamond Sutra* (300 verses) and the *Heart Sutra*. It is possible that the *Diamond Sutra* is earlier, and a copy of the *Diamond Sutra*, dated 868, is the oldest printed book in the world. These texts, as is obvious from the title, are concerned with '*Prajnaparamita*' or 'the Perfection of Wisdom'. This means the full and complete insight into the way things are. The emphasis on 'perfect' suggests a wisdom beyond the everyday assumption of most people, and beyond the earlier *Abhidharma* analyses of non-Mahayana Buddhists. It is the wisdom of the Buddhas. The central insight of this perfect wisdom is that all things are characterised by *sunyata* (S), pronounced shunyata, (emptiness). The term emptiness means 'empty of inherent existence'; in other words, nothing exists in and by itself, but only in relation to other things. Nothing possesses what Buddhists call *svabhava* (own-being), that is separate, eternal, existence. Nothing is in being through its own power, or possesses unchanging essence, substance or defining characteristics. This will remind the reader of the teachings of *anicca* (that all things are impermanent), *anatta* (that all things are without self) and dependent origination (that states of being come into existence dependent on conditions) in Pali Buddhism, and in fact the term 'emptiness' is found in the Pali canon eg 'the world is called empty, because empty of self' (*Samyuta Nikaya* 4.54).

The concept of emptiness in these Mahayana sutras is however seen as a deeper insight into the way things are than that of non-Mahayana Buddhism. Some non-Mahayana analysis had broken down experience into basic building blocks or *dharmas* (S) (see page 52). Whereas everyday language assumes the reality of things like persons and chariots, analysis shows that these are merely labels for a changing collection of impersonal events called *dharmas*. Some schools of thought (eg Sarvastivadins) had asserted that whereas words like self or chariot were mere labels without any corresponding reality, the basic dharmas, past, present and future, really existed. The constant theme of the Prajnaparamita *sutras* is that ALL *dharmas* are empty, lacking in inherent existence. Emptiness does not mean 'nothingness', nor is it a substance out of which all things are made, it is just that nothing whatsoever has ultimate or necessary being - including *nirvana*, Buddhas, perfect wisdom and emptiness.

> 'Beings are like a magical illusion...*dharmas* are like a magical illusion...Buddhahood is like a magical illusion...even *nirvana* is like a magical illusion' (*Prajnaparamita in 8000 lines* 2.38)

The concept of two levels of truth, the conventional and the ultimate, helps to make sense of this teaching. On the conventional level, we can talk of things like people and bodhisattvas and Buddhas existing, but on the ultimate level of possessing eternal, separate, non-relative existence they cannot be said to be; hence some of the difficult passages claiming that 'I neither see a *dharma* "bodhisattva" nor a *dharma* "perfect wisdom"' (*Prajnaparamita in 8000 lines* 1.5) after one has just decided that these are the two most important things in Mahayana Buddhism!

Moving between the two levels of truth means that certain passages seem on the surface to be paradoxical eg

> 'It is wonderful to see the extent to which the Tathagata (= the Buddha) has demonstrated the true nature of all these dharmas, and yet one cannot properly talk of the true nature of all these dharmas...even all dharmas cannot be talked about in any proper sense.' (*Prajnaparamita in 8000 lines* 18:348)

It depends whether we are speaking in conventional, everyday language, or looking at things from the ultimate truth. If this sounds difficult, it may be consoling that even listening gods found the *prajnaparamita* difficult to understand.

Two of the most famous *Prajnaparamita sutras* are the *Heart Sutra*, a brief condensed version of perfection wisdom teaching, and the *Diamond Sutra* .[2]

The *Heart Sutra* begins with worship of Perfect Wisdom personified as a goddess, a symbolic way of expressing its value. We pass on to the viewpoint of Avalokitesvara[3] - in his wisdom he sees no beings but only the five *skandhas*. So far, this is basic Buddhism. However,

Avalokitesvara's wisdom goes further than this. He sees that even the five *skandhas* (form, feeling, perceptions, impulses and consciousness) do not exist as separate entities, all are emptiness. This is addressed to Sariputra, the representative of Hinayana wisdom. Emptiness means that no *dharma* can truly be said to have come into being or ceased, or to be pure or impure, as no dharma exists absolutely.

'Avalokitesvara, the holy lord and bodhisattva, was moving in the deep course of the wisdom which has gone beyond. He looked down from on high, he beheld but five heaps, and he saw that in their own-being they were empty' 'Form is emptiness, emptiness is form...the same is true of feelings, perceptions, impulses and consciousness' 'all dharmas are marked with emptiness; they are not produced or stopped' (*Heart Sutra*)

This means that in terms of absolute, non-dependent, separate existence:

'There is no ignorance, no decay and death, no extinction of decay and death, no suffering, no origination of suffering, no stopping, no path' (*Heart sutra*)

Passing on to the *Diamond sutra*, from the ultimate point of view, it cannot be said that 'The Tathagata has fully known any *dharma*', that 'any being at all has been led to *nirvana*', that 'the *Tathagata* goes or comes' that 'the *Tathagata* demonstrated *dharma*'. What at first sight seems to be a total contradiction of Buddhist teaching, is to be understood as a way of teaching that none of these entities, though existing on a conventional level, possess own-being ie absolute, self-reliant inherent existence.

One further point on 'emptiness' in the *Prajnaparamita sutras*: if everything is 'empty', then as both *nirvana* and *samsara* are empty of inherent existence, there is no essential difference between them, as there is no essence to either. Therefore it can be said 'illusion and nirvana are not two different things.' (*Prajnaparamita in 8000 lines* 2.39) This idea was to have great importance, particularly in Chinese and Japanese Buddhism. Finally, if all things are empty, on the ultimate level, 'no one will grasp this perfection of wisdom...for no *dharma* at all has been indicated, lit up or communicated' (*Prajnaparamita in 8000 lines* 2.40) The other important concept introduced in the Prajnaparamita sutras is that of the *bodhisattva*, which will be dealt with separately. (see page 99)

The *Sukhavati Sutras*

There are two main *Sukhavati sutras*, smaller and larger, which are usually dated about the 2nd century CE. They concern the world of

Sukhavati (Happy land), which is one of many 'pure lands' or 'Buddha worlds' other than our own world system. The *sutras* represent the devotional rather than wisdom aspect of Mahayana Buddhism.

Shakyamuni Buddha is pictured talking to his disciple Ananda and telling stories of Buddhas of other ages and other worlds. In the time of one Buddha in ancient times, there lived a monk called Dharmakara who listened to his Buddha describing the wonderful qualities of the different worlds inhabited by the different heavenly Buddhas. As a result, he was inspired to aim for Buddhahood himself, and vowed to create a paradise better than all Buddhalands put together. He made a great *bodhisattva* vow to attain enlightenment in order to create this world for the sake of all beings, swearing that unless he achieves the creation of this world, he will forswear *nirvana* for ever. His vow consisted of forty-eight subsidiary sections referring to different wonderful qualities of his land, some highly spiritual (eg beings will be only one step from *nirvana*) and some down to earth (eg no one will have to wash any clothes). Of particular importance is the vow that if beings only believe in him, think of him and dedicate their merit towards being born in his land, he will come to them at their death and bring them to the Pure Land. The ancient Buddha predicts that what Dharmakara vowed will come about. Shakyamuni comments that this did indeed happen and Dharmakara is now a Buddha called Amitabha living in his fantastic paradise which is called Sukhavati or the Happy Land and is situated in the West. In that land there are also bodhisattvas, notably Avalokitesvara and Mahasthamaprapta. He describes the Pure Land in great and fantastic detail. It is very beautiful, with trees and flowers made of jewels, perfume and music in the air, fruit and flowers in abundance. No one has to cook or wash or sew or dig, everyone is beautiful, strong, healthy and contented. People are filled with Buddhist virtues and find it very easy to follow the Buddhist path - visions of Buddhas and sounds of the teaching are readily available. There are no difficult mountains or impassable rivers, but water will always be at the depth you want it. Everything is so easy that one is only one step from nirvana. After describing this land, Shakyamuni makes it visible to his audience in a vision and stresses that even one genuine act of faith in Amitabha can lead to rebirth in this land, although it should be accompanied by repeated devotions and prayers, meditation on the Pure Land and good works.

> This world Sukhavati, Ananda, which is the world system of the lord Amitabha, is rich and prosperous, comfortable, fertile, delightful and crowded with many gods and men. There are no hells, no animals, no ghosts...it is rich in a great variety of flowers

and fruits, adorned with jewel trees..' 'Everyone hears the pleasant
sounds he wishes to hear ie he hears of the Buddha, the Dhamma,
the Sangha... of emptiness... which brings about the state of mind
which leads to the accomplishment of enlightenment.' 'All beings
are irreversible from the supreme enlightenment if they hear the
name of the lord Amitabha, and on hearing it, with one single
thought only raise their hearts to him with a resolve connected
with serene faith.' (from the *Sukhavati-vyuha*)

The *Saddharmapundarika* or *Lotus Sutra*

The Saddharmapundarika or 'Lotus of the Wonderful Law' is one of
the most popular Mahayana scriptures, especially in China and Japan.
It puts forward some of the central concepts of Mahayana Buddhism,
that all beings are called not just to be *arhats*, but to be Buddhas, and
that Shakyamuni Buddha is a being with a lifespan far beyond the
brief story usually told.

The *sutra* is given by the glorious Shakyamuni (as seen by the eyes of
faith rather than as a mere human figure) to a vast congregation of
disciples and bodhisattvas. To the amazement of his audience, he
puts forward the idea that beings are called not to be arhats but to be
Buddhas. 'There are now here before me sons of the Buddha, who are
pure in all ways, wise, virtuous...I can announce to them that they
shall become Buddhas, for the benefit and out of compassion for the
world.' 'The way in which you walk is the *bodhisattva* way. By
gradually practising and learning all of you will become Buddhas.'

This announcement, that 'all of you shall become Buddhas' is so
astounding, and so different from what is normally taken as the
teaching of Shakyamuni Buddha, that the Lotus *sutra* has to explain
why the Buddha did not give this teaching to start with. The answer
is in the *upaya kausalya* (S) (skilful means) of the Buddha, whereby he
gives people the teaching that they are ready for, whatever they need
at this particular stage of development. Previously, he had spoken
about the goal of becoming an *arhat* or enlightened saint who achieves
nirvana, and of the *pratyekabuddha* or solitary Buddha, who becomes
enlightened independently but does not go on to teach. 'This is really
only a skilful device by which the Buddha wishes to prepare them for
the day when he can awake them to the cognition of a Buddha...the
Saviour speaks only after he has paid attention to the proper time for
doing so.'

The teaching about the path that leads to *nirvana* was given as a
preliminary teaching to encourage people to start out on the spiritual
path who were not ready for the final teaching. That they were not is

demonstrated by a large group of 5000 monks, nuns, laymen and laywomen who leave in disgust at this point. These represent all the Buddhists who cannot accept the Mahayana teaching.

In order to defend himself against the charge that the teaching of the way of the arhat and pratyekabuddha were misleading and that therefore the Buddha was a liar, he tells the parable of the burning house. The following is a summary.

'In some village or city there lived a rich householder. He was getting old but was very rich. His house was very large, but falling apart. One day it caught on fire, and the old man ran outside through the single door, but his sons were still within. The old man realised that the children did not realise the danger they were in, and made no effort to escape. So, he called out to them that the house was burning and they must escape, but they ignored him. Desperate to save them, he hit on the idea of promising them whatever toys they most wanted, if they would only run out. To some he promised goat carts, to others deer carts and to the rest bullock carts. The children ran out and were saved. When they asked for their carts, he did not give them the different carts they had asked for, but all had the very best type of cart, splendid carts pulled by white bullocks.'

Did the father lie to his sons when he promised them a variety of different carts, but in the event gave them all the same top-quality cart? The disciple Sariputra answers 'Not so, Lord. The man cannot be charged with speaking falsely, since it was only a skilful device by which he managed to get his sons out of that burning building.'

Thus the Lotus sutra explains the variety of Buddhist teachings. They are at different levels for different sorts of people, but all get to the same goal in the end. In the teaching of the Buddha, beings are offered three vehicles, that of the *arhat*, that of the *pratyekabuddha*, and that of the *bodhisattva*, who aims at the goal of Buddhahood for the sake of saving all beings. However, in truth, 'there is only one-vehicle, the great vehicle (mahayana)'.

The revelation that all are called to be Buddhas is compared in further parables to a son who left home and became destitute, eventually gaining employment as a servant in the house of a kind master, only to find out eventually that he was really the master's son, and restored to a place of honour. The master did not tell his son straight away, for fear that he would not be able to cope. Another image is that of the Buddha as a raincloud, which rains down upon all plants equally, whether large or small. Similarly, the *Dharma* is preached to all, according to their capacity. 'When I rain down the rain of the *Dharma*, then all this world is well-refreshed, each one according to their power to take to heart.' The second main message of the *Lotus Sutra* is also revealing *upaya* on the part of the Buddha. For the sake of beings, he tells them the story about his birth, enlightenment and death, but in truth 'it is many hundreds of thousands of myriads of aeons ago that I have awoken to full enlightenment' and 'even today my lifespan is not ended'. The birth, enlightenment and death was just a teaching device. The Buddha pretended to pass away into *Nirvana*, but in fact is still around, working to liberate beings.

This is again an amazing announcement, set among miraculous events. A wonderful jewelled *stupa* appears, a monument to a Buddha of long ago, and cracks open to reveal that this Buddha is not dead, but still alive. Similarly, it is later revealed Shakyamuni is in reality such a glorious, still-living being. Why did he go through the motions of birth, enlightenment, and passing into *parinirvana*? Because otherwise beings would not have realised the urgency of getting on with the spiritual path, and would have been lazy about following the *Dharma*, thinking that there was plenty of time. 'Therefore the Tathagata, though he does not in reality become extinct, yet announces his extinction'. Again this is illustrated with a parable. A doctor returns from his travels to find that his sons have drunk his poisonous chemicals. He makes up an antidote, which some take and recover, but others are too confused to take. For the sake of the latter, he leaves for another country and pretends to have died. This shocks them into taking the medicine, which is all that they have left of him. The father returns and all live happily ever after. Depending on the translation, there are two ways of taking this teaching about the Buddha. The Japanese translation portrays this very long life of the Buddha as meaning eternity, so that the Buddha is in the Lotus sutra announcing 'the Buddha's life is eternal' and that in reality the Buddha is 'Father of the world, self-born, the healer and protector of all creatures'. However, Paul Williams argues, from the Tibetan perspective, that there is 'an enormously long but still finite length to the Buddha's life' (Williams 1989 p151). Otherwise, how could beings become Buddhas? This reveals a philosophical difference in Mahayana Buddhism between those who teach that all beings are ultimately Buddha from all eternity and only have to realise it (Japanese tradition) and those who teach that this is to take a metaphor too literally (Tibetan understanding). Is the message of the Lotus Sutra that we are all to become Buddhas eventually, or that we are all already Buddhas? Similarly, are there several Buddhas, or are they all forms of the eternal Shakyamuni? Or is it all the same anyway? The concept of *upaya* in the Lotus sutra puts all teaching under suspicion of only being provisional - how far should we take it literally? Some have pointed out that in the Lotus Sutra itself, which presents itself as the final teaching, there is some suspicion about the final teaching as presented in the parable of the burning house. Is the wonderful bullock cart that all get in the end the same as that requested by one set of children, so that they (the Mahayana Buddhists) are completely right, or is the cart that all get even better than that?

Tantras

In the Chinese and Tibetan collections of scriptures, as well as the non-Mahayana *vinayas*, *sutras*, and *abhidharmas*, the Mahayana sutras and the philosophical treatises and commentaries, there are texts called *tantras*. These are a further form of Buddhist literature, which describe rituals and meditations used in a form of Buddhism known as Tantric Buddhism. This is sometimes seen as a third form of Buddhism, in addition to 'Hinayana' and Mahayana and referred to as the *Vajrayana* (Diamond vehicle), though in many ways it is a subset of Mahayana Buddhism. Vajrayana claims to be an express course in the *Dharma*, for advanced students, using all means available. It is considered to be dangerous and therefore it is vital to have a guru or personal teacher to guide the student. The tantric texts themselves therefore do not make much sense to a casual reader, but can only be understood in the context of a particular practice. The earlier tantric texts appeared about the 6th century CE in India, and Tantric Buddhism was practised in India until the demise of Buddhism in the 12th century. It has continued to be influential in Tibetan Buddhism, and in some schools of Far-Eastern Buddhism.

What exactly is *Tantra*? It is often considered very mysterious, as its scriptures are in cryptic language, its teachings passed down orally, and its rituals kept a secret to the initiated. Basically, *Tantra* is an experiential and practical form of Buddhism, stressing real experience of the Buddhist goal, achieved sacramentally and symbolically. It involves the physical body, the emotions, and the imagination as well as the intellect. In order to achieve genuine experience, it draws on a vast range of ritual practices, many of which are found also in Hinduism and thus represent ancient traditions in India. The *tantras* describe various rituals which have been adapted into a form of Buddhist meditation. Tantra lays particular stress on the need for individual tuition from a master or guru.

One common tantric practice is called 'visualisation' and involves vividly imagining a chosen *bodhisattva* or Buddha until he (or she) seems to appear before one. This being is worshipped in imagination with incense and flowers, sins confessed to him or her and vows - such as the *bodhisattva* vow - taken. Sometimes the meditator then identifies himself or herself with the Buddha or *bodhisattva*.

When the full ritual is practised with proper guidance, it can impart a real, if temporary, feeling of enlightened consciousness. The practice of visualisation is supported by other practices, involving the whole person in the attempt to maximise the value of the experience. These include the chanting of *mantras*, the construction of *mandalas*, the forming of *mudras*, physical *yoga* and the sacramental use of sexuality.

A *mantra* is a short chanted phrase in which the literal meaning of the words is less important than the inner meaning and the actual effect of the sound of the words on the human mind. Examples of *mantras* are: *Om mani padme hum* (sometimes translated, questionably, as 'Hail to the jewel in the lotus'), the *mantra* to Avalokitesvara, or *Om tare tuttare ture svaha* (the *mantra* to Tara). Protective chants are used even in Theravada Buddhism and chanting can be very calming, if nothing else. Another use of mantras is in visualising the written shape of syllables such as 'om' or 'hum'.

Mandalas are coloured diagrams, mostly circular, but sometimes square or triangular. These are used as a focus for meditation and either visualised or actually painted or made from coloured sands. Some mandalas are very complex, with representations of different Buddhas at the cardinal points. The theory of the mandala involves the idea of identification. It represents both the universe and oneself, which in Mahayana theory are interconnected. Thus the five main cosmic Buddhas (Vairocana, Amoghasiddhi, Amitabha, Akshobya and Ratnasambhava) are identified with the five *skandhas* which go to make up the human being, but also with the five material elements of fire, water, earth, air and ether. The contemplation of such correspondences in the mandala is designed to help you realise the 'emptiness' of all things.

A *mudra* is a symbolic shape made with the hand(s), as found in Indian dance and seen on statues of the Buddhas and *bodhisattvas*. For example, a hand held open and upright symbolises protection. Appropriate *mudras* can be formed when making offerings to the visualised being - one *mudra* represents the offering of the whole universe - or when trying to identify oneself with a particular Buddha or *bodhisattva*.

A form of physical yoga is practised, resembling Hindu practice, but given a Buddhist interpretation. The yogic theory about the body is very complicated, but in this Buddhist practice the controlling of 'inner breaths' leads to a feeling of power pervading the whole body, which is interpreted as the uniting of wisdom and compassion, leading to the 'thought of enlightenment' and then the bliss of *nirvana*.

The sacramental use of sexuality involves visualising the uniting of male and female as a symbol of the uniting of wisdom and compassion. The female represents wisdom and the male represents compassion, or its expression in skilful means. In some advanced tantric rituals, use is made of actual sexual practices. Other rituals involve the consumption of minute amounts of meat or alcohol. The vast collection of 'deities' (Buddhas, *bodhisattvas*, and other beings) employed in Tantric visualisations include both familiar figures like Amitabha Buddha, and frightening figures, which are said to be the Buddhas and *bodhisattvas* expressing their determination and power to overcome evil. The basic idea behind *Tantra* is to harness all things in the universe to the quest for Buddhahood, including the physical and what may appear negative. It is always stressed that this is dangerous material, and the expert guidance of a *guru* (in Tibetan, *lama*) is essential.

The Bodhisattva

In so far as there is a central, defining teaching of the Mahayana, it is that of the way of the *bodhisattva* (S) (being of enlightenment), whose aim is to reach enlightenment or Buddhahood, in order to save all beings. This is the goal that characterises the Mahayana and which separates it from the non-Mahayana Buddhists, who teach the goal of the *arhat* (which Mahayana sees as a lesser goal, concerned with the enlightenment of the individual rather than the salvation of all beings). It is sometimes said that the *bodhisattva* 'puts off' nirvana for him or herself until all beings are saved. However, as Paul Williams points out (Williams 1989 p52) if *nirvana* is defined as enlightenment, this would lead to absurd conclusions such as *bodhisattvas* being kinder than Buddhas, *bodhisattvas* never becoming enlightened because the supply of beings goes on forever, or nearly all beings being enlightened except the *bodhisattva*, who is hanging on for the last few! It is better, not to say that the *bodhisattva* 'puts off' nirvana, but the bodhisattva altogether rejects the *nirvana* of the *arhat*, which (according to the Lotus Sutra) was only a skilful device anyway.

The *bodhisattva* is a term found in all the Mahayana scriptures we have looked at. It can refer to one who understands the emptiness of all things; a heavenly companion of Amitabha Buddha in the pure land (and of course, the *bodhisattva* who became Amitabha Buddha); a 'deity' to be visualised and identified with in tantric practice; or the goal announced for all in the Lotus sutra. The concept exists also in non-Mahayana Buddhism, where it is used of Shakyamuni before he became a Buddha, and of the current status of Maitreya, the next

Buddha to appear in our particular world. The difference is that whereas in non-Mahayana Buddhism this career was only available to very rare beings, in Mahayana it is open to all.

The *bodhisattva* is one who has vowed to aim at the supreme and perfect enlightenment of Buddhahood in order to save all beings. A Mahayana Buddhist is one who has conceived this aim. In the *8000 verse Prajnaparamita*, the would-be *bodhisattva* is first moved towards this decision by reflecting on the sufferings of all beings. His (or her) reaction is to decide 'I shall become a saviour to these beings, I shall release them from all their sufferings!' (*8000 lines* sutra 22.403). In this same text, the bodhisattva is compared to a brave hero who finds himself in a forest of terrors with his family. He would not abandon them to save himself, but would reassure his family, use all his prowess to defeat the terrors and bring everyone safely home.

The *bodhisattva* is compounded of two elements fundamental to Buddhism - *prajna* (wisdom) and *karuna* (compassion). These traditional Buddhist virtues are pressed to their extreme limit -perfect wisdom and infinite compassion. The perfect wisdom aimed at by the bodhisattva is the total insight into reality spoken about in the Mahayana scriptures; the complete understanding of the total interdependence of all things, the realisation of the lack of self, the 'emptiness' of all things. The bodhisattva, then, aims at total knowledge, the 'supreme and perfect enlightenment' of a Buddha, far beyond the state that Mahayana ascribes to the mere *arhat*.

The infinite compassion of a *bodhisattva* means that he or she puts the happiness of all beings in the universe before his or her own, not resting until every being in the universe is saved. In order to accomplish this aim, he or she is willing to suffer anything, even if it means giving up his or her life for others over and over again. Not only is he or she willing to give up material welfare for the sake of others, but even spiritual welfare. Any *punya* (merit) that he or she earns from the performance of good works, is given to others so that they may benefit. If helping others turns out to involve earning bad *karma* (as in the situation where one might decide do kill a would-be murderer) then the *bodhisattva* is willing to suffer the consequences of hell, if it can help others towards salvation.

The complete selflessness of the bodhisattva is described in detail by Shantideva, an 8th century Mahayana monk. 'I take upon myself the burden of all suffering...to the limits of my endurance I will experience all the states of woe... it is surely better that I alone should be in pain than that all these beings should fall into the states of woe...I must not abandon all beings' (*Sikshsamuccaya* 280)

The conjunction of the two ideals of wisdom and compassion leads to a seemingly paradoxical situation. The *bodhisattva* aims to lead all beings to *nirvana*, while simultaneously gaining the enlightened insight that no separate beings or even nirvana actually exist as such.

In the Diamond Sutra we read 'Someone who has set out in the vehicle of the *bodhisattva* should think in this manner "as many beings as there are in the universe of beings...all these I must lead to *nirvana*...and yet although innumerable beings have thus been led to *nirvana*, in fact no being at all has been led to *nirvana*"'. On the conventional level, beings exist and the *bodhisattva* compassionately sets out to save them, while knowing that on the level of ultimate truth there are no beings (or *bodhisattvas* or *nirvana* for that matter) for all are empty of inherent existence and only relatively real.

Even imperfectly grasped, it is a useful antidote to the subtle forms of selfish pride that can attach themselves to the idea of aiding others less fortunate than oneself.

Many Mahayana writings describe what has become known as the career of the *bodhisattva*, the Mahayana equivalent to the eightfold path. Someone with aspirations to become a *bodhisattva* should begin by living the life of a good ordinary Buddhist. This means living life in accordance with Buddhist morality, helping others and worshipping the Buddhas and *bodhisattvas* who have achieved the goal, with great devotion and love. At this stage you do not really feel capable of leading others to salvation, you are in need of being lead, and turn to the Buddhas and *bodhisattvas* for guidance and help. If this way of life is followed with genuine dedication, there may come a point where a spiritual breakthrough occurs and one feels called to the vocation of *bodhisattva*. This is referred to as the arising or production of *bodhicitta* (the thought of enlightenment). This does not mean a vague notion that it might be rather nice to be a *bodhisattva*, but a revolution in one's consciousness like religious conversion; a sudden and profound understanding of the purpose of one's life brought about by the coming together of wisdom and compassion into a unified whole. It is the Mahayana equivalent to the '*Dhamma* vision' spoken of in the Pali Canon, which set the Buddha's disciples on the supramundane path to *nirvana*.

This 'thought of enlightenment' leads to the making of a solemn and binding vow 'May I obtain supreme and perfect enlightenment, promote the good of all beings and establish them in the final and complete *nirvana*.' This vow is a public declaration, ideally made in the presence of a living Buddha, as the future Shakyamuni vowed before the Buddha Dipankara, but more realistically made in the presence of the heavenly Buddhas and one's own human spiritual master. In the stories where would-be *bodhisattvas* take their vows in front of living Buddhas, the Buddha will then predict the time and place when one will achieve enlightenment. The gap between initial vow and actual attainment of enlightenment is said to be millions of years and countless lifetimes.

Various Mahanaya writings have attempted to systematise the *bodhisattva*'s subsequent career into various stages. They all have in common the practice of the six *paramitas* (perfections) - virtues which the *bodhisattva* must perfect in order to reach enlightenment. These are *dana* (giving), *sila* (morality), *kshanti* (patience), *virya* (vigour), *dhyana* (meditation) and *prajna* (wisdom). This is the Mahayana equivalent to the eightfold path of morality, meditation and wisdom.

Perfect giving is the expression of infinite compassion. The bodhisattva must be generous to all - his family and friends, the sick, poor, unfortunate and helpful, animals and the monastic order. He must give away material things, all his merit, and even his life if necessary. He must give spiritual gifts to others such as courage, guidance, education and most of all the teaching of Buddhist *dharma*. In order for this giving to be perfect, it must be done with judgment and with no sense of pride - thus giving cannot really be perfect without wisdom and the understanding that there is no distinguishing between giver and receiver.

Perfect morality means keeping the Buddhist moral rules. The Mahayana version of the precepts usually lists ten (also found in the Pali Canon). One must abstain from taking life, taking what is not given, sexual misconduct, lying speech, malicious speech, harsh speech, idle chatter, covetousness, ill-will and wrong views. Sometimes abstention from intoxicants is included and two of the forms of wrong speech counted as one. As well as avoiding evil, the positive counterparts must be developed, respect for life, generosity, etc. In order for morality to be perfect it must be neither legalistic nor selfish - in other words, one must be prepared to practice *upaya* and bend the rules if the situation requires it, having no thought of gaining merit for oneself from good actions. Both these qualities require wisdom in order to be able to judge and to have no thought of self. Thus only an advanced *bodhisattva* can really practice *upaya*.

Perfect patience is not just negatively enduring suffering but includes the joyful acceptance of difficulties if they are necessary for the goal, and acceptance in faith of doctrines you may not fully understand. Patience is only perfect, if you no longer distinguish between the one suffering and the ones causing the suffering or for whom the suffering is undertaken, and therefore requires perfect wisdom.

Perfect vigour means boundless enthusiasm in the quest of the *bodhisattva*, never tiring of helping others, studying Buddhism, etc. It is not perfect until one stops thinking of individual achievement, and therefore not until wisdom is gained.

Perfect meditation means becoming completely adept at all the practices of Buddhist meditation. However, it is not perfect if one sees this as a personal achievement, or meditates for one's own benefit. Thus, again, the perfection of wisdom is essential.

The final perfection, of wisdom, has already been described. It is the crowning perfection because without it, as we have seen, none of the other virtues can ever be called completely perfect.

Sometimes a further four perfections are spoken of: *upaya* (skill in means), vows, strength and knowledge. The most important one is *upaya*. This is the ability of the *bodhisattva* always to know the right thing to do to help beings towards salvation in any given circumstances. It represents compassion informed by wisdom, not just wanting to help, but knowing exactly what to do, avoiding the dangers of making things worse or selfish motives.

The *bodhisattva*'s career has been systematised into stages, and to make a neat pattern the perfections have been allocated to various stages. This is rather artificial as they are not really practised in isolation, but the general pattern of gradual progress is important. The most common pattern is one of ten stages.

Stage one is *Pramudita* (Joyful), named from the happy confidence of knowing your goal in life. The *bodhisattva* makes great vows for the future and particularly practices the virtue of 'giving'.

Stage two is *Vimala* (pure) because the *bodhisattva* pays particular attention to perfecting morality, and preaching to others about what he or she practices.

Stage three is *Prabhakari* (lightgiving) as the mind is cleared through study and meditation. The *bodhisattva* practices the virtue of patience and is devoted to working for the good of others.

Stage four is *Arcismati* (Radiant), with the energy of the perfection of vigour. The *bodhisattva* enthusiastically practices all the 37 principles conducive to enlightenment; the eightfold path; the four applications of mindfulness; the four right efforts; the five traditional virtues (faith, energy, mindfulness, concentration and wisdom), the five powers of these virtues, the four psychic powers (urge, energy, thought and investigation) and the seven factors of enlightenment (mindfulness, investigation of *dharmas*, energy, joy, tranquillity, concentration and even-mindedness). This traditional list of 37 exhausts all possible factors leading to enlightenment ever spoken of by the Buddha. In this stage, the *bodhisattva* is also an example to others.

Stage five is *Sudarjaya* (difficult to conquer), as the *bodhisattva* is really progressing and it would be difficult to stop him now. He becomes perfect at meditation and as a side effect gains magical protection.

Stage six is the decisive one, *Abhimukhi* (face-to-face) because the *bodhisattva* comes face to face with the truth. He or she fully understands reality and can be called enlightened in the lesser sense, gaining the perfection of wisdom. However, he or she does not rest in the enjoyment of this state, but presses on for the salvation of the universe. From this point, he or she is an advanced and holy being.

Stage seven is *Durangama* (far-going), because the *bodhisattva* has passed beyond existence as we can imagine it and having gained perfect wisdom can concentrate on *upaya*, finding endless ways and means of helping others to progress spiritually.

Stage eight is *Acala* (immovable) because the *bodhisattva* cannot turn back. As a result of perfect wisdom he or she has endless supernatural abilities to use in the task of helping other beings. Renewing his or her vow, now in a perfect way, he or she has the resources to fulfil it.

Stage nine is *Sadhumati* (good intelligence) as the *bodhisattva* achieves great knowledge and practices the perfection of power or strength.

Stage ten is *Dharmamegha* (the cloud of Dharma), in which the *bodhisattva* practices perfect knowledge and reaches the limits of glory. He or she has a glorious celestial body, is one with all the Buddhas, and has all the qualities required for the salvation of the universe.

The idea of the *bodhisattva* works on two levels in Mahayana Buddhism. It provides an ultimate goal to work towards, and it provides saviour beings for those in need of help. A Mahayana Buddhist both aims to be a *bodhisattva* and seeks help from *bodhisattvas*; looking up to those ahead on the path for help, and aiding those behind. To turn from the path of becoming a bodhisattva to the idea of bodhisattvas who are far advanced on the path, Mahayana Buddhism provides a colourful collection of beings who offer help to those who are in need of it. These are described in the language of mythology and imagined as heavenly beings dwelling in celestial realms.

Each *bodhisattva* has his or her particular characteristics, and stereotyped iconographical forms have developed, so that they are instantly recognisable in pictures. The ones most often mentioned include Avalokiteshvara, Manjushri, Maitreya, Mahasthamaprapta, Kshitigarbhha, Samantabhadra, Vajrapani and Tara. Avalokiteshvara is the bodhisattva of compassion, sometimes pictured with thousands of arms ready to help. Manjushri is the *bodhisattva* of wisdom, with a sword and book, (the *Prajnaparamita in 8000 verses*). Maitreya is the *bodhisattva* destined to be the next earthly Buddha, pictured with a flask of the elixir of life, and associated with friendliness. Kshitigarbha is shown with a staff and is concerned with the welfare of the dead in unhappy realms of hell and ghosts. Samantabhadra is pictured on a white elephant and specialises in powerful spells. Vajrapani is associated with the power of the will and is often pictured as fearsome, scaring away evil. Mahasthamaprapta and Avalokiteshvara dwell with Amitabha Buddha in his paradise land. Tara is a gentle saviouress, pictured as a young princess, but full of motherly love; she is particularly popular in Tibet.

Avalokiteshvara

The name of this *bodhisattva* possibly means 'the Lord who looks down'. In other words, the compassionate one who cares for suffering beings. In Chinese, the name is Kwan-Yin, the regarder of cries. The origin of the actual image is obscure and may have been influenced by that of some Hindu god (Shiva). In China, the concept of Avalokiteshvara may have been influenced by an ancient goddess of mercy, as Kwan-Yin is usually pictured as female. This popular *bodhisattva* is often pictured with thousands of arms ready to help everyone at once. He is said to be at the tenth stage of the *bodhisattva*'s career and so has unlimited amounts of merit to share, and supernatural abilities to work miracles. Chapter 25 of the popular Mahayana scripture the Lotus Sutra, is all about Avalokiteshvara. In this chapter the Buddha Shakyamuni endorses the worship of Avalokiteshvara, recommending it to all. To some people Avalokiteshvara has almost become the supreme being; he is referred to in one Mahayana work as 'the spirit of the universe and the saviour of the world'. He is believed to dwell with Amitabha Buddha and Mahasthamaprapta in a Western paradise, yet he does not enjoy the peace of this paradise but constantly busies himself in helping the world. He is sometimes thought of as male, sometimes female and sometimes both or neither.

Tibetan Buddhists believe he works through their religious leader, the Dalai Lama, who is therefore Avalokiteshvara's earthly instrument. Shakyamuni Buddha in the Lotus Sutra claims that Avalokiteshvara will help anyone in any sort of trouble, specifying sailors in trouble on the sea, disasters like floods and storms, attack by demons, swords or robbers, poison and temptations. He will set you free from prison, help you evade the death penalty, and is particularly kind to criminals and sinners. Childless women who pray to him will be granted sons and daughters. He will work miracles, and can appear in any form to help you, human, divine, man or woman, Buddha or non-Mahayana religious teacher. The Lotus Sutra even claims that calling on him is worth thousands of prayers to any other Buddha or bodhisattva. This mantra, given in another sutra, is: *'om mani padme hum'*.

Avalokiteshvara is a perfect illustration of Mahayana Buddhism, in that he shows how people of all types are catered for in the religion. He is a saviour figure, a being to imagine and relate to. He satisfies the emotions and is a being who loves and protects, that can be loved in return with devotion and worship. He is a figure deserving of worship having unselfishly devoted himself to the salvation of the whole world in his *bodhisattva* vows. Whether pictured as female or not, she adds a gentle, motherly dimension to the Buddhist religion.

The question is sometimes asked whether *bodhisattvas* such as Avalokiteshvara really exist, or whether they are part of the *upaya kausalya* (teaching devices) of the Buddha. Are we meant to take Avalokiteshvara literally, or is he a symbolic figure, a personification of the power of compassion? In one sense such a figure is a teaching device. One young monk explained to the author 'they are a big show put on by the Buddhas to attract and increase faith. They are not separate beings.' (Cush 1990) On the Mahayana understanding of emptiness, one can neither find, apprehend or see a *dharma* 'bodhisattva' in ultimate reality. However, it must be remembered that one cannot apprehend a *dharma* 'human being'; bodhisattvas are thus as real as we are. On the ultimate level, neither bodhisattvas nor human beings exist, but on the relative level of unenlightened beings, they are there to help.

The Philosophical Schools

Madhyamaka

Perhaps the most famous of Buddhist philosophers is the 2nd century CE Mahayana monk Nagarjuna, the founder of the Madhyamaka school of philosophy. Legend says that Nagarjuna recovered the Prajnaparamita texts from the Naga spirits, who had been guarding them since they were taught by Shakyamuni, waiting until the person came along who could understand them. The central ideas of

Madhyamaka are those of the Prajnaparamita literature, but expressed in a more philosophical, analytical and logical form.

The name 'Madhyamaka' means 'the middle position'. In putting forward the teaching of *shunyata* (S) (emptiness) - that things neither exist absolutely nor do not exist absolutely, but exist relatively - Nagarjuna claims that he is true to the original teaching of Shakyamuni 'neither eternalism nor annihilationism'. It would be useful for readers to remind themselves at this point of the teachings of the Prajnaparamita literature (see page 90ff). In the *Mulamadhyamakakarika* (verses on the fundamentals of the middle way) by Nagarjuna, we find the same concepts of 'emptiness', the denial of *svabhava* (ownbeing) as a characteristic of things, and the two levels of truth (conventional and ultimate).

Svabhava and emptiness

Nagarjuna defines *svabhava* as existence which is dependent on nothing else. But, as all things are dependent on causes and conditions to bring them about, there can be no such existants: all things are *shunya* (S) (empty) of inherent existence. 'The coming into being of own-being from conditions and causes is not possible' (15.1). In making this statement, Nagarjuna sees himself as simply restating the original teaching of the Buddha that all states come into being through causes and conditions 'it is dependent origination that we call emptiness' (24.18)

To call all things 'empty' is a way of trying to express that no individual thing is anything in and by itself, but only in relation to others. Emptiness denies that there is any entity, physical or non-material, which possesses what Buddhists call *svabhava* (own-being). In other words, nothing is self-existent, nothing has unchanging characteristics by which it is totally distinguished from all other things, nothing possesses an eternal, unchanging essence or substance, nothing exists separately, independently, unchangingly. Emptiness implies the interdependence of all things.

If we ask whether 'empty' things exist or not, the answer depends on what level of truth we are using. On the level of conventional truth, things exist, but at the level of ultimate truth (where to exist means to exist eternally and independently) they do not.

If asked whether things exist, one cannot say either 'yes' or 'no' as both would give the wrong impression. 'Yes' is too definite, implying (especially with the background of Indian thought) that things exist eternally, separately and independently. 'No' is too negative, implying that things do not exist in any sense. Thinkers like

Nagarjuna felt that they were following in the true footsteps of the Buddha in asserting a 'Middle Way' between the eternalism of existence and the annihilationism of non-existence. Things neither exist nor do not exist, they are 'empty' and exist relatively. Another way Buddhists express this is to speak of the *tathata* (suchness) of things - they simply are, in this relative way.

It might help to distinguish the meaning of 'emptiness' from what it is not. Despite its rather negative sound, emptiness does not mean 'nothingness' in the sense that nothing exists at all; things exist on a relative level, but we must not seek for a permanence that is not there. Emptiness is not some sort of material or substance out of which all things are made, as in some Hindu forms of non-dualistic teaching. Individual things are not cells of some larger organism which could then be said to exist in its own right. There is not actually a 'One' which all things are, or are part of. Things are dependent and interconnected.

Nagarjuna's method of argument was to take the idea of an opponent and, by analysing it, show it to be logically absurd. He rejected all speculative 'views' not based on experiencing the world as it really is. In particular, his view has been seen as a critique of the Sarvastivadin theory that although there are no 'selves', reality is made up of *dharmas*, these *dharmas* can be said to have own-being.

The Sarvastivadin Abhidhamma literature, like that of the Theravada, denied the Hindu concept of *atman* (unchanging self-substance) and put forward the idea that reality was made up of impersonal series of events called *dharmas*. One was advised to analyse everything, especially the human personality, into its component dharmas, and the truth of anatta would become apparent. Thus, the sentence 'I am hungry' is a poor representation of reality, because although there is a hungry feeling, there is no *dharma* corresponding to the word 'I'. There are no permanent, separate things in themselves like selves or chariots, just constantly changing series of combinations of *dharmas*. The Sarvastivadins taught that these basic *dharmas* could be said to be real, whereas the things they go to make up like 'me' were just labels. Madhyamaka philosophy claimed that this made *dharmas* unconditioned and absolute, and that Sarvastivadin philosophy did not go far enough in applying the Buddha's teaching of impermanence and 'no-self'; even *dharmas* are dependent, ever-changing and impossible to distinguish - in other words 'empty'. Thus one cannot properly assert that *dharmas* are either real or unreal.

> 'Since there is no *dharma* that is not dependently originated, there is no dharma that is not empty' (24:19)

Najarjuna also argues against critics, who claim that he is a heretic.

'If everything is empty, there will be neither arising or passing away... the four holy truths have no existence...the Dharma and Sangha and Buddha do not exist.' (24:1.5)

He argues that they have misunderstood emptiness, and the two levels of truth. On the contrary, it is those who deny emptiness that deny Buddhism, for in asserting the own-being of *dharmas*, they make it impossible for things to arise and pass away -things would be static and unchanging.

'If everything is NOT empty, then there is neither arising nor passing away... for YOU the four noble truths do not exist.' (24:20)

Causality

In teaching 'emptiness' Nagarjuna criticises the normally held view of causality, that 'really' existing things are brought about by 'really' existing causes. If things 'really' exist, (ie possess own-being) then they would either exist forever or not at all. It would be illogical for things possessing 'own-being' ever to be brought into being. 'No existing thing is produced, either from itself, from another, nor from both, nor from no cause.' (1:1)

Nirvana and samsara

One of the initially startling conclusions of Nagarjuna's teaching is that 'there is no distinction what ever between *nirvana* and *samsara*. The limit of *nirvana* is the limit of *samsara*. There is not the slightest difference between the two.' (25:19) What does Nagarjuna mean here?

Nirvana is said by Nagarjuna to be neither existent, non-existent, both nor neither. It is 'the calming of all apprehension and the blissful calming of false concepts'. In the teaching of emptiness, *samsara* has no inherent existence. Thus *nirvana* and *samsara* cannot be separated out as two separate and independent ultimate and opposed realities, rather 'the state of rushing backward and forward which is dependent or conditioned is taught as *nirvana* when not-dependent and not-conditioned' (25.9) *Nirvana* is seeing samsara for what it really is, empty.

If one can sort out the level of truth on which various statements are being made, the teaching of 'emptiness', that nothing exists separately and independent of other things, is an obvious truth. The problem is that although logical analysis can show that all things are empty, we talk and live as if things did have own-being. Our language contains concepts that we use as if they really did refer to independently existing objects (eg me and mine, you and yours, us and them). Our behaviour, in grasping after things as if they were permanent and unchanging and could bring happiness suggests that we believe that both ourselves and the things we desire possess 'own-being'. The perfect wisdom of the Mahayana involves not just intellectually accepting 'emptiness', but realising it in our attitudes and emotions. Here both meditation and morality can aid wisdom.

Yogacara

The major rival to the Mahyamaka philosophy is that known as the Yogacara (practice of yoga), Vijnanavada (teaching of consciousness), or Cittamatra (mind-only) school of thought. This was founded by Asanga and his brother Vasubandhu, Mahayana monks of the 4th century CE. It sees itself as an advance on Madhyamaka, which it criticises for being too negative and implying that nothing exists at all (a misunderstanding of Madhyamaka). The debate between the two has gone on throughout the centuries, although some thinkers have tried to combine the insights of the two, or claim that they are really saying the same thing in different ways.

Both schools agree that the perceived phenomena of the universe are wrongly attributed with *svabhava* (own-being) and need to be seen for what they really are. The Madhyamaka claims that they are really 'empty' (ie only relatively and dependently real). The Yogacara claims that they are mental constructions.

The basic texts of the Yogacara include some *sutras* which reflect this view, such as the Samdhinirmocana sutra and the Mahayana-abhidharma sutra together with the *shastras* (treatises) and commentaries written by Asanga and Vasubandhu such as Asanga's Mahayanasamgraha. The Lankavatara Sutra also reflects Yogacara ideas we well as other Mahayana tendencies.

The basic teaching is that although there appears to be a multiplicity of separate things and beings in the universe, an external world of solid objects and individual selves, this is only an appearance. The truth is that our minds impose these fixed interpretations on our experience, and what we perceive as really existing things are in reality mind-created. Some quotations from the Lankavatara sutra illustrate this:

> 'the world is nothing more than thought construction'; 'where there is false imagination there is multitudinousness of things'. What we think of as 'the real world' is compared to a mirage, a dream, an eye disorder, an echo, a reflection, a barren woman's child in a dream. (*Lankavatara Sutra* 90-96)

Phenomena such as dreams and mirages prove that it is possible to have experiences without there being any corresponding real objects.

'One may ask "How, in the absence of an object, can one experience desirable and undesirable impressions?" To remove this doubt, things are compared to a dream. In a dream also there is no real object, and yet pleasant and unpleasant impressions are felt.' (Asanga, *Mahayanasamgraha* 2.27 in Conze (1964) p215)

Yogacara teaches that there are three ways of understanding reality. The first way, *parikalpita* (imagined or constructed), is the belief that there are selves and objects that possess 'own-being', independent and separate. This is a delusion. The second way is the *paratantra* (dependent or relative). This is the actual flow of perceptions dependent on conditions; it is what we experience. The third is the *parinispanna* (perfected or accomplished). Reality is seen for what it actually is - the understanding that there are no separately existing subjects and objects.

So the *parinispanna* is the right interpretation of the *paratantra*, in contrast to the *parikalpita*, which is a delusion. There are no selves or external objects, but there is a flow of mental experiences that is mistakenly interpreted as the former.

The Yogacara goes on to explain how the false perception comes about. It puts forward eight types of consciousness, the six traditional Buddhist consciousnesses (the consciousnesses associated with the five senses, plus the mind, considered as a sixth sense), the *manas* (mind) and the *alayavijnana* (store consciousness). The store consciousness is like an underlying unconscious level of the mind which acts as a store for impressions caused by the actions we perform as a result of our craving and ignorance (*karma*). These are like seeds which grow into a flow of perceptions. The *manas* then wrongly organises and interprets these perceptions into separately existing persons and objects. These then become the focus of further cravings etc which cause further impressions to sink into the *alyavijnana*, to become the seeds of further delusions etc. The Yogacara thus has a theory of how *karma* works, and what it is that provides the continuity between one life and the next; the underlying store-consciousness. It explains how our deluded perceptions arise, and why it is so hard to escape from the cycle of *samsara*.

It also shows the way out; by realising that persons and objects are 'mind-only', one will no longer cling to them and form karmic seeds. 'When cognition no longer apprehends an object, then it stands firmly in consciousness-only, because where there is nothing to grasp there is no more grasping.' (Vasubandhu, quoted in Conze: 1964). Several questions arise in connection with Yogacara teaching. Are all other people figments of our imagination? As separate selves, yes, but as streams of perceptions, no. Other streams of perception can interact with our own, and the reason that many beings seem to experience similar 'realities', is that their karmic seeds are similar.

Both Yogacara and Madhyamaka would see themselves as true to the middle path between annihilationism and eternalism, but that the other had strayed too far over the line. To the Yogacarin, the Madhyamika is too negative, saying all things without exception are empty, which sounds too non-existent, but to the Madhyamika the Yogacarins are too positive about mind, seeing it as something that really exists, and possibly too negative about things, seeing them as totally illusory rather than relatively real.

Some further ideas: the *tathagatgarbha* and *hua yen*

In some Mahayana *sutras* and *shastras* (treatises), such as the Lankavatara sutra, the Srimala sutra and the Ratnagotravibhaga, a further idea is found - that of the *tathagatagarbha*. This is translated either as 'the embryo of the Buddha' or 'the womb of the Buddha', expressing the idea of the potentiality of Buddhahood in all beings. This idea is not the basis of a fully worked out philosophical school, as in the case of Madhyamaka and Yogacara, but has been an influential concept, especially in Far-eastern Buddhism. The idea is that all beings have this potentiality, the seed, embryo or womb of Buddhahood within them, but that in the unenlightened this is obscured by 'defilements'.

'In each being there exists in embryonic form the element of the Tathagata, but people do not look through to that' (*Ratnagotravibhaga*, in Conze (1954) p217)

This potential Buddhahood is compared in the Ratnagotravibhaga to a lovely Buddha statue covered over with dirty rags, to the unseen seed in a fruit, to gold in ore. As in these cases, the Buddha nature itself is pure and undefiled, but covered over by impurities. Thus enlightenment is not so much achieving something new, but uncovering what was already there. It is because of this Buddha potential that beings can follow the Buddhist path. There are two ways of understanding the concept. It can be seen as meaning only that all beings have the potential for Buddhahood, but have a long way to go before they are buddhas, or, if combined with Yogacara thought about the illusory nature of our perceptions, it can be understood as saying that all beings already are Buddhas, because the so-called defilements are illusory anyway, and only Buddha nature is real. The Tibetan tradition tends to the former understanding, and the Far-eastern tradition to the latter. Are all beings potential Buddhas or Buddhas already without knowing it?

Hua yen

The Avatamsaka sutra (in Chinese, Hua-yen, meaning 'flower garland') teaches a further idea 'the total interpenetration of all things'. This idea develops the idea of 'emptiness' in Madhyamaka, that nothing is anything in itself, but only exists dependently, and the ideas of Yogacara, that all is mind-only, to put forward the idea that as all things are interrelated in this way, then all things exist in total mutual interpenetration.

Each individual thing or person contains all other things. The universe is like a net of jewels wherein each jewel reflects every other one. This gives a great value to every person and even atom, and gives a basis for the more positive appreciation of the natural world found in Chinese rather than Indian Buddhism. The Avatamsaka sutra became the basis of one of the influential schools of Buddhism in China and Japan (see p132)

The Trikaya or Three Bodies of the Buddha

The word Buddha can be used in many ways in Buddhism. Most westerners think primarily of the historical man, Siddhartha Gautama, who lived on this earth and achieved enlightenment or buddhahood. However, even in Theravada Buddhism, it is taught that he was not the only such being. There were Buddhas in past ages, and there will be future Buddhas, such as the bodhisattva Maitreya, considered to be currently in his last life before the one in which he will achieve Buddhahood. There are also different ways of looking at the Buddha in Theravada - as he appeared to ignorant eyes, as an ordinary man, as he appeared to the eyes of faith, a glorious, shining being, with the 32 characteristics of a great man. There is also the famous saying of the Buddha in the Pali canon, that identifies the Buddha with the truth he taught: 'he who sees the Dharma sees me' (*Suttanipata* 3.120)

In Mahayana Buddhism, as we have seen, there are many more Buddhas, dwelling in other Buddha-lands, and all beings are potentially Buddhas. The Lotus sutra claims that Shakyamuni still lives and works for beings and that his birth, death and enlightenment were *upaya*. Nagarjuna and the Prajnaparamita texts talk of the two forms of the Buddha, the physical form, and the *dharma* body, or the perfect wisdom that the Buddha realises and taught. The important thing is not the physical body but the truth he taught.

The Mahayana understanding of the Buddha was systematised into what is known as the *Trikaya* (3 body doctrine), probably among thinkers of the Yogacara school. This doctrine puts forward that there are three aspects to Buddhahood - the *Dharmakaya* (Dharma body, truth body or essential body), the *Sambhogakaya* (glorious body, enjoyment body or body of bliss) and the *Nirmanakaya* (transformation body).

The *Dharmakaya* refers to that which ultimately makes a Buddha a Buddha - the understanding of the truth about the universe, the emptiness of all things, the underlying truth of the universe. According to the *tathagatagarbha* concept, it is present in embryonic form in all beings 'impure in ordinary beings, partly pure and partly impure in the bodhisattvas, and perfectly pure in the Tathagata' (*Ratnagotravibhaga* 47). The *Dharmakaya* is enlightened purified consciousness which sees reality for what it is. It cannot be described using ordinary language.

The *Sambhogakaya* refers to the glorious, heavenly Buddhas described in the Mahayana sutras. These are wonderful beings, with many powers which they employ for the salvation of beings. They live in their own Buddhalands (eg the pure land of Amitabha Buddha: see p92f), and have unimaginably long lifespans. It is usually said that the Mahayana sutras were preached by Shakyamuni Buddha in his glorious form. These are the Buddhas that form the focus of devotion in Mahayana Buddhism, and are depicted in artistic forms in paintings and statues. They are worshipped and visualised. It can be said that the *Dharmakaya* is the Buddha from the point of view of wisdom, and the *Sambhogakaya* from the point of view of compassion.

The *Nirmanakaya* (transformation body) refers to the Buddha manifested in earthly form, of which the best known example is Gautama. In Mahayana teaching, the lifestory of Siddhartha Gautama was like a drama, acted out for the benefit of beings by an emanation of the glorious Shakyamuni Buddha who was enlightened many ages ago. Transformation bodies do not have to take the form of earthly Buddhas, they can take on any form which will be of help to living beings, including animal form, gods or the religious teachers of other religions. The teachings of such *nirmanakayas* will be governed by *upaya kausalya* (skilful means) and be suited to the needs of whatever beings need help.

The three bodies of the Buddha are related, in that the *Nirmanakaya* are produced by the *Sambhogakaya*, and the *Sambhogakaya* are those beings who have realised the *Dharmakaya*. On the level of ultimate truth, only the *Dharmakaya* is real.

Tibetan Buddhism

Tibetan Buddhism is basically Mahayana Buddhism with Tantric
elements, and very similar to that which would have been found in
India between the 8th and 12th centuries CE. The Tibetan type of
Buddhism is also followed in Sikkim, Bhutan, certain parts of Nepal
and North-West India, in Mongolia and some areas of the former
Soviet Union.

History

Legend has it that Buddhism first came to Tibet in the 7th century CE,
when the King of Tibet sent a deputation to India to learn about
Buddhism. Buddhist texts were brought back to Tibet, a Tibetan
alphabet devised and the process of translation started. The King was
probably led to this interest in Buddhism by his two wives who were
both Buddhists, one Nepalese and the other Chinese. However, no
attempt was made to spread the religion to the common people until
the 8th century, when two famous teachers arrived in Tibet, a
Mahayana scholar called Shantarakshita and a tantric master called
Padmasambhava. Padmasambhava was particularly successful, and
legend claims that he managed to convert the local gods and spirits
who opposed the introduction of Buddhism. What this probably
means is that Padmasambhava's tantric type of Buddhism could more
easily blend in with the beliefs of the local people, and appealed to
them more than scholarly Buddhism. Padmasambhava is considered
to be a great saint and even a *nirmanakaya* of the Buddha, not born in
the normal way but found inside a lotus flower. He is credited with
great magical power and the authorship of *The Tibetan Book of the
Dead*. During his time the first monastery was built in Tibet, and the
first Tibetans became monks.

The next important event was a great debate or more likely, series of
debates in the late 8th century between an Indian Mahayana scholar
and a Chinese Ch'an (Zen) master. The main issue between the two
was whether the road to Buddhahood was the long and gradual path
of the bodhisattva or whether enlightenment could be gained instantly
(the Zen view). The Tibetans were more impressed by the Indian
arguments, and in general Tibetan Buddhism has followed India
rather than Chinese forms. However, some teachings do speak of the
'quick' way to enlightenment, and Ch'an ideas may have had some
influence.

In the 9th century CE there was a backlash against Buddhism, and a
King called Lang dar ma persecuted Buddhism, hoping to restore

Tibet to its traditional religion of Bon. Monasteries and scriptures were destroyed, monks exiled, and practising Buddhism was made a capital offence. After six years of the persecution, Lang dar ma was assassinated by a Buddhist monk disguised as a dancer. This daring escapade is a favourite Tibetan story, and is interpreted as an example of *upaya* - although killing is wrong, in this case it was the right thing to do in order to save the Buddhist religion and to save the King himself from earning even more bad *karma* than he already had.

With the restoration of the monarchy in the 10th century, there was a revival of Buddhism, and many Tibetans travelled to India to learn about Buddhism either in the great universities or with individual tantric masters. Upon their return, they set about translating texts and teaching what they had learned. This led to the formation of different sects of Buddhism, as different teachers stressed different aspects of Buddhism.

The **Ka dam pa** ('Bound by command') sect was started by an Indian scholar called Atisa, who taught doctrinal scholarship as well as tantric rituals. This sect stressed discipline and morality and played down the magical and tantric aspects. The monks had to keep strictly to the vinaya rules including celibacy and no alcohol. The worship of Avalokitesvara and Tara were popularised.

The **Sakya** sect, named after its main monastery, was started in the 11th century. The leadership of this sect is hereditary and it had great political influence in the 12th and 13th centuries.

The **Kargyupa** ('Transmitted command') sect was also begun at this time by Marpa. This Tibetan master studied in India under tantric teachers and claimed to be continuing a line of teaching revealed directly by a heavenly Buddha, Vajradhara, to an Indian teacher called Tilopa. This sect combines both scholarly Mahayana doctrine and advanced tantric practices. The early teachers such as the Indians Tilopa and Naropa, and the Tibetan Marpa are described as eccentrics, rather like Zen masters, and they stress that the teachings cannot be put into words, but must be transmitted directly from master to pupil. The successor of Marpa was Milarepa, 'the cotton clad', one of Tibet's best loved saints. Milarepa lived in the 11th century CE and turned to Buddhism in order to atone for his previous practice of 'black' magic. This he had used to get his revenge on an uncle who had deprived his poor widowed mother of all her property. After an arduous apprenticeship with Marpa, he lived as a hermit high in the mountains. His name refers to the fact that he lived a very ascetic life, wearing only a cotton cloth in the snow, having mastered the generation of heat through the power of meditation. He expressed his enlightened vision in beautiful poems which teach about Buddhism and also celebrate the joys of solitude and of the natural surroundings such as the mountains and wild animals. Milarepa's disciple, Sgam-po-pa, was more scholarly and composed a famous summary of the Buddhist path called *The Jewel Ornament of Liberation* which is still used today. His 12th century disciples formed four different branches of the Kargyupa sect. This sect was the first to recognise a *tulku* (earthly *bodhisattva*) who is deliberately reborn time after time in order to help suffering beings. Karmapa, the first *tulku*, has now been reborn sixteen times.

The name **Nying ma pa** ('old-style ones') was coined to refer to Buddhists who did not follow any of these new and organised sects, but had continued the practice of Buddhism through the dark age of the 9th century. These were distinguished from the newer sects by more emphasis on tantric and magical practices. Their lamas, or religious masters, included married clergy rather than celibate monks. They trace their teachings and practices back to Padmasambhava.

Buddhism seems to have been well established throughout Tibet by the 12th century CE. In the 13th century, the Sakya sect were supported by the Mongol Khans, which meant that this sect had political power in Tibet. The Mongols were influenced by Buddhism, and Tibetan-style Buddhism was brought to China during the Mongol rule of the 13th and 14th centuries. This was a time of great scholarship among Tibetan Buddhists, and the vast collection of Buddhist literature amassed by the Tibetans was organised into a canon of scriptures in the 14th century. The scripture is divided into two sections - Kanjur (the word of the Buddha including *vinaya* rules, Mahayana and Hinayana *sutras* and *tantras*) and Tenjur (commentaries and other works). The printed canon runs to well over three hundred volumes.

A further development of Tibetan Buddhism was brought about by Tsong kha pa, a famous saint who lived from 1357 to 1419. Tsong kha pa began a new sect of Buddhism called **Ge lug pa** (virtuous way), because of their stress on proper monastic discipline, celibacy, and scholarship. They are also nicknamed the 'yellow hats' which distinguish Ge lug pas from the 'red hats' of the earlier sects. This sect does not deny the truth or value of the *tantras* but considers many practices are for advanced students only, stressing that enlightenment is to be reached by a gradual, well-disciplined path and not by some instant secret ritual. The line of teachers started by Tsong kha pa developed into the institution of the Dalai Lama. As previously mentioned, Tibetans believe that certain holy men, being *bodhisattvas*, deliberately chose to be reborn in human form in order to help other suffering beings. What distinguishes Tibetan belief from the general belief of Mahayana Buddhism is that these reincarnated holy men can actually be pointed out. Thus, when the fourth patriarch of the Ge lug pa school died, his successor was claimed to be his second incarnation. The third incarnation claimed his identity from a very young age, and later converted the Mongols to Ge lug pa Buddhism. It was the Mongol ruler who coined the title 'Dalai Lama', *dalai* meaning 'ocean' in Mongolian, and *lama* meaning 'holy man' or 'religious teacher' in Tibetan. This was in the 16th century. Not only was the Dalai Lama the reincarnation of the 15th century holy man, but as a *bodhisattva*, an actual *nirmanakaya* form of the Buddha, more specifically an earthly manifestation of the heavenly bodhisattva Avalokitesvara (in Tibetan, Chen re zi). Although the most famous, the Dalai Lama was not the first *tulku* to be recognised, and there are many other recognised lines of incarnations. Whenever a Dalai Lama or other *tulku* dies, a search is made for a baby born after his death. The baby *tulku* is verified by various methods. He may recognise old friends, pick out belongings - for example, prayer beads - from among a collection of others, have the large ears of the Buddha, or his whereabouts may be revealed in a dream. *Tulkus* are always taken from their families, often poor and provincial ones, and educated as a monk as befits a holy *bodhisattva*.

The fifth Dalai Lama became the religious and political leader of Tibet in the 17th century and built the famous Potala palace in Lhasa. During the 18th and 19th centuries, the Dalai Lamas were caught up in political intrigue involving, among other things, the Chinese claim to sovereignty over Tibet. Some died young, possibly assassinated.

The 13th Dalai Lama (1878-1933) managed to rule as an independent monarch, attempted to bring Tibet up to date by selecting the useful aspects of Western civilisation, and is remembered with affection by the foreigners who met him.

The 14th Dalai Lama was born in 1935 and was only a teenager when the Chinese Communists invaded (or 'liberated') Tibet in 1951. At first an attempt was made to compromise with the invaders and combine political Communism with religious freedom. This proved impossible, as the Communists objected to religious practices, and many Tibetans objected to Chinese rule, and the consequent upheavals led to the Dalai Lama's flight in 1959 to India, where he now leads the Tibetans in exile. It has been estimated that there are about 100,000 Tibetans in exile, mainly in India but also spread throughout the world. Many of the *tulkus* and other leading monks escaped, which has meant that Tibetan Buddhism has had many gifted teachers for missionary endeavours; meanwhile, the Communists of the 60s attempted to destroy everything to do with religion in the 'Tibetan Autonomous Region of the People's Republic'. More recently, Chinese policy has denounced this destruction of cultural heritage and there is some evidence of religion reviving. Cynics, however, say that Buddhist temples in China are just outward show for propaganda purposes, and although often invited, the Dalai Lama has not yet returned to Tibet.

Beliefs and Practices

Tibetans, like other Buddhists, believe in the Four Noble Truths, the three marks of life, *karma*, rebirth, enlightenment and compassion. These basics are continually brought to mind by the popular picture known as the 'Tibetan Wheel of Life' depicting the six possible states of rebirth, the twelve links of dependent origination, and the greed, hatred and delusion (symbolised by a cockerel, snake and pig) that keep the wheel of samsara turning. Death, pictured as a monster, holds the wheel in his grasp and the Buddha points the way out. Dazzled by more exotic aspects of Tibetan Buddhism, Westerners sometimes forget that all its practices are firmly rooted in the Dharma taught by Shakyamuni. Tibetans are also Mahayana Buddhists and thus accept the philosophies of 'emptiness' and 'mind-only', the *Trikaya* doctrine of Buddhahood and the ideal of the *bodhisattva*. They have been heavily influenced by *tantra* and so their rituals are very complex, involving a multitude of heavenly beings, visualisations, *mandalas*, *mantras*, *mudras*, and more esoteric forms of yoga; but all of these are firmly geared to traditional Buddhist goals.

Buddhism became the foundation of all Tibetan society, and the huge monasteries had great influence, wealth and political power.

It has been estimated that one in six of all Tibetan men were monks, and they had a variety of religious and social roles. There were (and are) also nuns in the Mahayana tradition, though not so numerous as the monks. Tibetan monks wear robes dyed in shades of burgundy rather than the bright orange of Theravada countries. The word *lama* does not mean monk, but refers to a holy man who acts as a *guru* or religious master or teacher, and who is often a monk but may also be a layman and married, like Marpa and the Nying ma pa clergy.

Tibetan lay Buddhists combine Buddhist belief with local beliefs in spirits, magical rituals, etc. They spend more time on outward forms of ritual worship - visiting temples, giving offerings to statues, chanting prayers and going on pilgrimages, than on inner meditation. For the lay people the monks provide religious rituals, education, and supernatural protection, while the lay people give the monasteries material support and their sons. Among the services provided by the monks are funerals, which traditionally in Tibet involved not cremation but the dismemberment of the body, which is left out in the wilds for animals and birds to consume. This was suitable in a country with little firewood or depth of soil. Lamps are kept lit for 49 days to aid the departed spirit through the intermediate state into its next life. There are also festivals to celebrate the days of the Buddha's birth, death and enlightenment. In Spring, there is a New Year Festival, which involves prayers, special offerings in the temples such as huge sculptures out of butter, dance dramas, religious debates, and games such as horse races. On special occasions like these Tibetans give each other white silk or muslin scarves which may be draped around the statues of the Buddhas or *bodhisattvas* as offerings.

Among the distinguishing features of Tibetan Buddhism are the vast variety of supernatural beings, the beliefs about the Bardo (an intermediate state between one life and the next), the elaborate variety of rituals and the belief in *tulkus*.

The colourful mythology of Tibetan Buddhism includes all the heavenly Buddhas and *bodhisattvas* of Mahayana Buddhism. Favourites in Tibet are Avalokitesvara, patron *bodhisattva* of Tibet, Tara and Manjusri. In addition, there are the *bodhisattvas* and Buddhas of the *tantras* and countless demigods and spirits taken over from the previous religion and made into 'protectors of the Faith'. To add to the complications, each *bodhisattva* is provided with a female consort (from tantric symbolism) and can appear in two forms. There is the 'peaceful aspect' where the *bodhisattva* appears in the form of a kindly deity, and the 'wrathful aspect' where the *bodhisattva* appears as a frightening monster, surrounded by flames. These fierce figures - and each has its own name - are not evil, but the destroyers of evil, and appear hostile because of their enmity to all things evil. The actual form of the 'wrathful' *bodhisattvas* may have been influenced by ideas about spirits in the local religion, or possibly by Hindu beliefs, as gods such as Shiva and the goddess Kali have this double nature. The Tibetans are great artists and love to portray these mythological beings; a favourite art form being the *thanka* or painting on cloth, a practical, portable art form for nomadic people or travelling teachers.

The Tibetan Book of the Dead describes the *Bardo* or intermediate state of 49 days between one life and the next. Although not believing in a soul in the sense of a Hindu *atman*, Buddhists have often tried to identify the means of continuity between one life and the next. Strict Theravada doctrine denies the intermediate state, considering the last act of consciousness in one life directly conditions the first act of consciousness in the next; but in practice they have not been so sure; as is shown by the Burmese custom of leaving a branch for the 'butterfly spirit' to rest on for seven days. The Pali Canon speaks of a mysterious *gandhabba* (P), *gandharva* (S) (spirit), which, together with the male and female gametes is necessary for the formation of new life.

According to *The Tibetan Book of the Dead*, the first experience after death is that the spirit, (or life force, or whatever) remains close to the dead body, not realising that it is dead, and frantically tries to communicate with grieving relatives. After a while, the earthly scene fades out and one experiences a clear, white light. This is actually one's own consciousness in its fundamental, pure, enlightened state, where it is identical with the emptiness of all things, and the *Dharmakaya* of Buddhahood. If one can recognise this for what it is, and without belief in a separate self, submerge oneself in the light, one can win through to enlightenment and Buddhahood without need of any rebirth. Most people are confused and frightened and perceive the white light and themselves as two separate things. As a result, the second stage of the Bardo dawns. One seems to exist in the form of a subtle body, like a ghost, and visions appear. For seven days the Buddhas and *bodhisattvas* appear in their peaceful forms, beautiful and shining. One should realise that these are symbolic manifestations of Buddhahood, pray to them, and then be reborn in a pure paradisal Buddhaland instead of in the world of suffering. For the next seven days, if that chance is missed, the Buddhas and bodhisattvas will appear in their wrathful form like demons threatening to kill. One must try to realise that these are just creations of one's own mind, that there is no duality, or if nothing else, worship them as kindly bodhisattvas. Most people do neither, paralysed with fear, and pass to the next stage of the Bardo, seeking rebirth.

The first event is an illusion that one is being judged by Yama, the mythological Lord of the Dead and that one's good and bad deeds are being weighed. It is all a creation of one's own mind and *karma*. After this judgment one is dragged off by monsters and realises that one is dead. This causes a feeling of great misery and a craving for more life. It is described as feeling like being tossed about and driven by a wind and squeezed into cracks in rocks. As a result of craving, one will see six beckoning lights, leading to the six places of rebirth. A white light leads towards the temporary heavens of the gods, a red light towards the jealous gods, a blue light towards human life, a green light towards animal life, a dull yellow light towards the life of a preta or miserable ghost, and a dark smokey light leads towards the hells. All of one's previous ethically significant choices (*karma*) cause one to be particularly attracted towards one of these lights. The desire for rebirth feels like a terrible thirst and like pursuing demons. One sees possible parents around and feels a desire to enter one particular womb. Before you know it, you have been born again in *samsara*!

When a person is dying, a monk will read *The Book of the Dead* in an attempt to communicate with the departing spirit and explain what is happening to it. The idea is either to realise that none of this is real, and achieve enlightenment, or if, like a *tulku*, you actually want to be reborn, to have conscious control of the whole process and choose your rebirth. At least you might be able to influence the process a little, and avoid the worst rebirths.

Tibetan religious rituals are very varied and complex; Tibetan Buddhism prides itself on its variety of 'skilful means' for aiding people towards liberation. Tibetan teachers try to encourage people to make the effort by stressing the rarity of obtaining human birth, and the potentiality of Buddhahood in everyone, which can only be realised in human form. Further encouragement is the debt you owe to all beings. In Tibetan thought, in endless samsara, all beings have probably at one time been your Mother, and striving for enlightenment is the best thing you can do to pay them back. There is great stress on individual progress and the need of an individual *guru* or *lama* (spiritual master). This master may allocate to you a particularly suitable 'deity' or *yidam* (ie a Buddha or *bodhisattva* to concentrate on in your practice). The central practice is the tantric one of visualisation, *mudras*, *mandalas*, and chanting *mantras*. Complex visualisations are usually confined to monks or laypeople seriously seeking to practice meditation. However, even ordinary worshippers make great use of *mantras* in particular.

Mantras such as **om mani padme hum** are chanted all day long, written on flags and stones and wheels driven by wind, water, or hand which are then considered to be saying the mantra for you. This is a skilful device for reminding people of spiritual realities wherever they look. Worshippers may also make offerings of flowers, incense, food (special cakes), water, lights and white scarves, together with *mantras*, *mandalas* and *mudras*, to statues of the Buddhas and *bodhisattvas* in the hope that their prayers will be answered. Others may see this as a form of meditation, or perform the offerings in the imagination only. Rituals may involve taking the three refuges, full length prostrations on the ground, and confession. The confession ritual involves praying to a Buddha named Vajrasattva, confessing one's sins and chanting his *mantra*. Vajrasattva may be imagined as absolving one from all sins, a useful psychological preparation for further meditation. There is also a ritual involving eating small pellets of blessed bread which is performed to ensure 'long life', especially of the bodhisattvas and Buddhas who can offer help. Tibetan communal rituals are performed with the accompaniment of drums, bells, gongs and trumpets made from thigh bones.

There are also secret rituals known only to advanced practitioners of meditation, but partially described in books. One ritual involves going to a deserted place alone, visualising a crowd of Buddhas, *bodhisattvas* and demons and performing a visualisation that one is sacrificially dismembered by these beings and eaten by them. It is used as a means of destroying the attachment to 'self'.

The Kargyupa sect has six advanced practices known as the six doctrines of Naropa. These involve complex yoga exercises, visualisations and secret teachings, but are said to result in the abilities to produce heat by the power of the mind, realise the illusory nature of the body, have complete control over the mind in dreams, learn to recognise the 'clear light', learn to recognise Bardo experiences, and most strange of all, the ability to remove the consciousness from the body and transfer it into other forms. That advanced meditation can lead to magical or psychic powers has been claimed by Buddhism from its beginning, but this aspect is always played down; 'powers' attested by foreign visitors included the melting of snow by the yoga of heat, and traversing the mountains at great speed while in meditational trance.

Another Kargyupa advanced practice is the direct realisation of the *mahamudra* (enlightened consciousness) by emptying the mind of all discursive thought. The aim is to reach the natural state of the mind when it is free from the normal coverings of imagining, thinking, analysing, meditating and reflecting. Many people have commented that this is similar to 'sitting meditation' in Chinese *Ch'an* (Zen) Buddhism.

Other advanced tantric practices included the sacramental use of sexuality; but since Tsong kha pa, this has been considered unsuitable for most people. However, Tibetan art still uses the image of a male and female *bodhisattva* in sexual embrace, called *yab/yum* (father/mother) as a symbol for the unity of wisdom and compassion in ultimate enlightenment. Yet another symbol found in Tibetan-type Buddhism is the concept of the *adi-Buddha* (original Buddha), a personification of the basic reality underlying the universe of multiplicity, which is the nearest Buddhism has ever got to a theistic-style God.

Buddhism in the Far East

The Buddhism of China, Japan, Korea and Vietnam is suitably studied together, for although each country has made its individual contribution to the Buddhism tradition, Japan, Korea and Vietnam received Buddhism from China (directly or via Korea) and most of the influential sects in these countries are of Chinese origin.

China

When Buddhism spread to China around the 1st century CE, it encountered what it had not encountered before - an advanced foreign literate civilisation with highly developed philosophical and religious systems of its own. Buddhism did not replace these systems but developed alongside them. Sometimes there was conflict, but the 'three religions of China' also influenced one another.

The Chinese trace their history back to the Shang dynasty of 1766 BCE. Practices which have been influential since these ancient times include the cult of spirits, especially those of dead ancestors, the quest for harmony between heaven and earth, and divination. At roughly the same time as Siddhartha Gautama was preaching in India, the two most influential Chinese systems, Confucianism and Taoism, developed in China.

Confucianism

Confucius (Kung fu tze) lived from 551-479 BCE. His teaching was basically a system of moral behaviour which would result in harmonious living on earth. He put forward the idea of the noble man whose conduct resulted in the best possible results for society; thus, the virtues he admired were respect, courtesy, hard work and social concern. Good manners were very important, as was education and a sense of one's place in society - children must always respect parents, wives their husbands, employees their employers, subjects their rulers. Yet, Confucianism was not just the outward observance of etiquette but also a genuine loving kindness for one's fellow men. All the lesser pieces of advice could be summed up in the Golden Rule 'Do not do to others what you would not like them to do to you'. Confucius did not have much to say about any reality beyond the human realm; he did not mention any reward or punishment for moral behaviour in an after-life; and although he recommended keeping up the traditional rituals of honour of ancestors and powers of nature, this seems more for the unifying effects it can have on the living rather than any real contact with superhuman powers. However, he always referred to his teaching as that of *T'ien* (heaven), in which he placed his trust when things seemed to be going wrong on earth. Thus, Confucius seems to have believed in some ultimate meaning in human life, but that man's concern was not to speculate about this, but to get on with living a good and worthwhile life. Later

Confucians would develop his ideas in either a religious or humanistic way - Mencius in the 4th/3rd century BCE had a definite belief in heaven, whereas Hsun-tzu in the 3rd century BCE was a rationalist and atheist. By the 2nd to 1st centuries BCE Confucianism took over many elements in Chinese tradition not in the original teachings of Confucius, notably ceremonial sacrifices and funeral rites, divination, and the theory of 'Yin' and 'Yang'. Divination is represented by the 'Confucian' classic, the *I ching*, which uses a method of divination based on 64 hexagrams, or different possible combinations of six lines, either divided or undivided, each of which has a special meaning. The theory of Yin and Yang refers to the idea that life must be a harmony between two fundamental principles. Yin stands for darkness, passivity, feminity, etc and Yang for light, activity, masculinity, etc. Imbalance between the two leads to disharmony and applies to all areas of life, even food.

Eventually, under the Sun dynasty (960-1279), Confucianism became the official state cult in a form, heavily influenced by the ancient folk religion, Buddhism and Taoism, referred to as 'neo-Confucianism'. Advancement in government service required thorough knowledge of the 'Confucian classics' tested by public examination. It remained the major influence on the ruling classes until the Communist takeover in 1949.

Taoism

Taoism (pronounced Dow-ism) is supposed to have been started in the 6th century BCE by the philosopher Lao-tzu, although there is doubt about his historical existence. The ideas of Taoism are to be found in two books, the *Tao-te-ching* which has been dated around the 4th century BCE and the *Chuang-tzu*, from the philosopher of the same name in the 4th/3rd centuries BCE. The basic belief put forward is the concept of the *tao* (way), the unity that underlines the plurality of existence. This eternal principle is to be found in nature and in quiet contemplation. Thus, Taoism tended to stress the aspects of life opposite to those stressed by Confucianism. Behaviour should be natural and spontaneous, rather than artificial etiquette. The individual is important rather than society, and one does better to withdraw peacefully from the world rather than meddle with trying to improve it. Taoism had little time for governments and law and order, feeling that people fared best when left to their own devices, and thus it has been seen as a kind of anarchism. It stresses peace and quiet, putting forward water as the model of achievement, through taking the path of least resistance, and was against all use of violence by governments or individuals. It was not specific about life after death, but as it considered life a dream and death a natural change rather than a tragedy, it did leave room for hope. This vagueness left the original Taoist philosophy open to developments. By the 2nd century CE it combined with elements from the folk tradition to form a religion with divinities, temples, rituals and priests. The stress of this 'religious Taoism' was upon the quest for immortality, healing and forgiveness of sins and it appealed to a wider range of people than the more philosophical Taoism. Though Taoism and Confucianism seem opposite in theory, in practice the Chinese incorporated both currents of thought into their understanding of the world.

Buddhism in China

Buddhism first arrived in China from India via Central Asia somewhere around the 1st century CE. It was not an immediate success, as the Chinese considered their own traditions superior to those of 'barbarian' races. Although it had some features in common with Taoism, several aspects of Buddhism were considered to be unacceptable to the Chinese. It was foreign, it undermined the family by advocating monastic celibacy, it showed disrespect to one's ancestors by mutilating the body (shaving heads), it was morbid in its stress on the sufferings of life rather than happiness, selfishly concerned with individual salvation rather than contributing positively to society, and had strange new beliefs like rebirth. In spite of this, Buddhism did have attractions for some, and between the 2nd and 3rd centuries some Buddhist texts were translated into Chinese and Chinese people began to join the *sangha*. The initial attraction of Buddhism seems to have been twofold; philosophers, especially Taoists, found its ideas interesting to speculate about and relate to Taoism; more practically-minded people hoped that its rituals and meditative techniques might enrich the Chinese store of magic. Thus, the first Chinese Buddhists had a rather distorted view of Buddhism, which was not helped by the poor quality of the first translations, which tended to put Buddhist concepts into Taoist terminology - for example, *nirvana* was *wu wei* (non-activity). Even so, the ideas of Buddhism gradually filtered into the Chinese world and by the 4th century CE there were 24,000 monks and 1786 monasteries recorded by the Eastern Chin dynasty. Two important 4th century monks helped establish a Buddhism that was properly understood. Kumarajiva made many improved translations of Mahayana *sutras*, and Tao-an organised a properly disciplined monastic order.

From the 4th to the 6th centuries CE Buddhism developed in both Southern and Northern China. In Southern China it was more independent and intellectual. In Northern China it was more practical, related to popular needs, and under the control of the ruler.

If Buddhism displeased a Northern ruler, it would be punished, as in the persecutions of 446 and 574-77.

The 6th to the 9th centuries CE were the golden age of Chinese Buddhism. Although individual rulers might favour Taoism, Buddhism was the dominant religion of the people. The *sangha* became very powerful and wealthy, and monasteries became a part of Chinese society. As well as centres for religious study, meditation and temple rituals, they functioned as hospitals, dispensaries, guest houses and banks. Many monasteries owned rolling mills and oil presses which were used by local peasants, and monks were involved in social projects such as road-building, bridge-building, irrigation and tree-planting. The people celebrated Buddhist festivals such as Buddha's birthday in February and the festival for the dead in July.

This period also saw the development of different Buddhist sects. These grew up because of the complexity and diversity of Indian Mahayana Buddhism, and the method by which Buddhism was gradually introduced to China by different teachers using different translations of different scriptures. Some sects followed one particular school of Mahayana philosophy, others concentrated on one particular scripture or practice, others tried to make sense of the whole Buddhist heritage by organising the various scriptures and practices into one unified system. The important schools that developed in China include the **San Lun** or Madhyamaka school, **Fa hsiang** or Yogacara school (both established in the 6th century); the **Lu** or Vinaya school which stressed monastic discipline; **Tien t'ai** and **Hua yen** which both attempted to synthesise the different aspects of Buddhism; **Ching t'u** which concentrated on Amida Buddha; **Ch'an** which concentrated on meditation, and **Chen yen** which was tantric. The teachings of these schools will be discussed later. Most of them followed the Hinayana *vinaya* until the Ch'an sect modified the rules in the 8th century CE. During this period, several Chinese Buddhists travelled to India and left records of their adventures, such as Hsuan-tsang and I tsing.

In 845 there was a great backlash against Buddhism inspired by Taoists, and Buddhism was suppressed throughout the Chinese Empire. As in other such persecutions, the motives were not just religious but political and financial, the Buddhist monasteries had become very wealthy and powerful. Although Buddhism continued after this time and was outwardly quite successful -for example, the full Chinese Canon was printed in the 10th century - it gradually lost its dominance over Chinese life. Most of the different schools disappeared, apart from Ch'an and Ching t'u which were not so tied to large monastic institutions, libraries of scriptures and the support of the Chinese intellectual class. The latter gradually turned back to the traditions of Confucianism, especially after the systematic neo-Confucianism of Chu Hsi (1130-1200 CE).

The Mongol dynasty (1280-1368) introduced Tibetan-style Buddhism into China but this did not have a great effect on the character of Chinese Buddhism, which remained either Ch'an or Ching t'u. Apart from a brief period of revival in the 19th and early 20th centuries, Buddhism was already declining in influence before the Communist takeover in 1949. As in other Communist countries, Buddhism was attacked as an other-worldly fantasy which wasted resources and manpower. The 'Cultural Revolution' of the 1960s destroyed much of the Buddhist heritage in China as well as Tibet. There are signs recently of a revival of religion, in that there are functioning Chinese Buddhist temples and visitors to China report open Buddhist practice among ordinary people. Whatever the situation in mainland China, Chinese Buddhism continues among Chinese communities in places like Taiwan, Hong Kong, Malaysia and Singapore, and the Chinese forms of Buddhism were also spread to Korea, Vietnam and Japan. Although the different sects have many different teachings and practices, Chinese Buddhism in general, when compared to Indian Buddhism, has a tendency to be more positive and life-affirming. Both Indian and Chinese Mahayana Buddhism are based on the belief in the non-duality of *nirvana* and *samsara*, but, whereas the Indian tendency is to stress *nirvana* and the consequent emptiness of *samsara*, the Chinese tendency is to stress *samsara* and its consequent pureness. If the Buddha nature is present in all beings, to the Chinese it makes all beings precious rather than negligible, and the things of everyday life gain a spiritual importance. The positive nature of Chinese Buddhism is captured by the well-known pot-bellied 'laughing Buddha', who is really an amalgamation of the future Buddha Maitreya and a 10th century eccentric called Pu-tai, who loved clowning and playing with children.

Japan

When Buddhism came to Japan in the 6th century CE, it came along with Chinese civilisation to a relatively underdeveloped country. Thus, there was less resistance to the religion than in China. There was already a local religion which is known as Shinto and which has continued alongside Buddhism up to the present day. However, it did not present Buddhism with an intellectual challenge in the way that Confucianism did. The Shinto religion is based on belief in and worship of the *kami*, rather vaguely conceived divinities, spirits or gods. The kami dwell all around in nature, animating such objects as mountains, trees, waterfalls and including the spirits of certain

ancestors. There is no chief *kami* corresponding to the idea of God, but
the sun goddess Amaterasu has some prominence as the line of
emperors were said to be descended from her. The religion has no
strict doctrines or written scriptures and is more a matter of intuitive
feeling - the *kami* represent powerful forces in the world, or a sense of
local community. There are sometimes said to be eight million *kami*
altogether, which are not represented by images but by symbols like a
mirror, sword or jewel. It is felt that the *kami* can influence human life,
so prayers and offerings are made at their shrines. Devotees clap their
hands to attract the *kami*'s attention, and write their petitions on pieces
of wood which are then hung in the shrine. At home, the family may
have a '*kami* shelf' where symbols of the *kami* are kept. The religion is
an optimistic life-affirming one, celebrating the beauty of nature. In
modern times, *kami* is sometimes interpreted in a vaguely generalised
way as something equivalent to God. Throughout most of Japanese
history, Shinto and Buddhism have been seen as forming, together, a
complete religion for the Japanese.

The first Japanese contact with Buddhism came in 539 when a Korean
ruler sent a deputation to seek an alliance with a Japanese ruler, and
with the party came Buddhist monks, scriptures and images. Some of
the ruling class became interested in this new religion, and it was
enthusiastically supported by Prince Shotoku (574-621) who is
considered to be the father of Japanese Buddhism. Shotoku
welcomed both Confucian and Buddhist ideas, built temples,
established monasteries and practically made Buddhism a state
religion. During the 7th century, several Chinese Buddhist sects were
introduced such as **Sanron** (Sanlun), **Hosso** (fa hsiang) and **Kegon**
(Hua yen). At this time the capital was Nara, and the importance of
Kegon in particular is attested by a huge statue of Vairocana Buddha,
symbolising the cosmic Dharmakaya Buddha, the inter-relationship of
all things. In the 8th century the capital moved to Heian (Kyoto) and
two other sects became most influential, the **Tendai** (Tien t'ai) school
introduced by Saicho, a comprehensive type of Buddhism and
Shingon (Chen yen) introduced by Kukai which was based on Tantric
practices. Both had centres in mountain monasteries. Although these
two schools were partly rivals, the all-embracing nature of Tendai led
to Shingon practices being incorporated in its system, so that by the
11th century tantric, magical Buddhism was widespread.

The 12th and 13th centuries were a time of social change and several
new sects developed. The situation favoured simplified faiths that
could appeal to people, rather than scholastic systems. The schools
that emerged at this time were **Jodo**, 'Pure Land', (in Chinese, Ching
t'u) popularised by Honen, **Jodo Shinshu**, 'True Pure Land', started
by Shinran, **Rinzai Zen** (Lin chi Ch'an) introduced by Eisai, **Soto Zen**

(Ts'ao tung Ch'an) introduced by Dogen and a new Japanese form of Buddhism started by Nichiren.

The 14th and 15th centuries were unsettled and monasteries, particularly Zen ones, conserved the teachings of Buddhism and Confucianism. In the 16th century the mountain centres of Tendai and Shingon were destroyed in civil wars, leaving Zen and Jodo as main forms of Buddhism; although, unlike the situation in China, Hosso, Kegon, Tendai and Shingon have continued to this day.

The 17th century saw the beginning of the practice of having to register with a particular sect, whether one was actively religious or not. This was introduced to prevent people remaining Christian after the expulsion of Christian missionaries and the banning of Christianity. It resulted in there being many nominal Buddhists whose only contact with the religion was a funeral.

During the 19th century, Shinto was seen as the state religion and symbol of nationalism with Buddhism as a secondary power. Since 1945 Japanese society has gone through rapid changes. Traditional forms of Buddhism survive and function rather like Christian denominations, providing services - especially funerals - and social events. Most Japanese clergy are married rather than celibate monks, especially in the Pure Land tradition. There is a certain amount of secularisation and turning away from religion altogether, as is happening in many countries, but also new forms of Buddhism and other new cults are developing. Even now about two thirds of Japanese people would be counted at least nominally as Buddhists, possess a Buddhist altar through which they revere ancestors in their home, and join in traditional celebrations. July 15th is the festival of O bon which combines Buddhism with traditional Chinese and Japanese respect for dead ancestors. The Buddhist story behind the festival is Maudgalyayana's vision, through his psychic powers, of his own mother in a hell world, and her release through the Buddhas's compassion. The custom is for everyone to return to the family home for O bon and offer fruit and flowers for departed ancestors. This is combined with enjoyment, like fairs and dances. The two equinoxes, September 21st and March 21st, were traditionally dangerous times in ancient Chinese tradition when the powers of Yin and Yang exchange dominance. In Buddhism, they are called *Higan* ('the other shore', or *nirvana*), festivals with a theme of harmony, balance and peace. People visit temples and family graves and pour water out as a symbol of offering merit to the dead. On New Year's Eve (December 31st), Buddhist temples ring in the New Year with a lucky peal of 108 bells. April 8th is Shakyamuni Buddha's birthday, celebrated with a flower festival as he was born in a garden. This festival is called

Hanamatsuri. Images of the baby Buddha, standing upright, are bathed with perfumed tea as a sign of worship, and people generally enjoy themselves.

Buddhism, then, has been part of Japanese culture since the beginning of its written history in the 6th century CE and is still a powerful force in Japanese society today.

Some Schools of Far Eastern Buddhism

Several different schools of Buddhism have been mentioned in the course of this historical outline of Buddhism in China and Japan. Apart from at the very beginning, these schools have all been forms of Mahayana Buddhism. Some followed schools of philosophy found in India, others concentrated on one particular scripture or practice in Mahayana Buddhism, and others tried to organise all aspects of Buddhism into a comprehensive synthesis. Further schools, or subschools, developed as reform movements by particular individuals, and the 20th century quest for 'new religions' has led to even more new sects being formed today. The character of the movements as separate sects rather than just lineages of teachers was emphasised more in Japan than China, although the Japanese schools are nearly all developments from Chinese schools. The most important schools are in the following list, with the Chinese name given first and Japanese name in brackets: Fa hsiang (Hosso), San lun (San ron), Hua yen (Kegon), Tien t'ai (Tendai), Chen yen (Shingon), Ching t'u (Jodo), Ch'an (Zen) and Nichiren (only in Japan).

Fa hsiang is the Chinese school based on the Indian Yogacara school which taught 'mind-only'. It was established as a school of Buddhism in China in the 7th century CE by Hsuan-tsang, the most famous of the monks who travelled to India in search of scriptures. It was introduced to Japan as Hosso within the same century. Fa hsiang died out in China during the persecution of 845 CE, but Hosso has continued as a small sect in Japan up to today.

San lun is the Chinese version of the Madhyamaka school in India. It was introduced in the 5th century CE when the famous Kumarajiva translated three Madhyamaka treatises by Nagarjuna and Aryadeva, the founders of the Madhyamaka school. The teaching of 'emptiness' had some appeal for those used to Taoist terminology, and the Madhyamaka idea of two levels of truth, the ultimate and the conventional was also found useful. In Japan, San ron was seen as an academic philosophy to study rather than as an actual sect. The sect died out in China in 845 CE.

Hua Yen (Kegon), like Tien t'ai, represents one of the Chinese attempts to synthesise all Buddhist scriptures and practices into a comprehensive system. In order to do this, the various scriptures of Mahayana and Hinayana Buddhism were seen as a progressive revelation by the Buddha, beginning with simplified teachings for the unintelligent and gradually working up to the final and full revelation which Hua Yen believed was contained in the Hua yen or *Avatamsaka sutra*. (The name means 'Flower garland'). Hua yen was founded as a school of Buddhism by Tu Shun (557-640) but its most influential teacher was Fa tsang (693-712). The basic teaching of the school is a form of Mahayana philosophy which asserts the unity of all things yet the importance of individual phenomena. As in Madhyamaka thought, individual entities are empty of separate existence, and, as in Yogacara all things are manifestations of the One Mind. Yet this does not mean that individual people and things are nothing - each individual phenomenon is a total manifestation of the universal principle and so utterly valuable in itself. All things are one, but the one is in each thing; all the Buddhas, *bodhisattvas* and worlds in each grain of dust. The 'one' cannot be separated out from the 'things' but all *dharmas* are said to have risen simultaneously in total interdependence. Fa tsang tried to illustrate this by two images, that of a lion made of gold, and of multiple reflecting mirrors. In the image of the lion, the gold represents the underlying unity and the lion the multiple manifestation of the Buddha nature in the diverse phenomena of the universe. The mirrors each stand for one individual entity which in itself reflects the whole. This more positive valuation of the phenomenal universe is typically Chinese, yet stays within the general direction of Mahayana thought. The underlying principle of the universe was symbolised in Hua yen by the figure of Vairocana Buddha, the shining Buddha, who is said to have revealed the *Avatamsaka sutra* through the earthly body of Shakyamuni. The order in which the various strands of Buddha's teaching were revealed are considered to be as follows: first, the Hinayana scriptures, drawing our attention to the non-existence of separate selves by analysis into *dharmas*; second, the basic Mahayana schools of Madhyamika and Yogacara which stresses the emptiness and oneness of all *dharmas*; third came the Tien t'ai teaching which Hua yen interprets as the teaching of the Buddhahood of all beings, stressing unity; fourth, Ch'an and the sudden insight into the truth, grasped intuitively rather than in words, and finally, Hua yen's full realisation of the unity in diversity and diversity in unity of all things, their total interpenetration in perfect harmony.

Hua yen teaching was taken to both the uneducated masses and the upper classes, notably the Empress Wu (625-705), and its general ideas filtered through into other forms of Buddhism, especially Ch'an. In China it disappeared as a separate sect in the 845 CE persecution, but it had been introduced to Japan during the early Nara period (8th century), where it was quite influential and exists as a separate school (Kegon) up to the present. Kegon was particularly influential on the Japanese view of society where individuals are important yet must strive to work as one in harmonious interdependence. The figure of Vairocana Buddha appealed as a symbol of Cosmic unity, as more positive than concepts like 'emptiness'. The shining Buddha was , according to traditional Japanese ideas, the real form of Amaterasu who appeared as the sun goddess in Japan, and was sometimes related to the emperor, as a representative of this power on earth.

T'ien t'ai (Tendai), like Hua yen, is an attempt to synthesise all Buddhist teachings into a comprehensive system. Although it expresses its teachings in slightly different concepts, and ranks the Mahayana sutras in a different order, in the end its basic teaching is pretty much the same - the total interdependence of all things, so that the Buddha nature is in all things and that the whole universe is contained in each particle of dust or moment of thought. The T'ien t'ai sect is named after a mountain in China which became the headquarters of the sect, which was very influential in China between the 7th and 9th centuries. It was founded by Chih-kai (538-597) who had been taught by Hui ssu (514-577). Chih-kai believed that the fullest and most perfect statement of Mahayana Buddhism was to be found in the *Lotus of the Wonderful Law* (Lotus Sutra, see p94) with its announcement of the eternal nature of the Buddha and the Buddhahood of all beings without exception. Like Hua yen, T'ien t'ai teaches that the phenomenal world is a manifestation of the single absolute mind, which is in all things and behind all things. Yet this does not deny the value of individual entities because the absolute mind is present in its entirety in each individual entity down to a single particle of dust. All things are not one in the sense of cells in a larger organism or bits of clay added together to make a lump, but the divine Buddha essence is manifested in totality both in individual beings and the material world. To give a value to *samsara*, T'ien t'ai explained that although all beings are empty and therefore non-existent in a sense, they also exist temporarily and therefore have a relative value. This is seen as a 'middle way' philosophy and follows Madhyamaka thought.

T'ien t'ai believes that the Buddha deliberately revealed a variety of doctrines because of the variety of human capabilities, and has a great tolerance for all teachings, even Hinayana, as simply different paths to the same goal. The T'ien t'ai ranking of teaching is as follows: The first teaching of the Buddha was Hua yen, which is the full truth, but expressed in a way too difficult to understand. Next, the Buddha, realising human limitations, taught Hinayana Buddhism; this led on to the basic Mahayana teachings such as the bodhisattva ideal, and then to the deepest of Mahayana thought, the Prajnaparamita literature and its 'emptiness' teaching. Finally, the full and total revelation was contained in the Lotus scripture, announcing the eternity of the Buddha and the Buddhahood of all beings. Although this scripture says pretty much the same as Hua yen, it does so in a way that can be understood by everyone, symbolising the eternal oneness in the attractive figure of Shakyamuni, the loving father-Buddha, and explaining the Buddhahood of all in parables. The practical outcome of T'ien t'ai teaching was that all forms of Buddhist practice were considered valid ways to the same goal. No one form of Buddhist practice should claim superiority, as all are ways to the same end, most perfectly expressed in the Lotus Sutra.

T'ien T'ai was introduced into Japan in the 8th century by Saicho (Dengyo Daishi) (767-822) who built a small temple on Mount Hiei. This gradually expanded into a huge monastic settlement of three thousand temples and became a very powerful influence in Japan. Japanese Tendai was perhaps even more comprehensive than Chinese T'ien t'ai as it welcomed tantric rituals, Zen meditation practices, Pure Land prayers to Amida, and even tried to encompass Shinto, explaining the *kami* as *bodhisattvas* who had compassionately prepared the minds of the Japanese people for the true religion of Buddhism. In the 12th and 13th centuries several Tendai monks left to form new sects of Buddhism, often mantra-based. The Mount Hiei complex was destroyed in the 16th century, but Tendai has continued as a small sect up to the present. In China it died out after the 845 CE persecution.

Chen-yen (Shingon) ('true word', or *mantrayana*) is the Chinese name for Tantric Buddhism (see p97). This was brought to China in the 8th century CE by Indian tantric teachers such as Amogavajra who died in 774. It never became an actual sect in China, and gradually disappeared after the end of the 8th century. However, it was during this brief time when *tantra* was fashionable, that a Japanese monk named Kukai (Kobo Daishi, 774-835) visited China and was taught by the Chinese master Hui kuo (746-805). Kúkai returned to Japan to form a tantric school, known in Japanese as Shingon. Like T'ien t'ai, it was based on a mountain headquarters, Mount Koya, and became very powerful and influential. As a Mahayana sect, Shingon taught the total inter-relation of all things, which was symbolised by the images and rituals of *tantra*. As in Indian and Tibetan *tantra*, many different Buddhas and *bodhisattvas* were used as images for visualisations, but Shingon laid particular stress on Vairocana Buddha, as the personification of the cosmos itself - of the

Dharmakaya body of the Buddha. Vairocana took central place in the Shingon mandala, or diagram of the universe. Shingon made use of other tantric practices such as chanting *mantras*, visualisations, forming *mudras* (symbolic gestures), initiation ceremonies and the secret transmission of the teaching from master to pupil. *Tantra* can be seen as an acting out in body, speech and mind of the insight put forward in Chinese theories like those of Hua yen and T'ien t'ai - that the whole universe is one, and that this universal principle is present in each phenomenon of the material world. Thus, the material world and the human body can be used as a vehicle of the spiritual. Kukai stressed the importance of beauty and harmony in his rituals, and the spiritual value of art forms such as painting, sculpture, music and literature. All beautiful things convey to us something of the Buddha nature, helping us to have an intuitive glimpse of what cannot be expressed in logical philosophy. This aesthetic and intuitive approach to religion seems to appeal to the Japanese character, as can be seen from the Shinto religion and Zen. Both Shingon and Zen emphasised that enlightenment can be attained 'in this very body' without waiting through many rebirths.

Kukai expressed his teachings in a polished literary style and, like Hua yen and T'ien t'ai, attempted to rank the various schools of religious teaching in order of their gradual understanding of the truth. Starting from total ignorance, Kukai saw a gradual increase of insight in Confucianism, Taoism, Hinayana Buddhism, Hosso, San ron, Tendai, Kegon and the final revelation in the esoteric teachings of Shingon. Shingon was popular in Japan between the 8th and 11th centuries, and was even practised on Mount Hiei, the centre of Tendai Buddhism. It continues as a sect in its own right up to the present.

Pure Land Buddhism

Ching t'u (Japanese, *Jodo*), means 'Pure Land', and refers to the type of Buddhism based on the worship of the Buddha Amitabha (Amida) who dwells in a paradisal, pure Buddhaland known as 'Sukhavati' or 'the Happy Land'. Amitabha and his Pure Land are described in an Indian Mahayana sutra called the *Sukhavati vyuha* (see p92f), in which Shakyamuni Buddha tells Ananda the story of a *bodhisattva* monk named Dharmakara (in Japanese, Hozo), who in a past aeon vowed in the presence of a living Buddha that he would create a perfect paradise out of compassion for suffering beings. Dharmakara made 48 (or 46, depending on the version of the sutra) vows which refer to the beauty of this land, its pleasant lifestyle, the presence of *bodhisattvas* and, most important of all, that beings only have to think of him in trusting devotion and he will take them to this land upon their death. He made his vows on pain of forfeiting enlightenment for ever, and, as

Shakyamuni taught that Dharmakara did become a Buddha called Amitabha (Infinite Light) and dwells in a paradise land in the West, people can have confidence in the efficacy of his vows. There are two versions of the Sukhavati scripture, the longer one includes the merit of a moral life, as well as faithful devotion, as the methods for gaining rebirth in the Pure Land.

Amitabha is accompanied in the Pure Land by two *bodhisattvas*, Mahasthamaprapta and Avalokiteshvara. In Far Eastern Buddhism, Avalokiteshvara is Kwan yin (Chinese) Kwannon (Japanese) and since the 10th century is usually pictured as female.

The founder of Chinese Ching t'u is often said to be Hui Yuan, who, in the 4th century, organised a group who met regularly to recite the invocation of Amida. As an actual school, it seems to have started with Tan lu'an (476-545), who was inspired by a vision of Amitabha and taught that meditation on the infinite qualities of Amitabha Buddha and chanting his name was an unfailing path to salvation for all but the worst of sinners (ie those who murder mother, father, or a saint, strike a Buddha or deliberately cause schism in the monastic community). Other important Chinese teachers include Tao-cho (562-645), a T'ien t'ai monk who taught that the method of praying for rebirth in the Pure Land was the only one suitable for most people in this present age of decay, when hardly anyone can manage the difficult path of personal holiness. Tao-cho used to teach the value of hundreds of invocations, counted with beans. Shan tao (613-681) taught that the aspiration for rebirth in the Pure Land was like a narrow path across a torrent of water and fire, which would lead us to unending bliss. This aspiration should be formulated by reciting Amida's name, reciting the Mahayana sutras, meditating on the wonders of the Pure Land, offering worship to statues of Amitabha and singing his praises. Such invocation of Amida Buddha is known as *nien fo* and although it originally included these five practices, it eventually refers to the simple recitation of the name - 'namo Amito-fo' (Chinese), 'namu Amida Butsu' (Japanese), 'I bow to Amitabha Buddha!' Tzu min (680-748) attempted to combine the *nien-fo* with a traditional Buddhist life of discipline, meditation and scholarship, but as it spread among the ordinary people, it tended to be limited to the *nien-fo*. The idea of salvation by the power of Amida had great appeal to the uneducated working people who had not the time or inclination for Buddhist philosophy or meditational practices, or were involved in morally questionable tasks, like fishing. After the persecution of 845 CE, Pure Land and Ch'an were the only forms of Buddhism that prospered, as they do not need vast libraries of scriptures, temples full of artistic images or complex monastic organisation. Pure Land in particular became the religion of the masses, and influenced even Ch'an practice; whereas the upper classes reverted to Confucianism. In the 1930s, between 60% and 70% of Chinese Buddhists were of the Pure Land variety.

The recitation of the name of Amitabha seems to have been first practised in Japan as one of the many methods used by the eclectic Tendai sect based on Mount Hiei. Several Tendai monks were attracted by the idea of spreading Buddhist teaching to the ordinary people, and found the Pure Land tradition the most effective way of doing this. Kuya (903-972) used to dance through the streets, singing songs about Amida and his parables and teaching ordinary people the recitation of Amida's name. Ryonin (1072-1132) also composed songs, and tried to encourage people to recite the name for the sake of all beings as well as themselves. Genshin (942-1017) tried to spread the Pure Land message by contrasting the bliss of Amida's Pure Land with the terrors of the hell worlds to which sinners would surely go if they did not call on Amida to save them. The hells and the paradise became favourite subjects for artists.

The 12th century was a time of social upheaval in Japan, and many reformist Buddhist groups developed. One of the most important figures of the Pure Land tradition was Honen (1133-1212), whose followers made Pure Land an actual sect in conscious opposition to other Buddhist sects. He began his career as a Tendai monk on Mount Hiei, having been orphaned at an early age. He felt that both Japanese society and the Tendai Buddhist religion had become corrupt, and after being very impressed by the vow of Amida, began to teach that faith in Amida was the only hope for people. Though respecting other religious practices, very few are capable of saving themselves through the traditional path of personal holiness in the present state of the world (*mappo*, age of spiritual decline). We must rely on the grace of Amida, have faith in him, concentrate our thoughts on his paradise land, repeat his name, and try our best to live a decent moral life. Honen himself seems to have been a kind person, as he looked after a young unmarried mother, despite the scandal this might cause. However, his criticism of other religious practices led to opposition by other Tendai monks who burned his writings. In 1206, at the age of 74, he was disrobed and sent into exile because of rumours about the influence of some of his followers over young ladies of the retired emperor's court. Honen's reaction was to welcome the opportunity to spread the gospel of Amida in outlying districts among uneducated people. Honen's school of Buddhism is referred to as Jodoshu (Pure Land Sect) and has continued to today.

At the same time as Honen, a disciple called Shinran (1173-1262) was also exiled. Shinran was also an orphan, and after leaving the monastery of Tendai, decided to get married, apparently after a vision of Kwannon which advised him on this course of action. Shinran's followers eventually formed a sect of Buddhism called Jodo Shin Shu, or True Pure Land Sect, as they felt that he was the only one to have really understood Honen's teaching. Shinran taught that sinful humankind, himself included, could do nothing to earn salvation for themselves and must throw themselves totally on the mercy of Amida. He criticised the attitude of trying to earn merit through keeping moral rules, and performing ritual practices, considering a sinner nearer to Amida Buddha than a so-called good man who may be proud of his own achievements. Honen had expressed the mercy of Amida in the following saying:

'Even a bad man will be received in Buddha's land, how much
more a good man'.

Shinran preferred to say:

'Even a good man will be received in Buddha's land, how much
more a bad man'.

The idea of merit simply leads to false self-importance whereas one should rely totally on the power of Amida in the humble opinion that one can do nothing for oneself. To guard against any form of self-assertion creeping in, Shinran stressed that even a single act of faith in Amida was sufficient; repeating his name on subsequent occasions earned no extra merit but was merely a way of expressing thanks to Amida. Even faith would be a temptation to pride for some people, and Shinran stressed that faith in Amida is a gift from Amida and not something we achieve for ourselves. It seems that for Shinran, the Pure Land was the final goal, equivalent to *nirvana* or Buddhahood, rather than a step on the way there.

'Shin' Buddhists are taught to lead a humble life, fitting in with people around them, and not marking themselves out as different and superior by any special customs. Ordinary family life is the pattern rather than monastic celibacy, and the organisers of the sect form a kind of married clergy for simple ceremonies, the office being hereditary rather than based on any personal qualification. The worship of other Buddhas and *bodhisattvas* is discouraged, and Shakyamuni is seen as merely an earthly representative of Amida. However, Shin Buddhists are taught not to criticise other religions or sects. This attitude of humbly following the 'Shin' path without advertising it or criticising others was particularly stressed by the 15th century teacher Rennyo.

Shin Buddhism was particularly appealing to ordinary, busy people. It attracted the outcaste members of society, women and others who were excluded by traditional monastic Buddhism. It can seem a long way from the original teaching of the Buddha, but it can be explained as a form of *upaya* - one of the many skilful means employed by the Buddhas to save beings. There have been several attempts to harmonise the teachings of the Pure Land with other forms of Buddhism. Praying to Amida can be seen as drawing on the Buddha nature within oneself rather than to a separate divinity, and the Pure Land as a state of consciousness rather than a place. Shinran's insistence on eliminating any trace of self-pride in total reliance on Amida, can be seen as an alternative way of expressing the basic Buddhist teaching of *anatta*, 'no self'. The Zen scholar Suzuki suggests that the importance of reciting the *nembutsu* (namu Amida Butsu) is its effect on the consciousness. *Mantras* are often used in meditation as a technique for stopping discursive thought and achieving mystical experience. Thus, Suzuki feels that it can achieve the same goal as Zen practices, such as meditation on the *koan*. However, this is not the traditional way in which the *nembutsu* is understood.

Shin Buddhism is the most popular forms of 'mainstream' Buddhism in modern Japan, as it is possible to combine it with a busy industrial life, and it offers the hope of happiness after death.

Zen (Ch'an)

Ch'an (Chinese) and *Zen* (Japanese) translate the Indian word *dhyana* (meditation). Ch'an Buddhism is a form of Buddhism based on meditation; not in the sense of practising all of the techniques practised in India, but in the general sense of purifying the mind in order to directly experience reality. Thus, although called 'meditation' Buddhism, Ch'an could appropriately be called 'wisdom' Buddhism, as it stresses the need for the intuitive grasp of reality called *prajna*. Ch'an claims to represent a special line of transmission of the Buddhist tradition directly from Shakyamuni. **'A direct transmission of awakened consciousness outside tradition and outside scripture'** is the traditional Zen summary attributed to Bodhidharma. It is passed on not in words but directly from mind to mind, teacher to pupil. It is also in many ways similar to Taoism (see p125) in its stress on wordless teaching, nature, spontaneous behaviour and lack of respect for tradition, and has often been seen as an amalgamation of Indian Buddhism and Chinese Taoism. Yet, on the other hand, there is little in Ch'an that cannot be found in the teaching of Indian Mahayana Buddhism. The experience sought by Ch'an is the perfect wisdom which intuitively grasps the empty, non-dual nature of reality spoken about in the Perfect Wisdom literature or the One Mind spoken of in Yogocara philosophy. Madhyamaka philosophy had already shown how the mind can be tricked into false views by words and arguments; the *Lankavatara Sutra* had already spoken of the Buddha nature hidden within all beings; and the *Avatamsaka Sutra* of the total interpenetration of all things, so that all things are one, while each individual thing has its own special meaning. *Tantra*, in its own way, had already pointed out the value of the things of *samsara* as vehicles for experiencing spiritual truth. Thus, although Zen is sometimes spoken of as something completely revolutionary, it is really a form of Mahayana Buddhism expressed in a Far-Eastern way. In practice, it has sometimes been characterised by severe discipline, and completely spontaneous, almost anarchic behaviour. These seeming opposites have attracted a variety of types of people. Japanese warriors admired the former, and American 'hippies' admired the latter. Zen combines discipline and spontaneity, which are not seen as opposites, but two sides of the same coin; one cannot act freely without discipline, and discipline eventually leads to complete spontaneity and naturalness. Chinese and Japanese art forms tend to express this strange combination of 'disciplined casualness', which is captured in art better than in words. The stress on wisdom and the inadequacy of words has attracted intellectuals, in the way that Pure Land Buddhism attracted the less educated. Like Pure Land, Ch'an is an 'instant' path to enlightenment, rather than a gradual structured one, and these two forms of Buddhism proved to be the most successful in the countries of the Far East.

The History of Zen

In Zen tradition, the legendary history of Zen goes back to Shakyamuni Buddha, who is said to have once taught the *Dharma* by holding up a single flower and turning it in his hand. Only one of his disciples, Kasyapa, understood the message and smiled. This direct grasp of reality was passed down from master to pupil in India as an alternative tradition to that recorded in the *sutras*. Eventually, in 520 CE, an Indian master named Bodhidharma came from India to China and began the line of Chinese Ch'an masters.

Bodhidharma is a partly legendary figure, who is said to have commenced his preaching by meditating facing a wall for nine years, until his legs fell off, and to have insulted the emperor by telling him that his sponsoring of Buddhist monasteries and scriptures gained him no merit at all. These symbolise the Ch'an opposition to a Buddhism that is just words and outward observances, and the need of great exertion in the quest of the truth. Bodhidharma is pictured by later Zen artists as a fierce, severe man with staring eyes who is at the same time comical. Both fierceness and humour are characteristics of Zen. It is said that he cut off his eyelids to keep himself from dozing off during meditation. Bodhidharma probably was a historical figure, but historians feel the traditional date may be wrong, and a more correct date around 480 CE. Bodhidharma is said to have particularly liked the *Lankavatara Sutra*, which teaches the non-dual nature of reality, and 'mind only' philosophy, and the embryo of Buddhahood within all beings. He founded the famous Shao-lin monastery.

The second in line was Hui k'o, of whom it is said that he sat outside Shao lin temple in the snow, begging Bodhidharma to admit him, and finally cut off his arm to convince the master of his determination. Such stories are possibly invented or exaggerated but express the tough determined attitude of Zen so admired by Chinese and Japanese warriors.

The third teacher was Seng t'san who composed a famous poem on the non-dual nature of ultimate reality, called 'On believing in Mind'. In Conze's translation, the last two verses read:
'One in All, all in one
If only this is realised
No more worry about not being perfect.
When Mind and each believing mind are not divided
And undivided are each believing mind and Mind
This is where words fail;
For it is not of the past, present and future.' (Conze 1959 p175)

The fifth patriarch was Hung jen (601-675). Towards the end of his life, according to the Platform Sutra, he suggested a poetry competition to decide which of his disciples had the best grasp of the Buddhist truth, and therefore, deserved to be next in line. The learned chief monk, named Shen hsiu, composed a poem and wrote it on a wall which was about to be decorated.
The body is the bodhi tree
The mind is like a clear mirror
At all times we must strive to polish it
And must not let the dust collect.'
This verse expressed the traditional view that enlightenment was achieved by purifying the mind from the obstructions of ignorance, and that the place where this process takes place is in human bodily life. The image of mind as mirror was a traditional one in both Taoism and Buddhism. This verse was considered reasonable, but not outstanding. The news of the competition came to a lowly novice working in the kitchen, called Hui neng. According to the story, Hui neng was a poor illiterate firewood seller who had been attracted to Buddhism when hearing some of his customers discussing the Diamond Sutra, but who had up to now merely been employed in the monastery kitchen, pounding rice. This illiterate kitchen servant

composed his own poems and asked a friend to write them on the wall next to Shen hsui's. Hui neng's poems read as follows:

'The Bodhi tree is originally not a tree
The mirror has no stand
Buddha nature is always clean and pure
Where is there room for dust?

'The mind is the Bodhi tree
The body is the mirror stand
The mirror is originally clean and pure
Where can it be stained by dust?'

These poems showed a much deeper grasp of Zen truth. From the eternal enlightened view of reality the individual mind and the Buddha nature cannot be separated, and therefore both are eternally pure and not confined to any time or place. The 'dust' of *karma* produced by ignorance and craving is really only illusory, and so to strive to remove it, shows that you have not understood its nature.

According to Hui neng's followers, he was secretly summoned to Hung jen's presence and taught the Diamond Sutra, which expresses the idea of the emptiness of all things. Hui neng was thereupon enlightened and made the sixth patriarch.

A late 8th, early 9th century master named Huai hai, introduced the idea of the value of manual work into Ch'an practice. This, together with the fact that Ch'an needed no libraries of scriptures, temples full of images or elaborate organisation helped Ch'an monasteries to be self-sufficient and survive the persecution of 845 CE.

During the 9th and 10th centuries, the Ch'an tradition split into five different lineages or sects, which stressed different aspects of Ch'an. The two which proved of lasting importance were **Lin chi** (Japanese, Rinzai) and **Ts'ao tung** (Japanese, Soto). Lin chi was started by I hsuan from Lin chi, who died in 867. Lin chi emphasised the tradition of eccentric teaching methods, such as shouting and beating, riddle-like sayings and tough discipline. It was he who uttered the famous saying 'If you come across the Buddha in your path, kill him', emphasising the need to be free of all external forms of religion and mental constructs such as the idea of the Buddha as a being separate from oneself. The Buddha is 'killed' when one realises that, like all things, he is empty of inherent existence. This tough, sometimes shocking form of Buddhism was particularly attractive to the Chinese warrior class, and through this connection Lin chi Ch'an became involved in politics and nationalism.

Ts'ao tung was started by Lian Chieh from Tung Shan (807-869) who felt the dramatic eccentricity of Lin chi could easily degenerate into self-assertiveness and intellectual 'mind games'. Eccentric actions could be mere showing off and could seriously undermine the morality of ordinary folk who might think that they could go about breaking the normal moral rules at whim. Ts'ao tung stressed a more quiet, unassuming approach involving decent moral behaviour, study of the scriptures, no worldly political involvements and long sessions of quiet sitting meditation.

After the 10th century, Ch'an became more institutionalised. Lin chi monks, in particular, became very involved in government matters. Instead of inventing their own methods of conveying the truth, the custom became that of studying the sayings and actions of previous Ch'an teachers. These are known as *Kung an* (Japanese, *koan*) which means an old case or public document and are usually in the form of a story or a question and answer session (*mondo*) between a master and a disciple. Two large collections of kung an's were made, the Pi yen in the 11th century and the Wu men kuan in the 12th century.

It was in the 12th century that Zen became popular in Japan, although Zen meditation practices had been known since the 7th century. The pioneer of Japanese Zen was Eisai (1141-1215), originally a Tendai monk who travelled to China and brought back the Lin chi (Rinzai) tradition. As in China, this type of Buddhism was very attractive to the Samurai or warriors, and is characterised by toughness, practice of martial arts, political nationalism, eccentric masters, dramatic methods of teaching such as shouting and beating, and striving to understand the paradoxical *koans*. Mere quiet meditation will never bring the flash of intuitive insight called enlightenment. Eisai also popularised the use of tea in Japan, advising the shogun that it would be much better for him than alcohol - 'Whenever one is in poor spirits, one should drink tea.' (de Bary 1972 p.367). Meditating monks also found it helpfully refreshing.

Dogen (1200-1253) was another Tendai monk who, although from a noble family, had been orphaned and lived as a monk from the age of 13. He was at first attracted by Eisai's teaching but, not quite satisfied, travelled to China himself and brought back the Tsao tung (Soto) tradition. Dogen is considered a great saint. He taught that the true Buddhist life is a simple, selfless one, and that we do not have to go to dramatic extremes to realise Buddhahood, for all beings are already, eternally Buddha. He taught that the best way to realise this Buddhahood was simply to sit in quiet meditation, doing nothing but just sitting, letting thoughts fade away without being obsessed by pushing them away. We should have no desires, even for Buddhahood, and should not be seeking any great 'mind-blowing' experience. Simply sitting was in itself the goal of Buddhism and our Buddha nature would gradually unfold itself to us in a natural, undramatic way. This method of meditation is called *zazen* or 'sitting meditation', for which Dogen left detailed instructions called 'zazen rules', still in use by Soto Zen Buddhists today.

Dogen criticised some of the practices of other Zen teachers; eccentric behaviour could become self-assertive, as could too much intellectual striving, or involvement in worldly politics. Instead, one should live a quiet, decent, simple life, with faith in the Buddha and one's teacher, practising zazen faithfully without looking for results. His monks should live a traditional humble life of poverty and begging. He felt that teachers who did away with scriptures altogether were foolishly throwing away a useful tool. The scriptures should be studied without losing sight of their purpose. If one fails in the Buddhist life, one should make a sincere act of repentance to the Buddha and try again.

Rinzai and Soto Zen have often been contrasted; the former seeks an instant understanding of the truth gained by a sudden revolution of consciousness brought about by dramatic methods and severe discipline; the latter feels that the truth will dawn on you gradually as you sit in quiet meditation and live a good, decent life - it is nothing special, in that it has really always been there. Although perhaps the actual personal experience in the two traditions might feel different as a result of the difference in method, they can also be seen as different ways to the same goal suited to different types of personality. The Japanese view is that Rinzai is for the general, Soto for the farmer.

During the civil unrest of the 14th and 15th centuries in Japan, Zen monasteries became havens of peace in a troubled world. It was at this time that the tea ceremony was developed, combining Zen naturalness with Confucian politeness into an oasis of calm.

During the 16th and 17th centuries, Zen declined somewhat into formalism, as it became part of the establishment. However, Hakuin (1685-1768) was a great Rinzai teacher who gave Zen a new impetus after he was enlightened when hit on the head with a broom. Hakuin spread the Zen message among all sections of society, rejecting a mere nominal Buddhism. He himself invented new *koans* such as 'What is the sound of one hand clapping?' and expressed Zen truth in paintings as well as writing. Since his time, Zen has had to resist becoming just another religious sect with an organisation and members engaged in merely ritual activities. This led a modern Zen teacher, D T Suzuki, to suggest that the real living Zen tradition is found more in America, where it is still new and exciting, than in Japan where it has become traditional.

Main teachings of Zen

1. As in all forms of Buddhism, the goal of Zen is enlightenment, seeing the world as it really is. For Zen, this is seeing the non-duality of all things, a *nirvana* which is not separate from *samsara*, but simply *samsara* seen in its true light. Zen draws on different Buddhist terminology to describe this reality 'emptiness', 'Mind' or 'the total interpenetration of all things', which originally came from distinct Buddhist philosophies. Unlike the idea of some Mahayana schools that this insight only comes at the end of a long *bodhisattva* career, Zen teaches that it is available here and now, as in the time of Shakyamuni. This enlightenment experience comes all at once, like getting a joke and is referred to as *wu* in Chinese and satori in Japanese. The 'instant' nature of *satori* is stressed more by Rinzai than Soto Zen. Hakuin compared it to the sudden shattering of a block of ice. Descriptions of *satori* sound like classic mystical experiences - great unity, great peace, a feeling of really knowing the truth, of having transcended time and space, reaching a higher state of consciousness, which is impossible to describe in normal words. It is hard to know whether the *satori* claimed by Zen masters is really the same experience as the *nirvana* of Shakyamuni; there seem to be different levels of insight, so that satori may be more accurately compared to the 'Dharma vision' gained by Shakyamuni's followers, or the temporary foretaste of *nirvana*, obtained in *samadhi*, than the supreme and perfect enlightenment of Buddhahood. Zen practitioners who claim to have experienced *satori* would not claim to have achieved full and complete Buddhahood, except in the sense that even the ordinary, everyday consciousness is really Buddha consciousness in the end.

2. Zen likes to stress this identity between oneself and Buddha, teaching that the Buddha nature dwells within all beings, and that one does not have to become Buddha because one always has been. This idea that there is nothing to achieve is stressed in Hui neng's poem, and the Zen saying 'Seeing into one's own nature and realising Buddhahood.' Your own everyday mind is the Buddha mind, a point stressed by the Soto teaching - that sitting in *zazen* is Buddhahood, not a way to Buddhahood.

3. As in most Chinese and Japanese forms of Buddhism, the non-duality of *nirvana* and *samsara* is interpreted as giving a spiritual value to everyday life and the material world. There is a great love of nature in Zen, expressed in art and poetry; possibly the influence of Taoism, but also of Hua yen (see p132) belief that every grain of dust contains the whole universe. I hsuan claimed that Zen was really 'only everyday life with nothing to do', eating when you

were hungry and lying down when tired. Carrying fuel and drawing water are spiritual activities. Along with this appreciation of nature and of the everyday activities is the idea that behaviour should not be a slavish following of normal rules, but natural and spontaneous. This again has been seen as Taoist influence, and can easily be misunderstood as childish behaviour, following unrestrained whims. However, what it really means is behaviour springing directly from the Buddha nature within us, so that the correct thing is always done at the appropriate time, *upaya kausalya* 'skill in means'.

4. As pointed out by mystics everywhere, Zen believes that the truth cannot be put into words, but can only be passed directly from mind to mind. This is expressed in the sayings attributed to Bodhidharma: 'A direct transmission outside tradition and outside scripture; no dependence on words; directly pointing to the human heart; seeing into one's own nature and realising Buddhahood.' Because of this, Zen has been critical of over-reliance on the scriptures. Te Shan (780-865) burned all the scriptures as soon as he reached enlightenment and Han Shan (16th century, China) used to go round reading a blank scroll. Scriptures are just symbols, even 'emptiness' or 'Buddha' is just a mental concept and these can get in our way of understanding the truth directly. Dogen felt that this 'burning scriptures' attitude could go too far and stressed that the scriptures can be very useful tools. The Zen criticism of scriptures is not that they are useless but that it can be easily forgotten that they are just tools, as are all religious practices, rituals, moral rules, etc. Religion seems to be in constant need of reminding that its symbols are not the reality itself. This criticism of being tied down to actual words is also found in Taoism, 'The Tao that can be named is not the eternal Tao'. Chuang-tzu said, 'Where can I find a man who has forgotten words - he is a man I would like to talk to.' We should try and experience reality directly instead of at second hand through our mental constructs. In a similar way, Zen is iconoclastic with regard to symbols of Buddhism like Buddha statues. One Zen master made a fire of a wooden statue when he was cold, another showed that his pupil's golden Buddha had become a snake. Such symbols can be a hindrance as well as a help if taken as sacred in themselves.

Zen Practice

If the truth cannot be put into words, it must be conveyed somehow. Zen has several methods of its own whereby the transmission of truth can be achieved 'from mind to mind':

1. The master-pupil relationship is very important in Zen for only a person already enlightened knows how best to arrange for another to experience reality. A zen master is called a *roshi* in Japan and pupils are expected to submit without question to the master's authority. It is traditional to have periodic private interviews with the master, who will question the pupil and gauge his development. In Rinzai Zen, these can be traumatic experiences, as the master may perform some eccentric act like hitting or shouting at the pupil - one even cut his pupil's finger off. There are many stories of eccentric acts performed by Rinzai masters. One rather shocking one is the story of Nan chuan who killed a cat when none of his disciples gave the right answer to his question. When another disciple arrived, he was asked what he would have said; this disciple put his sandals on his head and walked out, causing the master to exclaim, 'If you had been here, the cat need not have died.' Such stories make little sense out of the context of the particular relationship between master and pupils, and led to Soto's criticism of Rinzai as dangerous. In Soto Zen, one simply has quiet faith in one's teacher and the *zazen* method.

2. In the master-pupil interviews of Rinzai Zen, the pupil may be asked to explain a *koan*. These are paradoxical riddle-like sayings, or sets of questions and answers, usually drawn from the collections of the sayings of Zen masters of former times. *Koans* may be questions like: 'What is the sound of one hand clapping?' or 'Why did Bodhidharma come from the West?' They may be statements like 'Bodhidharma is an old bearded barbarian'; 'Shakyamuni is a dung heap coolie'; or 'Buddha preached for 45 years yet his tongue never moved once'. They may be questions with answers provided like: 'What is the Buddha? Three pounds of flax'; 'Is the Buddha nature in a dog?' - answer 'wu' (nothing). Lastly, they may be stories about the old masters such as the one about Bodhidharma and the monk who sought peace of mind. 'Bring out your mind', said Bodhidharma, 'and I'll give it peace.' On finding that he could not produce a mind, Bodhidharma exclaimed that the monk no longer had a problem. Another story is that of a master who was asked about the relationship between the body and the lifeforce of a person and replied that it was windy outside.

   With some of these riddles and surreal conversations it is possible to attempt an explanation. For example, there is no such thing as the sound of one hand clapping because clap is a word to describe the sound of two hands being brought together. However, the idea is not to come up with an intellectual explanation, but to realise that words and concepts are things that we impose upon reality and which get in the way of our seeing it. As the pupil struggles over the *koan* and pushes his mind to the limit, the intellect is exhausted and the pupil may break through into an intuitive grasp of the truth.

3. The method stressed by Soto Zen is quiet sitting meditation known as *zazen*. Following Dogen's rules, particular attention is paid to getting the posture just right, normal sitting in the lotus position, with a straight back and palms together. *Zazen* is practised staring at a wall with eyes open, because Zen does not reject the material world. The idea is just to sit, rather than to sit and think, which will lead to the direct experience of Buddha-reality. Helps towards this are concentration on breathing and the observation of thoughts, trying neither to hold on to them nor obsessively ignore them. Simply sitting, with no thoughts or desires, even for Buddhahood, is not just the means to the Buddhist goal but the goal itself.

Soto Zen advises long periods of *zazen*. To prevent meditators drifting off or falling asleep, the master may patrol behind them with a stick, ready to strike any who seem drowsy. To avoid getting cramp, *zazen* is alternated with *Kin hin* (walking meditation), where the idea is to 'just walk', in a circle with the other meditators.

4. The monastic discipline of Zen is strictly organised. The would-be monk is usually turned away at first to test his commitment, as was Hui k'o. Once admitted, the first few weeks may be spent at manual tasks like preparing food or cleaning. Manual work is considered a good discipline in Zen Buddhism, and all monks spend some time during the day working. The monastic routine is very structured. The day is marked out by bells and everything done at the correct time. Meals are taken in silence, with a few grains of rice always left for the *pretas* (spirits of the dead). As well as periods of work, there are lectures, periods of scripture study, periods of meditation, interviews with the master and periods of chanting *sutras* to the accompaniment of drums. The begging round is continued, not out of necessity, as Zen monks can grow and cook their own food, but as a good discipline. Great stress is placed on personal hygiene, and monasteries will always have a bath house. The monasteries themselves should be kept spotless and with an atmosphere of simple calm. The ritual etiquette is a combination of traditional *vinaya* rules and Confucian politeness, together with the Zen idea that only through discipline can one be free to act naturally.

5. Zen monks often practice arts such as calligraphy, music painting,
   poetry, and gardening. These are seen as methods of penetrating
   directly into reality; the measure of good Zen art is whether it
   manages to convey experience rather than being pretty but
   meaningless. Art can often take us where philosophy cannot. All
   Zen art forms have the characteristic of 'disciplined casualness',
   being simple and yet just right. This attitude has influenced
   Chinese and Japanese art in general and not just art produced by
   monks. Paintings and calligraphy influenced by Zen are simple
   combinations of a few strokes of an ink brush, black on white, yet
   each stroke is very effective. Poetry influenced by Zen is simple
   but disciplined, notably the Japanese *haiku* or poem of seventeen
   syllables. Within this strict limitation, a real experience is
   captured. Basho was a famous 17th century *haiku* writer who
   captured feelings directly:

'Violets -	'Has it returned,
how precious on	the snow
a mountain path!'	we viewed together?'

   In Ikebana (flower arranging), the very idea is artificial yet the skill
   is to follow the natural line of the flowers and twigs. Zen-
   influenced gardens are simple yet precise arrangements of rocks
   and raked sand with a very peaceful effect.

Zen monks also practised martial arts such as kung fu, karate, archery
and fencing. These were seen as forms of meditation, and also
strengthened the connection between Rinzai Zen and the warrior
class. In Japanese martial arts, courage comes from having no belief in
yourself as a separate being and so no fear of death. Success in martial
arts is not due to strength or striving, but in using the natural
properties of matter and precise timing. In archery, the arrow leaves
the bow naturally only when you stop trying too hard.

The tea ceremony turned drinking a cup of tea into a form of
meditation. Ideally, the ceremony takes place in a special hut, in a
special garden, all designed with the utmost simplicity. Inside the hut
there is only a simple scroll and a few flowers, and the implements for
making tea. The process of making, serving and drinking tea is
carried out with extreme formality and total concentration. There
may be incense and soft music. The conversation should be light and
polite, may be admiring the tea, and perhaps the tea cups. The whole
effect is one of great peace and delight in the simple things of
everyday life.

Finally, humour is very important in Zen. The eccentric Zen masters
and their odd sayings can be amusingly absurd, and many Zen

pictures are comic ones like the Buddha as a bullfrog. Laughter helps to stop us taking ourselves and our ideas too seriously and thus is a valuable guard against the ever-present danger of idolising religious symbols. A good example is the laughter caused when a monk, who had successfully kept for 30 years a vow of not leaving his hermitage gates, accidentally did so when saying goodbye to his friends. Zen even laughs at itself - when a monk had thoroughly learned the teaching that all things are mind only, he commented that a rock he was looking at really existed in his own mind rather than as a separate reality. His friend replied that he must have a heavy head. Humorous lines and absurd behaviour can lead us to see something we had missed, if it is real and not forced. Perhaps enlightenment is when one suddenly 'gets' the joke that is the universe.

Nichiren

Nichiren (1222-1283) was a man from a poor, low class background, who became a Tendai monk of Mount Hiei, and, like Honen, Shinran, Eisai and Dogen, left to form his own school of Buddhism. The time in which these men lived was one of social change and civil disruption in Japan, as well as a decline in quality of the Tendai school of Buddhism. There was a widespread feeling of living in the age of *mappo* (spiritual decline). Tendai Buddhism was particularly comprehensive and, by the 13th century, had embraced tantric practices, Zen meditation techniques, Pure Land's chanting to Amida and Shinto elements. Nichiren felt that both Japan and Buddhism were 'going to the dogs' and that he was the one destined to save both. He had a strong sense of mission and was convinced that only he understood the real truth of Buddhism - a rather untypical attitude for a Buddhist. The name he adopted, Nichiren (sun-lotus), suggests the vital importance he felt he had for Japan, the 'land of the rising sun'.

Nichiren taught that he had come to recall Buddhists to the original teachings of the Tendai sect, which had become corrupted by those of Zen, Pure Land and Shingon. This true teaching was to be found in the main scripture of the Tendai sect *The Lotus of the Wonderful Law* (see p94) This scripture in Japanese translation clearly teaches the eternal nature of the Buddha Shakyamuni and the wonderful secret of the Buddhahood of all. Shakyamuni Buddha is pictured as the eternal Father, who tenderly cares for all beings from all eternity, gradually leading them to Buddhahood. Other forms of Buddhism, according to Nichiren, had neglected the true Buddha, Shakyamuni, who appears on earth to teach us in his 'transformation body', to follow imaginary Buddhas like Amida and Vairocana.

Nichiren replaced the rituals of Pure Land and Shingon with his own.

Instead of chanting the name of Amida, his followers chanted the name of the Lotus Sutra *'nammyoho rengye kyo'*, Japanese for "Reverence to the 'Lotus Blossom of the Profound Truth'". As a *mantra*, this chanting can be understood on many levels. It can be taken simply as a declaration of allegiance to a particular scripture, or more deeply as 'tuning in' to the profound truth which underlines the universe, the cosmic Buddha, the Buddha nature within everyone. Or it can be held that the actual meaning of the words is irrelevant, and it is the actual sound that has a beneficial effect on one's consciousness. Nichiren formed the Japanese characters that make up this phrase into a *mandala* or meditation diagram to replace the tantric mandalas of Shingon.

Nichiren spent his life enthusiastically preaching the message of the Lotus Sutra. He considered himself to be a reincarnation of a *bodhisattva* in the *sutra*, and that, therefore, he had been present at the original preaching of the Lotus Sutra. He felt that other forms of Buddhism had neglected the *bodhisattva* idea of making huge efforts for the salvation of others, and particularly denounced Honen's reliance on Amida rather than Shakyamuni.

Nichiren was often persecuted because of his attacks on all other Buddhist sects, and his denouncing of the rulers for supporting them. He was once nearly executed, but somehow managed to escape, which he considered a sign of the correctness of his message. He was however exiled to a remote island. Nichiren welcomed these sufferings as a chance to expiate the bad *karma* of evil deeds from previous lives. Like an Old Testament prophet, Nichiren foretold the downfall of Japan because of its refusal to listen to him and specifically foretold the invasion of the Mongol army. Ten years later, in 1268, the Mongol ships sailed to Japan and demanded tribute. However, they left without causing great havoc, their fleet destroyed by a 'divine wind'.

Nichiren combined Buddhism with an intense nationalism. He felt that Japan had a sacred destiny as the 'ordination platform for the world'. People from all lands would come to Japan and acknowledge the truth of its Lotus religion. He looked to a time when state law and Buddhist truth would be united and a Buddhist Japan lead the world into salvation.

Nichiren's six main disciples formed their own branches of Nichiren Buddhism, and followed in his footsteps of energetic missionary work throughout Japan. Nisshin (1407-1488), a later Nichiren Buddhist, was severely tortured for his faith and a cooking pot jammed over his head in a desperate attempt to silence him.

Several modern Japanese groups follow the teachings of Nichiren, as well as those established earlier. The most important ones are Reiyukai, Rissho-kosei-kai and Soka Gakkai. Reiyukai, the 'Spirit's Friend Society' combines Nichiren's teaching with traditional concern for dead ancestors. Ceremonies of prayer and merit transference are held for dead relatives, and it combines ancient animism with modern spiritualism. This sect was started in 1923 by a lady who claimed to communicate with spirits.

Rissho-kosei-kai, the 'Society for establishing righteousness and fellowship', was originally formed as a breakaway movement from Reiyukai in 1938. It now preaches a modern Buddhism in which traditional Buddhist teachings like the Four Noble Truths and the Lotus Sutra are applied to 20th century life. They are involved in socially useful projects like building schools, hospitals and orphanages and in 1964 built a huge Meeting Hall in Tokyo. Their membership is several million and one notable characteristic is their technique of having small discussion groups or group counselling sessions, where each member shares his or her experiences with the others and together they decide the correct Buddhist course of action to take. Rissho-kosei-kai also worships Shakyamuni Buddha and recites the Nichiren lotus *mantra*, and provides for the spirits of the deceased with daily prayer at household shrines. In some ways, it functions as a club and members wear a sash and prayer beads. They are keen on contact with other religions, and allow that Buddha and God are simply different words for the same thing. The group has made a link with the Christian 'Focolare Movement', based in Italy, which, like Rissho-kosei-kai has a universalistic idea of world peace and unity.

The Soka Gakkai, or 'Society for creating values', started in 1937, is perhaps the most successful of the new movements, with about ten million members in Japan alone. Rather like their hero Nichiren, the Soka Gakkai are enthusiastic proselytisers. It is a society for lay Buddhists, originally within the Nichiren Shoshu (True Nichiren Sect), but recently separated, and presently headed by Daisaku Ikeda. They teach a Buddhism based on daily chanting the Nichiren *mantra*, which, it is taught, will bring material as well as spiritual rewards - health, success in business and personal happiness. Soka Gakkai is very well organised with different sections for different age groups. There is much stress on group activity, like sport, music and dancing, youth clubs, etc. Nichiren himself is viewed as the Buddha of the present age 'Nichiren Buddha'. They have large financial resources and have built a huge temple headquarters for the Nichiren Shoshu. Prior to the split, Japanese members would visit this once a year, as well as reciting the *mantra* and possessing a *gohonzon*, or scroll of Nichiren's mandala. They have their own schools, university and religious examinations and well-organised publicity. They have much influence in the 'Komeito' or 'Clean Government Party', which was the third largest political party in the 1960s. Other Buddhists, including followers of Nichiren, have criticised Soka Gakkai for its heavy propaganda, money-making activities and materialistic outlook. Some members seem to see the *mantra* as a magic spell to bring material prosperity. Enemies even claimed to detect undertones of Fascism in such elements as hero-worship, nationalism, heavy propaganda, and stress on organised group activities. However, Daisaku Ikeda maintains that Soka Gakkai is working for world peace, a goal which they hope to accomplish before the end of the century.

Soka Gakkai followers defend their chanting for material benefits by pointing to the Buddha's desire to reduce suffering for all beings, and claim that the practice of chanting, even if started for selfish reasons, will gradually purify the mind to look beyond self to working compassionately for others.

They do not have Buddha images, because this would suggest that the Buddha was a separate being to be worshipped as a god, rather than a potentiality within everyone.

Another Nichiren based group is the Nipponzan Myohonji, which is dedicated to world peace and disarmament. They can often be seen at peace rallies and marches of organisations such as CND. They are responsible for building 'peace pagodas' throughout the world, two of which can be found in England: one in Milton Keynes and the other in Battersea Park, London, overlooking the river Thames.

---

1.   Williams 1989 p25.
2.   can be found in Conze 1959 pp162-168.
3.   See page 105.

CHAPTER FIVE

BUDDHISM IN THE WEST
WITH PARTICULAR REFERENCE
TO BRITAIN

Since the last century, but particularly the last few decades, Buddhism has become a noticeable presence in the religious traditions open to Westerners. Even those who know nothing of Buddhism in Britain may have noticed the peace pagoda by the Thames, listened to the Dalai Lama being interviewed on television, or laughed at 'Ken, the part-time Buddhist monk' in the TV comedy 'Citizen Smith'. Not so well known may be the beautiful purpose built temples (the Thai temple in Wimbledon, the Tibetan temple in Dumfriesshire, and the Japanese temple and tea house in Suffolk) and the hundreds of local Buddhist groups that meet in converted buildings or private houses throughout Britain. There is a Buddhist school for Japanese children living in Britain, and plans for schools for children of British Buddhists. Buddhism is similarly established in the USA, Australasia, most European countries, both west and east, growing in South America and with some centres in African countries. It can thus be said to have become a worldwide religion.

Interest in Buddhism in the West has grown rapidly and new Buddhist centres open every year. In the case of Britain, the Buddhist Society could list 76 groups in 1981, 107 groups in 1983, 188 in 1987 and 214 in 1991 - and this is without counting the Nichiren Soka Gakkai which is one of the fastest growing movements at present. Since the 1970s, it has been possible to study Buddhism as part of Religious Education at school in Britain. The leader of Tibetan Buddhism, the Dalai Lama, has become a well-known and respected world figure, and there have even been Western boys identified as *tulkus*, or reincarnations of holy lamas, such as the young Spanish boy, Lama Osel, born in 1985 (Mackenzie 1988). All traditions of Buddhism are represented in the West. In Britain, of the groups listed by the Buddhist Society, about 25-30% are Theravada, 20% Tibetan, 15% Zen, 14% Western Buddhist Order and the rest mixed. There are one or two Pure Land groups, a group following the Indian Buddhist movement of Dr Ambedkar (see p 158), and a growing number of Nichiren groups. Of the Tibetan groups, all four schools are present, but the majority are either Gelugpa or Kargyupa. Soto Zen is more

popular that Rinzai Zen. The patterns are different in different
Western countries, depending on colonial connections, immigration
patterns and other factors. For example, there are relatively few
Theravada centres in the USA, with far more Tibetan and Zen centres.
Germany has more Theravada centres whereas France has more
Tibetan centres. In Britain, the earlier contacts with Theravada
countries has given a bias towards Theravada as representing 'pure'
Buddhism in some textbooks and examination syllabuses, which
needs to be guarded against.

History

A hundred or even forty years ago, for all but an elite few, Buddhism
was hardly heard of in the West, and would not be considered
seriously as a faith to live by. Yet the name of the Buddha was known
from early times. We do not know what became of the missions to the
West sent by King Ashoka (see p42) in the 3rd century BCE, but
Alexander the Great reached India in the same century, so it would
have been possible for an inhabitant of the Mediterranean world to
have heard of the Buddha. The first written mention is by a second
century CE Christian writer, Clement of Alexandria, who mentions the
Buddha among what were to him pagan idols.

Marco Polo reached the Court of the Mongol rulers of China in the
13th century, and Jesuit missionaries, such as St Francis Xavier,
worked in China, Japan and even Tibet in the 16th and 17th centuries.
However, apart from these few contacts, no serious study was made
of Buddhism by Westerners until the 19th century, and no one
seriously considered it as a religion to live by until the 20th century.

The British made contact with Buddhism when, in the late 18th and
early 19th centuries, the Empire expanded to include Buddhist
countries like Sri Lanka and Burma and contacts were made with
countries like Nepal. Some of the first people to study Buddhism
seriously were British Civil Servants stationed in these countries such
as B H Hodgson in Nepal and Turnour in Sri Lanka. The French also
colonised Buddhist countries including Vietnam, Cambodia and
Laos, French Indo-China. The most famous early French scholar is
Eugene Burnouf, who wrote an introduction to Buddhism in 1845 and
translated the Lotus Sutra. In 1879, Edwin Arnold, who had been
teaching in India, published a poem based on the Buddha's life called
'The Light of Asia' which helped to spread the Buddha's name among
English speaking people. Serious scholarship began in Britain in the
late 19th century with the formation in 1881, by T W Rhys Davids, of
the Pali Text Society. Rhys Davids, like many others, first came across

Buddhism and Pali while in the Ceylon Civil Service. The Pali Text Society collected, published and translated books from the Theravada Scriptures and first made them available for academic study. Other translations were made by Rhys Davids and the German scholar H Oldenberg for Max Muller's Sacred Books of the East series. In 1904 Rhys Davids became the first Professor of Comparative Religion at Manchester University.

As well as oriental scholars, certain Western philosophers, artists and poets of the nineteenth century were interested in Buddhism. The German philosopher Schopenhauer (1788-1860) made many references to Buddhism, which he admired, and Van Gogh painted a self portrait as a Buddhist among his Japanese pictures. The American writers Emerson and Thoreau were influenced by Buddhism as well as Hinduism. Meanwhile, Chinese Buddhists emigrated to the west coast of America for work connected with the 'gold rush' of the mid nineteenth century, though these lived in a different world to the scholars and writers, and carried out their Buddhist practices in the privacy of local 'Chinatown'.

Many of these early nineteenth century writers on Buddhism have been criticised for dreaming up a Buddhism of their own, rather than learning from Buddhists themselves. Scholars working from texts, put forward an over-rational, intellectual view of Buddhism and poets put forward an over-romanticised orientalism which gave Buddhism an exotic image. Neither presented Buddhism as a faith to live by.

The first step towards actually learning from Buddhists was probably the World Parliament of Religions, held in Chicago in 1893, which had representatives of both Theravada and Zen Buddhism.

One organisation which can be accused of romanticising and possibly distorting Buddhism, but not of failing to mix with Buddhists from traditional Buddhist countries, is the Theosophical Society, which did much to introduce Buddhism to a wider public. This was founded in 1875 in New York by Colonel Olcott and Madame Blavatsky and was based on a mixture of spiritualist, occultist, Hindu and Buddhist ideas. Colonel Olcott and Madame Blavatsky may well have been the first Westerners to formally become Buddhists, as they took the 'refuges and precepts' in Sri Lanka in 1880. Colonel Olcott designed the Buddhist flag (red, orange, yellow, blue and white) and encouraged Dharmapala to form the Mahabodhi Society (see p72).

The beginning of the twentieth century saw the first Westerners to follow Buddhism as a living religion, and the first to be ordained as monks. A young man named Alan Bennett had decided he was a Buddhist and travelled to Sri Lanka and Burma. In Burma, he was ordained as a Theravada monk, Ananda Maitreya, in 1902, and the first 'Buddhist Society' in Britain was formed in 1907 to welcome his arrival in 1908. This small group of people interested in Buddhism tended to be from the more educated class. The Theosophical Society supported this small Buddhist movement, and in 1924, a separate 'lodge' of Buddhist Theosophists was formed. This included Christmas Humphreys who went on to become president of the Buddhist Society. A further impetus was given to Buddhism by the arrival in England in 1926 of the Sri Lankan Anagarika Dharmapala, who started the Mahabodhi Society of England, himself sponsored by the Theosophical Society. A handful of Sinhalese monks settled in England. In 1926, the Society was formed which in 1943 became the Buddhist Society, whose President was Christmas Humphreys (1901-1983) for most of its existence. When the society started, its interest was mostly in Theravada Buddhism, then Zen, but it has always had a non-sectarian outlook, open to people 'just interested' in Buddhism as well as committed Buddhists. The Buddhist Society supplies information about all Buddhist activities in Britain. The bias towards Theravada during this early part of the century was simply because the countries of the British Empire, Sri Lanka and Burma were Theravada, and because the scriptures made available by scholars were from the Pali Canon. In 1927, the Japanese scholar, D T Suzuki, published *Essays in Zen Buddhism* in the English language, allowing the Buddhist Society to add Rinzai Zen teachings and practices to its knowledge of the Buddhist tradition.

In the same early decades, the first Buddhist Societies were formed in Continental Europe; German groups in 1903 and 1924, and in France in 1929. A German who ordained in Sri Lanka in 1903 under the name of Nyanatiloka became a prolific writer on Buddhism, as did his German pupil Nyanaponika. The first Western Buddhist 'nun', was a German ordained in 1926. The French explorer, Alexandra David-Neel had adventurous travels in Tibet in the 1920s, as did the German Govinda, who later formed a Tibetan Buddhist group in Germany, the Arya Maitreya Mandala. In the USA, the World Parliament of Religions had stimulated the formation of Buddhist groups, especially Zen. The Buddhist Society of America was formed in 1930.

The Second World War had a variety of consequences for Buddhism throughout the world. Many British people found themselves stationed in Buddhist countries and gained an interest in Buddhism. After the war, contact with Japan led to an increase of interest in Japanese Buddhism, especially Zen. Christmas Humphreys published popular paperbacks on Zen and on Buddhism in general in 1949 and 1951, making the teachings available to a wider public. D T Suzuki worked in America and visited Britain in 1953. The ideas of Zen became quite fashionable among certain sections of society, such as the so-called 'beat generation', and can be found in the books of the American writer Jack Kerouac, like *On the Road* or The *Dharma Bums*. More serious students of Zen, like Alan Watts, born in Britain but living in America, criticised this 'beat Zen' as a superficial fad. In his opinion, the 'beatniks' picked out the ideas they liked, such as eccentric spontaneous behaviour, and had no real understanding of the true meaning of Buddhism.

Other events in the 1950s included the mass conversion to Buddhism in 1956 of many ex-untouchables in India, who were followers of Dr Ambedkar. This group is represented in Britain and also associated with the Western Buddhist Order in Aid work in India. Theravada Buddhism was more firmly established, with a Sinhalese Vihara set up in 1954. In the same year, one of the first British men (William Purfhurst also called Richard Randall) ordained as a monk in Thailand as Kapilavaddho, and returned to form the English Sangha Trust, the first organisation to ordain British monks in Britain. A Thai Vihara was established in 1966, and the same group built the beautiful Buddhapadipa temple in Wimbledon in 1987. For Burmese Buddhists, a vihara opened in Birmingham in 1978.

For Americans, the wars in Korea and Vietnam meant further contacts with Buddhism, and there are examples of ex-servicemen becoming monks, for instance in Thailand.

The 1960s and 1970s brought a further interest in Buddhism for a variety of reasons. The Chinese invasion of Tibet in 1951 and subsequent flight of the Dalai Lama and other leading monks in 1959, led to the establishment of Tibetan Buddhism in Britain, America, Europe and Australia. This coincided with the general enthusiasm for all things Eastern shown by young Western people belonging to the so-called 'counterculture' of the mid 1960s. The colourful rituals and art of Tibetan Buddhism with its multicoloured mandalas and incense appealed to the 'hippies' (for want of a better word), though, like the beatniks before them, they did not always have a serious commitment to the religion. A typical example of the 'hippy' interest in Buddhism is Dr Timothy Leary, the pioneer of the drug LSD, who claimed a direct connection between the experiences induced by psychedelic drugs and those described in the Tibetan Book of the Dead. As a result, many Buddhist groups have had to stress that their monasteries or centres are not places for indulging in 'sex and drugs and rock and roll', but centres for serious meditation and hard work. However, several of today's serious Buddhists in Britain, Europe, America and Australia, first met Buddhism while on the 'hippy trail' through India and Nepal.

The first Tibetan centre in Britain was Samye Ling in Dumfriesshire, started by the Kargyupa lama Chogyam Trungpa, who also opened a centre in the USA in 1971. The first Gelugpa centre was the Manjusri Institute in Cumbria in 1976, and since then several centres of all four Tibetan schools have opened.

Reverend Master Jiyu Kennett became the first woman to train in a Japanese Soto temple. She founded Shasta Abbey in California in 1970. This organisation is the most significant Zen group in Britain, with Throssel Hole Priory opening in Northumbria in 1972.

Theravada Buddhism in the West gained a new impetus from the followers of the Thai teacher Ajahn Chah (died 1992) of the 'forest dwelling' tradition (see p 83), notably the American Ajahn Sumedho who was ordained in Thailand in the mid-sixties, was abbot of Wat Pah Nanachat, the international monastery in Thailand in 1974, and came to England with Ajahn Chah to establish a Western Sangha in 1977. Several monastic centres have been opened, notably Chithurst in West Sussex in 1981 and Amaravati in Hertfordshire in 1985.

The Western Buddhist Order, a specifically Western Buddhism, was started in 1967 by an English monk called Sangharakshita (see p160).

The latest Buddhist group to gain popularity in the West is the Nichiren Buddhism of the Soka Gakkai (see p 152). Introduced into the USA in the 1960s and to Europe and Britain in the 1970s and 1980s, it is growing fast and currently something of a fashion amongst celebrities from the worlds of pop music, film and television. The emphasis on practical, material results from chanting as well as spiritual development may account for some of its attraction. There has recently been a schism between Soka Gakkai and its parent sect, the Nichiren Shoshu, with what practical results remains to be seen.

In addition, a sizeable number of Western Buddhist groups consist of people interested in Buddhism but with no particular affiliation. The typical Buddhist group will organise meetings, talks, discussions, retreats and practice meditation and ceremonies of worship; some are monastic centres and others simple groups of friends who meet in houses.

Adaptations to Western Culture

Buddhism has always been very flexible, and just as it adapted to the culture of Tibet or China without losing its essential core, there is no reason why it should not adapt to Western cultures. Some Buddhist groups have assimilated themselves to the pattern of Christian churches, providing ceremonies for the birth of babies and marriages, as well as the traditional funeral. Some Zen monks have taken to wearing clerical collars so that they can be easily identifiable as religious ministers. There have been relaxations in the rules for monks so that they can wear clothes more suited to a Northern climate, carry pocket money and mix more freely with women. The attitude to work has had to change - even Theravada monks have found themselves helping with renovation work and gardening; and as most serious meditators also have an ordinary job, work has had to be given a more positive value.

A certain amount of 'demythologising' is observable in accounts of Buddhism written for Westerners - they will not be required to believe literally in the six states of rebirth, but may perhaps interpret animal life, hell, gods, etc as symbols for different human states of mind. Thus if a British person finds it hard to believe in reincarnation, she may be told to interpret it as referring to the way we change from day to day in this life. This can be seen as an example of 'skilful means'. Some Buddhist groups have tried to find more scope for women; particularly in America, where Roshi Jiyu Kennett is an important Soto Zen leader. Festivals may be rearranged for Sundays in order to fit in with Western work patterns and Sunday schools arranged for children. Finally, Buddhist groups have been involving themselves in positive social actions such as involvement in education and social work, and have been noticeable in peace movements like the campaign for nuclear disarmament. Such social action is often referred to as 'engaged Buddhism'.

In his books of the 50s and 60s Christmas Humphreys suggested that we might see the birth not just of a culturally British form of Buddhism but of a 'navayana', a 'new vehicle' which took advantage of modern scholarship and communications to combine the best elements of all the different types of Buddhism which previously developed in isolation.

Friends of the Western Buddhist Order (FWBO)

This movement was started in 1967 by Venerable Sangharakshita. Born in 1925 as Denis Lingwood, he was a member of the Buddhist Society, London, as a young man, and found himself stationed in India and Sri Lanka during the Second World War. In the 1940s and 1950s, he remained in the East and was ordained a Theravada monk. He also received the teachings of Tibetan and Ch'an teachers and worked with the Ambedkarite Buddhist movement for ex-untouchables in India. As a result of his experience he was convinced of the basic unity of

Buddhism and the need to detach its essential message from cultural accretions. He was also critical of formalism among Buddhists in lands where Buddhism was traditional, such as monks who feel free to smoke tobacco because there is no specific vinaya rule against it. Sangharakshita's Buddhism stresses the essentials and unity of Buddhism, taking the spirit rather than the letter of Buddhism. It is eclectic like T'ien tai' (see p133).

In 1967, he decided to form a Buddhist movement suited to Western society, combining the 'best' elements from the traditions he had studied, namely Theravada, Tibetan and Zen. He felt that the traditional monk was not very well suited to Western society, and in 1968 ordained 12 people into the Western Buddhist Order. There are now over 500 order members who are highly committed Buddhists who take serious vows but are not monks or nuns. The title *Dharmachari* (Dharma-farer) was coined to describe their status, followers of the Dharma. Dharmacharis take on a new name, take the refuges as a serious commitment, and keep the ten precepts of Mahayana morality - not to take life, steal, misuse sex, speak falsely, speak harshly, speak idly, slander, covet, harbour ill will or hold wrong views. Order members do not wear robes, but have a stole (called a kesa) for ceremonial occasions. As well as fully-fledged ordained Order members, there are *mitras* (friends) - committed and meditating Buddhists - and other people called 'Friends', who are 'just interested'. The whole movement is therefore known as the 'Friends of the Western Buddhist Order'.

FWBO stresses that the essence of Buddhism must be removed from the 'exotic novelty' of oriental trappings whether people find them attractive or offputting. A Buddhist life must be one of morality, meditation and wisdom as in the beginning. Buddhist morality means keeping the precepts, not slavishly, but in spirit, stressing the positive side of morality - loving kindness, generosity, contentment, stillness, truth, kind and helpful talk, love for all and wisdom. Buddhism as a whole is interpreted in a very positive way, rather as in Far Eastern Buddhism: not so much talk of suffering, death and no self, but of Buddhism as a way to true happiness, and the genuine positive development of our personalities. Against the exotic image of Buddhism, FWBO stresses the value of Western culture - Buddha statues have European faces, and the symbols of Western artists and poets are used to express Buddhist truths in a Western way.

Against the idea of Buddhism as an interesting intellectual theory, FWBO stresses that it is a whole way of life involving emotional commitment and right livelihood. This is helped by the practice of living with other FWBO members - most commonly in single sex communities, which were found to work best - and being involved in one of the Order 'Right Livelihood Co-operatives' earning a living in an organisation run by the Order, such as a vegetarian restaurant, gardening firms, or bookshop. In meditation, FWBO starts with the two basic and most positive forms - mindfulness of breathing and the meditation on love. Only later do they practice other forms, drawing on the whole range of Buddhist practice, *zazen*, *kin hin*, visualisations, *samatha* and *vipassana*. Great stress is laid on *puja* (worship) as a way of involving the emotions of devotion in the gradual development towards Buddhahood. This takes the traditional form of offerings and prayers to a Buddha or *bodhisattva*, chanting *mantras*, confessing faults and sharing merit. There are ceremonies for babies, funerals and festivals - Buddha Day, Dharma Day, Sangha Day and Buddhist saints days (eg Padmasambhava Day). FWBO is actively involved in helping poorer countries, especially through its contacts with the Ambedkarite Buddhists in India.

In ceremonies and everyday life there is a positive appreciation of the arts, and of beauty and elegance rather than being morbidly ascetic. However, FWBO does not see itself as in any way watering down the Buddhist message to make it more acceptable to Westerners, and they do not hesitate to criticise aspects of Western society which they do not like. Two areas which have been heavily criticised have been traditional Christianity and its moral and psychological consequences, and the nuclear family. FWBO members live a variety of lifestyles; as well as single or married, single sex communes, homosexual partnerships, homes for women and children are all acceptable. Some members are celibate, others not, depending on personality. The rule against mis-using sex is interpreted not legalistically but as advice to be unselfish and content with one's own sexuality.

The Future of Buddhism in the West, and elsewhere

The number of Buddhists in Britain is certainly growing, judging by the statistics published by the Buddhist Society, and a similar growth is observable in the rest of Europe, America, and Australia. Being a Buddhist is becoming more acceptable, and people are gaining a better understanding of what Buddhism is. Since the momentous events of 1989, Buddhism was begun to make inroads into the ex-communist countries of Eastern Europe. The Buddhist Society now lists groups in Prague and Moscow, and the author saw advertisements for the visit of a Tibetan lama whilst in Romania.

However, committed Buddhists are still a tiny minority in the 'Western' world, which does not seem to be about to convert to Buddhism en masse in the foreseeable future. Both in Western countries and in its traditional homelands, there are many competitors for the minds and hearts of the population. There are the other major world religions, with Islam and Christianity currently leading the field. There is Marxist Communism, which although failing in Europe, has done much to destroy Buddhism in China, Tibet, Vietnam, Cambodia and Laos. Perhaps most corrosive of all is the secular materialism of capitalism, which is weakening the influence of Buddhism in Sri Lanka, Thailand and Japan, and makes it unlikely to become the major faith of the West.

What does seem to be happening is that Buddhist ideas and practices are permeating into world culture and having a subtle influence on people's thinking and practice, without them actually becoming Buddhists. There are those who retain their allegiance to another religion, or none, who find Buddhist meditation techniques useful, or some Buddhist teachings helpful, without accepting the whole package. Buddhist references are to be found in popular culture, such as novels, films and songs. Some Buddhists welcome this, but others are worried that Buddhism will not be taken seriously and will lose its distinctive message and therefore the power to save beings from samsara. There has been recent concern among some Buddhist groups about the influence of New Age thinking, which has been blamed for portraying Buddhism as one path among many, all open to individual choice in a postmodern world, and for people taking Buddhist ordination without taking it seriously. A vague, relativist, facile universalism, which sees all religions as equally valid, is quite a common attitude among those who find aspects of Buddhism attractive, from the nineteenth century Theosophists through beatniks and hippies to contemporary New Age adherents. It is also quite common among students and schoolchildren in Religious Studies classes. There are some Buddhists who see such interest as a step in the right direction, and others who see it as more insidious a threat than either capitalist or communist materialism.

One Buddhist teaching which seems indisputable is that all things are slowly but surely always changing. Perhaps new Buddhist movements will develop in addition to the FWBO. Perhaps modern communications will lead to an increasingly 'ecumenical' Buddhism as the different traditions come together. Perhaps Buddhism will spread rapidly, or perhaps genuine Buddhism will die out altogether so the world will have to wait for the coming Maitreya. Who knows what will happen in the future?

CONCLUSION

As stated in the preface, the original motivation for writing this book was to help students studying Buddhism at A level or similar. It attempts to be a brief but comprehensive survey of Buddhism by a sympathetic outsider. The sources used by the author include far more than those listed in the bibliography, and include scholarly works, published and unpublished theses, Buddhist scriptures in translation, books by modern Buddhists, children's books, and conversations with Buddhists from both traditionally Buddhist countries and 'Western Buddhists'. There are bound to be misunderstandings, errors and things that could have been explained much more clearly. However, it is offered in the spirit of the parable of the raft - a book that might help students understand Buddhism a little better, to be discarded when they progress beyond it. Struggling with the first draft in 1985, and the final draft in 1992, certainly helped the author to clarify several aspects of Buddhism, so it may have been of use in two ways.

The eighth century monk Shantideva begins his book, the Bodhicaryavatara, with the following words which seem applicable;

> 'There is nothing really original here, and I have no skill in literary composition. I have composed this...to clarify my own mind'.

He ends his book by dedicating the merit gained by writing the book to the benefit of all beings, with some touching wishes;

> 'May all...have oceans of joy...may those in hell enjoy paradise...may animals lose their fear of being eaten...may all have food and drink...may travellers be safe...may magic work...may nuns be accepted as equal...and those who would find Buddhahood not break their vows'.

In a similar spirit, may those who read this book be helped to understand Buddhism a little better, and if there is any merit in its composition, may all beings share in this merit, especially those who have taken the trouble to read this book.

GLOSSARY

All words in this glossary are followed by a letter which indicates their language of origin: C = Chinese, E = English, J = Japanese, P = Pali, S = Sanskrit, T = Tibetan, Th = Thai.

Abhidhamma (P) 'higher knowledge', a section of the Pali Canon

Ajivakas (S) a type of ascetic with particular beliefs at the time of the Buddha

Alaya-vijnana (S) store-consciousness in Yogacara

Ajahn (Th) title for teacher in Thai Theravada

Amida (J) or *Amitabha* (S) a (non-historical) Buddha

Anagarika (P) in English Theravada, a stage half way between lay and monastic

Anatta (P) 'no self', without individual essence

Anicca (P) impermanence

Arhat (S) enlightened person

Ashoka (S) important 3rd century BCE emperor of India

Asala (P) Theravada festival celebrating the first sermon of the Buddha

Avalokitesvara (S) bodhisattva of compassion

BCE (E) Before the Common Era. Equivalent to BC but without the Christian doctrinal statement

Bhikkhu (P) monk *Bhikkhuni* (P) nun

Bodhicitta (S) thought of enlightenment, decision to take the
        bodhisattva path

Bodhidharma (S) legendary founder of Zen.

Bodhisattva (S) 'being of enlightenment' 1. a being who dedicates
        himself or herself to obtaining enlightenment not for
        themselves but in order to help others. 2. Gautama Buddha in
his life/lives previous to enlightenment

Brahmin (E) Indian (Hindu) priest or priestly class

Buddha (P,S) 'enlightened one', 'enlightened being' (literally: 'awakened one')

CE (E) Common Era. Equivalent to AD, but without the Christian doctrinal statement

Ch'an (C) 'meditation', Chinese Buddhist tradition = Zen

Chen-yen (C) Chinese Tantric school of Buddhism = Shingon

Chenrezi (T) bodhisattva of compassion = Avalokitesvara

Cittamatra (S) mind-only, central concept of Yogacara

Dalai Lama (T) 'ocean lama' religious leader of Tibetan Buddhists.

Dana (P,S) 'giving'

Dengyo Daishi (J) founder of Tendai in Japan

Dhamma (P) *Dharma* (S) Truth, Teaching, Law, Buddhism

dhammas (P) elements of existence

Dharmakaya (S) the ultimate body of the Buddha, the truth
Dogen (J) founder of Japanese Soto Zen
Dorje (T) vajra or thunderbolt. Ritual implement
Dukkha (P,S) suffering, unsatisfactoriness
Gelugpa (T) a tradition of Tibetan Buddhism
Gohonzon (J) scroll containing mandala of Nichiren's mantra
Guru (S) teacher who passes on religious tradition
Guru Rinpoche (S&T) 'precious guru', a title for Padmasambhava
Haiku (J) poem of 17 syllables
Hinayana (S) 'small vehicle' Mahayana term for non-Mahayana Buddhist traditions
Hua-yen (C) 'Flower Garland' Chinese school of Buddhism teaching the total interpenetration of all things = Kegon
Jataka (P) stories of previous lives of the Buddha
Jewels, three (E) the Buddha, Dharma, and Sangha
Jhana (P) meditative state
Jodo, Jodo Shinshu (J) Pure Land and True Pure Land school of Buddhism
Kami (J) Japanese divinities
Kargyupa (T) tradition of Tibetan Buddhism
Karma (S) 'actions' the law of cause and effect. Good actions bring happiness, bad actions bring unhappiness
Karuna (S) Compassion
Kathina (P) ceremony of presenting special robe
Kegon (J) = Hua-yen
Khandha (P) factor of a person's life, of which there are 5
Kin hin (J) walking meditation
Kshatriya (S) Indian warrior class
Koan (J) 'case' saying of a Zen master
Kwannon (J) Japanese form of Kwanyin = Avalokitesvara
Kwanyin (C) Female bodhisattva of compassion = Avalokitesvara
Lama (T) Tibetan name for guru
Lung (T) ritual transmission of a sacred text
Madhyamaka (S) 'Middle path' an important Mahayana school of philosophy
Magha Puja (P) Thai festival celebrating the sangha
Mahayana (S) 'great vehicle' one of the two main wings of Buddhist tradition
Maitreya (S) the next Buddha
Mala (S) prayer beads
Manas (S) mind
Mandala (S) diagram
Manjusri (S) bodhisattva of wisdom
Mantra (S) a sacred syllable or short series of these
Mappo (J) the last age, age of spiritual decline
Marks of Conditioned Existence, three (E) anicca, dukkha and anatta
Meditation (E) concentration, any technique which trains the mind, usually in a religious context
Merit (E) the result of skilful action
Metta (P) loving kindness, friendly love
Mindfulness (E) awareness, a meditation practice
Mitra (S) a friend (a term used in FWBO)
Mudra (S) a symbolic shape made with the hands
Nagarjuna (S) the founder of Madhyamaka

Nembutsu (J) repetition of the Buddha Amida's name

Nibbana (P) 'blown out' the state where all greed, hatred and delusion are ended. Eternal peace?

Nichiren (J) 13th century monk who started Nichiren Shoshu

Nichiren Shoshu (J) a Japanese Buddhist tradition

Nirmanakaya (S) transformation body, or earthly manifestation of a Buddha

Nirvana (S) Sanskrit for nibbana

Nying ma pa (T) tradition of Tibetan Buddhism

Padmasambhava (S) a famous enlightened person, who established Buddhism in Tibet

Pagoda (J) Japanese form of stupa

Pali (P) description of language used in Theravada scriptures

Pali Canon (P&E) the scriptures of Theravada Buddhism

Paramita (S) perfection, or perfect virtue, of which there are 10

Paticcasamuppada (P) dependent origination

Parinibbana The Buddha's final passing into nibbana

Patimokkha (P) The monastic code

Pirit (P) chanting sections of the Pali Canon as a blessing

Poson (P) Sri Lankan festival

Prajna (S) Wisdom

Prajnaparamita (S) perfection of wisdom. Also a series of Mahayana scriptures

Pratimoksha (S) the monastic code

Pratyekabuddha (S) solitary non-teaching Buddha

Puja (S) devotional ceremony

Pure Land (E) a purified place when the Dharma can be practised easily; used of a tradition of Buddhism centred on devotion to Amida

Rebirth (E) the doctrine that we pass through many lives in the cycle of samsara

Refuges, three (E) pledging commitment to the three jewels

Rinzai (J) tradition within Zen

Sakyamuni (S) see Shakyamuni

Sakyapa (T) tradition of Tibetan Buddhism

Samadhi (P,S) state of concentrated meditation Samantha (P) calm meditation

Sambhogakaya (S) glorious body of the Buddha

Samsara (S&P) the cycle of existence, rebirths into unsatisfactory states, ordinary unenlightened life.

Sangha (S&P) 'assembly' the Buddhist community, in Theravada this is sometimes restricted to the community of monastics only

Sanskrit ancient Indian language of Hinduism and many Mahayana scriptures

Satori (J) Zen word for moment of enlightenment

Shakyamuni (S) wise man of the Shakya tribe. Another name for the Buddha Siddhartha Gautama. Used commonly by Mahayana Buddhists

Shastra (S) a religious treatise

Shingon (J) = Chen-yen

Shunya, Shunyata (S) empty, emptiness, an important concept in Mahayana Buddhism

Siddhartha Gautama (S) *Siddhatta Gotama* (P) personal name of the historical Buddha

Sima (P) ritual boundary of monastery

Soka Gakkai (J) a Japanese lay movement associated with the Nichiren Shoshu

Soto (J) a tradition within Zen

Stupa (P) monument over Buddhist relics

Sukhavati (S) The Happy land of Amitabha Buddha

Sunya, sunyata (S) see Shunyata

Sutra (S), *Sutta* (P) scripture

Tantra (S) scriptures of Vajrayana Buddhism and parallel movements in Hinduism

Tantric (E) Buddhism based on tantra texts and related practices

Tathagata (S) the thus-gone one, another word for Buddha

Tathagata-garbha (S) womb or embryo of Buddhahood, Buddha-potential

Tara (S) a female bodhisattva

Tendai (J) a Japanese tradition of Buddhism related to Chinese Tien tai

Thangka (T) Tibetan religious painting on cloth

Theosophical Society (E & Greek) a religious organisation founded in the USA drawing on ideas from eastern religions

Theravada (P&S) 'the way of the elders' one of the two main wings of Buddhist tradition

Thero (P) A senior monk of over ten years in the robes

T'ien t'ai (C) An eclectic Chinese school of Buddhism

Trikaya (S) Mahayana doctrine that Buddhas has three forms, human, glorious and absolute (nirmanakaya, sambhogakaya and dharmakaya)

Tulku (T) a bodhisattva in human form, taking several rebirths which can be identified

Upaya (S) 'means' (short for upaya kausalya) 'skilful means') the ability to know exactly what to do for the best in all situations. If absolutely necessary, this may involve 'bending the rules' or 'being economical with the truth'

Vairocana (S) The shining one, the cosmic Buddha

Vajra (S) 'diamond' or 'thunderbolt' ritual implement used in Vajrayana

Vajrayana (S) 'diamond or thunderbolt vehicle' name used to distinguish Tantric Buddhism from other forms of Mahayana. Sometimes seen as a third, separate 'yana' of Buddhism and sometimes applied rather loosely to the whole of Tibetan Buddhism

Vassa (P) the three months rainy season retreat

Vihara (P) Buddhist monastery or temple

Vinaya (P) the discipline section of the Pali Canon dealing with rules for monks

Vipassana (P) insight meditation

Visualisation (E) meditation technique, focusing on a particular mental image

WBO (E) Western Buddhist Order, a new adaptation of Buddhism to Western conditions.

Wesak (P) Theravada festival celebrating the birth, enlightenment and death of the Buddha

Yidam (T) chosen deity for visualisation

Yogacara important Mahayana philosophical school

Zazen (J) sitting meditation

Zen (J) tradition of Buddhism

BIBLIOGRAPHY

General

Harvey, P *An Introduction to Buddhism* (CUP 1990) A comprehensive introduction for students at degree level.

Robinson, Johnson: *The Buddhist Religion* (Third Edition) (Wadsworth 1982)

Bechert and Gombrich ed: *The World of Buddhism* (Thames and Hudson 1984) An expensive but beautifully illustrated reference book on Buddhism, a survey of Buddhist civilisation.

General books for pre-A level students which could prove useful for beginners

Chryssides G *The Path of Buddhism* (St Andrew's 1988)

Connolly H & P: *Buddhism* (Stanley Thornes 1992) for GCSE, but a useful way in for older students.

Theravada

Rahula W: *What the Buddha Taught* (Gordon Fraser 1982). Straightforward account of basic Buddhist doctrine by a Theravada monk, with a selection of scripture.

Gombrich R: *Theravada Buddhism* (Routledge 1986). A social history of Theravada Buddhism.

Mahayana

Williams P: *Mahayana Buddhism* (Routledge 1989) A very helpful survey of the doctrinal foundations of Mahayana Buddhism, but with little on Zen.

Suzuki D T: *Outlines of Mahayana Buddhism* (1907/1963 Schoken Books NY) Rather old now, but a useful survey of main beliefs that characterise Mahayana in general from a Japanese Zen perspective.

Anthologies of scriptures

Conze E: *Buddhist Scriptures* (Penguin 1959)

de Bary: *The Buddhist Tradition* (Vintage 1972)

Beyer S: *The Buddhist Experience* (Wadsworth 1974)

Woodward: *Some Sayings of the Buddha* (OUP 1973)

Ling T: *The Buddha's Philosophy of Man* (Dent 1981)

Sangharakshita: *The Eternal Legacy* (Tharpa 1985)

The Life and times of the Buddha

Carrithers M: *The Buddha* (OUP 1983)

Nanamoli: *The Life of the Buddha According to the Pali Canon* (BPS, Kandy 1978)

Thomas E: *The Life of the Buddha as Legend and History* (Routledge 1975)

Ling T: *The Buddha* (Pelican 1976)

Saddhatissa: *The Life of the Buddha* (Unwin 1976)

Pye *The Buddha* (Duckworth 1979)

Theravada Countries

Gombrich R :*Precept and Practice: Traditional Buddhism in the Rural Highlands of Ceylon* (Clarendon 1971)

Spiro M: *Buddhism and Society: a Great Tradition and its Burmese Vicissitudes* (Allen and Unwin 1971)

Tambiah: *Buddhism and the Spirit Cults in North East Thailand* (CUP 1984)

The Bodhisattva

Dayal H: *The Bodhisattva Doctrine in Buddhist Sanskrit Literature* (Routledge 1932, Delhi 1970)

Matics M: *The Bodhicaryavatara of the Buddhist poet Shantideva* (Allen and Unwin 1971)

Tibetan

Guenther H: *The Jewel Ornament of Liberation* translation of Gampopa (Shambala 1971)

Trungpa C: *Cutting Through Spiritual Materialism* (Shambala 1973) By a lama who escaped from Tibet.

Snellgrove and Richardson: *A Cultural History of Tibet* (Praeger 1968)

Chang: *The Hundred Thousand Songs of Milarepa* (Harper 1970)

Evans-Wentz: *Tibet's Great Yogi, Milarepa* (OUP 1974)

Trungpa C: *Born in Tibet* (Allen and Unwin 1979) Autobiography of a lama who fled to the West.

Zen

Watts A: *The Way of Zen* (Penguin 1962) By a famous 'western' follower of Zen.

Kennett, Roshi Jiyu: *Zen is Eternal Life* (Shasta Abbey 1976) History and practice of Zen by a leading western female Zen master.

Suzuki D: *An Introduction to Zen Buddhism* (Rider 1949/1983)

Ethics

Saddhatissa: *Buddhist Ethics* (Allen and Unwin 1970)

Jones K: *The Social Face of Buddhism* (Wisdom 1989)

Festivals

Brown A ed: *Festivals in World Religions* (Longman 1986)

Connolly H & P: *Buddhism through festivals* (Longman 1989) A children's book, but useful.

Ordination

Silcock: *A Village Ordination* (Curzon 1980)

Pilgrimage

Russell: *The Eight Places of Buddhist Pilgrimage* (Wisdom 1981)

Buddhism in the West

Cush D: *Buddhists in Britain Today* (Hodder and Stoughton 1990) based on interviews with practising Buddhists from a variety of traditions: an easy way into Buddhism as a living faith. Also gives a comprehensive list of children's books on Buddhism, visual aids and useful addresses.

The Buddhist Society: *The Buddhist Directory* (1991)

Snelling J: *The Buddhist Handbook* (Century 1987)

Guy Claxton: *Buddhist Lives* (Oliver and Boyd 1989) A children's book but includes an interesting life of Alan Watts.

Subhuti: *Buddhism for Today* (Element 1983) A history of the FWBO.

The above bibliography contains suggestions for the most useful further reading rather than representing the books used in preparing this text, which were far too many to list.

INDEX